The
WOMEN'S BUSINESS
RESOURCE GUIDE

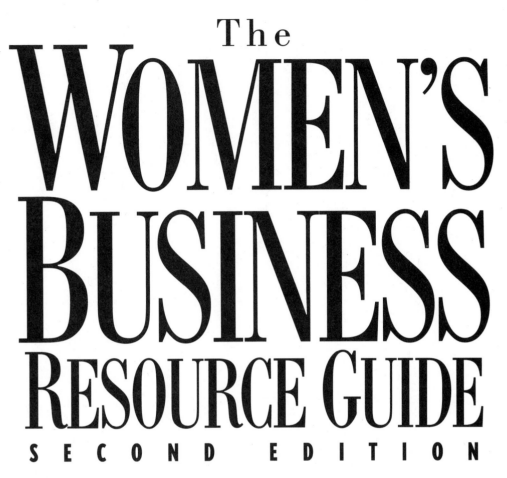

The
WOMEN'S
BUSINESS
RESOURCE GUIDE
SECOND EDITION

A NATIONAL DIRECTORY OF MORE THAN 800 PROGRAMS, RESOURCES, AND ORGANIZATIONS TO HELP WOMEN START OR EXPAND A BUSINESS

Barbara Littman

CONTEMPORARY BOOKS
A TRIBUNE COMPANY

Library of Congress Cataloging-in-Publication Data

The women's business resource guide : a national directory of more than 800
    programs, resources, and organizations to help women start or expand a
    business / Barbara Littman [compiler]. — 2nd ed.
            p.   cm.
        ISBN 0-8092-3166-2
        1. Women-owned business enterprises—United States—Directories.
    2. Women in business—United States—Directories.   3. Women—Services
    for—United States—Directories.   I. Littman, Barbara.
    HF5035.w66   1996
    338.6′422′082—dc20   96-17511
                                                                        CIP

Cover design by Scott Rattray
Interior design by Nancy Freeborn

Copyright © 1996, 1994 by Barbara Littman
All rights reserved
Published by Contemporary Books
An imprint of NTC/Contemporary Publishing Company
Two Prudential Plaza, Chicago, Illinois 60601-6790
Manufactured in the United States of America
International Standard Book Number: 0-8092-3166-2
10   9   8   7   6   5   4   3   2   1

Contents

Acknowledgments

I would like to thank the hundreds of individuals in private and government offices and organizations who graciously sent material about their programs, answered questions, and enthusiastically encouraged the completion of this project. If there are any errors of fact, I take complete responsibility for them. I also want to thank the following individuals, who generously gave their time to review and comment on an early draft of the first edition of this book: Brenda Black, Women's Business Specialist for the U.S. Department of Commerce; Harriet Fredman, Senior Project Manager for the SBA's Office of Women's Business Ownership; Geraldine Larkin, author, entrepreneur, and former Manager for Emerging Business Services with Deloitte & Touche. Special thanks are due Brenda Black and Harriet Fredman for their willingness to spend the extra time needed to carefully review descriptions of federal programs.

I want to thank my agent, Denise Marcil, and my editor, Susan Schwartz, for their enthusiasm about the book and recognition of its value. And with special appreciation, I thank my husband (former coauthor and business partner) for his patience and support while I worked overtime to complete the second edition.

Introduction

WHY THIS BOOK?

Women are going into business in record numbers. According to government sources, women are starting businesses at two to five times the rate of men, and they currently own 30 percent of all businesses in the United States. By the year 2000, that number is expected to reach or surpass 50 percent.

The businesses women start often grow more slowly than those started by men, but statistics indicate that woman-owned enterprises have a 75 percent success rate, compared with only 20 percent for businesses overall. As the owners of more than 7.5 million businesses and the employers of more than 15 million workers in this country (35 percent more than are employed by Fortune 500 companies), women are making significant contributions to the U.S. economy.

These women entrepreneurs face special challenges. Money and knowledge (and often respect) don't come easily. And succeeding in business can be a tough proposition for anyone, but the special challenges women face can often mean working overtime just to get to square one.

This book is designed to level the playing field a little by helping women entrepreneurs get started faster and move on sooner to the growth and stability that ensure success.

ABOUT THIS GUIDE

This guide covers resources available across the country to help women start, stabilize, and expand their businesses. Although it emphasizes special opportunities just for women, it also includes other resources that are too good to be ignored.

The book focuses primarily on programs available nationally, but it directs you to offices or people in your local area whenever possible. The sections on state resources are an exception to this approach. The goal was not to provide a state-by-state directory of resources, but rather to give you a place to start discovering what your state has to offer.

Chapter 5, about selling to the government, is included in the hope that it will encourage more women business owners to look seriously at often-overlooked opportunities in government contracting. The federal government and many state governments have programs designed to encourage and assist women in this area.

SCOPE

Following are brief summaries of the seven chapters in this book.

1: Business Women Talk

Interviews with successful women business owners give readers insight into what it takes to succeed. Owners of large and small businesses, representing a variety of products and services, speak frankly about their experiences. They describe the challenges, fears, and rewards of being an entrepreneur.

2: Information Sources

Listed in this chapter are offices, agencies, books, magazines, and government publications where you can find practical information on a wide range of specific business topics.

3: Training, Technical Assistance, and Counseling

Described here are government and private sources of counseling, mentoring, training, and consulting.

4: Business Financing

This chapter provides general information on types of financing available and describes specific financing programs—from microloans to venture capital and everything in between.

5: Selling to the Government

A primer on tapping into the huge market represented by state and federal governments, this chapter lists publications, databases, and assistance centers with programs specifically for women.

6: Membership Organizations

This directory of women's business and professional associations (and other general business organizations) includes descriptions of professional development opportunities and other benefits available to members.

7: Resource, Program, and Agency Listings

Contact information is provided for the more than eight hundred organizations, offices, programs, and agencies referred to throughout the guide.

HOW TO USE THIS GUIDE

The interviews with women business owners in Chapter 1 are a good place to start your reading. These stories will inspire you. They provide excellent role models in the form of women who used resources—from loan programs to free counseling—to start and expand their businesses. Next, skim Chapters 2 through 6 to identify areas that interest you most. In some cases, contact information will be included with a program description, but you will probably need to use Chapter 7 to find phone numbers and addresses of some of the programs and organizations that interest you.

STRUCTURE AND CONTENT

This guide is designed to make it easy for you to get an overview of resources on particular topics. Long listings of agencies and offices are grouped together in the last chapter for convenience. Once you know what you want to follow up on, it's easy to find the correct agency or program you want by using cross references in the chapter you're reading or by using the *Quick-Find Guide* on the second page of Chapter 7.

Every effort has been made to provide accurate and complete information for each listing. During the research phase, we requested and reviewed printed material from the programs and organizations included and, in many cases, followed up with phone calls to verify or clarify information. We verified all phone numbers and addresses to ensure that you spend as little time as possible looking for information and as much time as possible working on building a successful enterprise.

Despite our efforts, however, some phone numbers and addresses may have changed between the time we checked our data and the time the book came off the press. If you find incorrect information, please let us know by using the form at the end of this book.

LOOKING AHEAD

When the first edition of this guide was released, stories documenting the explosive growth of women's entrepreneurship were just hitting the popular media. At that time, we expressed hope that each edition would be bigger and better than the preceding one. As awareness of the unique needs and contributions of women business owners has increased, this hope has been fulfilled. New programs and agencies have emerged—some to study and report on the trend, others to support and serve this growing population.

In the short time between publication of that edition and this one, momentum has gathered. Lenders are beginning to consider women-owned businesses good risks. Purchasing agents are becoming aware that women-owned businesses offer a diversity of needed products and services. And, perhaps most encouraging of all, the business world in general is acknowledging—and modeling—the effectiveness of women's leadership and management styles. This book will continue to be updated and released on a regular basis. You can help businesswomen by sending us information about any program or organization you would like to have considered for inclusion in future editions. A form for directory submissions is included at the back of the book.

A GUIDE TO FEDERAL AGENCIES

The federal programs and resources described in this guide are made available by three key agencies:

The Small Business Administration (SBA), including the SBA's Office of Women's Business Ownership

The Women's Bureau of the U.S. Department of Labor

The U.S. Department of Commerce

The Small Business Administration (SBA)

The Small Business Administration (SBA) is the only federal agency whose sole responsibility is to assist small businesses. The SBA has been around for forty years, offering a cornucopia of free and low-cost assistance to small business owners throughout the country. Of particular interest to women is the Office of Women's Business Ownership (OWBO), which focuses on the special needs of women entrepreneurs. (OWBO is described in the next section.)

The SBA is organized around a head office in Washington, D.C., and a variety of regional, district, and other field offices around the country. The field offices are the workhorses of the agency, delivering services and programs customized to meet local and regional needs. Staff specialists in these offices—including a cadre of women's business representatives—work directly with business owners, offering counseling, referral, problem-solving expertise, and education. In addition, SBA staff members in the field work with local and regional businesses and agencies to present seminars and workshops targeted to the needs of business owners in their geographic area.

Contacting your regional SBA office is a good way to start finding out about the resources available to you. To locate the office that serves your area, see page 189.

The Office of Women's Business Ownership (OWBO)

OWBO is the place to call for almost any kind of business assistance. Geared to start-ups as well as stable and expanding businesses, the office provides one-stop shopping for guidance, training, referral, and information resources for women. OWBO does its job through a central office in Washington, D.C., and a network of women's representatives in local SBA field offices.

The OWBO office in Washington, D.C., serves as a clearinghouse for information on women's business ownership issues and develops programs that can be offered through its national network of women's representatives. The programs developed at the head office are designed to meet the special needs of business women in all areas and stages of business development.

The job of local women's representatives is to help women become successful business owners by coordinating the head office's efforts out in the field. Representatives customize programs to meet local needs; help women take advantage of programs and opportunities developed by the SBA, OWBO, and other federal agencies; and steer women to appropriate state and local resources.

A call to the women's business representative who serves your area is definitely worth the time. You'll most likely come away with a list of appropriate people to call, agencies to contact, and workshops to put on your calendar. To locate the number of the representative in your area, see page 192.

For more information about OWBO at the federal level, contact:

Office of Women's Business Ownership
Small Business Administration
409 Third St. SW, 6th Floor
Washington DC 20416
(202) 205-6673

The Women's Bureau (U.S. Department of Labor)

The Women's Bureau is the only office in the federal government whose sole mission is to study issues of women and work. Through its network of ten regional offices, the Women's Bureau acts as an advocate for working women (including self-employed women) by disseminating information, working to change government policies, and providing training and educational opportunities for women across the country. To locate the regional office that serves your state, see page 221.

For more information about the national office, contact:

The Women's Bureau
U.S. Department of Labor
200 Constitution Ave. NW
Washington DC 20210
(800) 827-5335 (automated information request)
(202) 219-4486 (reception and voice mail)

The U.S. Department of Commerce

A key function of the U.S. Department of Commerce is to help make federal resources available to the business community by providing information and assistance through its various bureaus such as the Minority Business Development Agency, the International Trade Administration, the Office of Business Liaison (OBL), and the Office of Small and Disadvantaged Business Utilization. Commerce also initiates efforts to assure purchasing from women-owned businesses.

To get an overview of the Commerce Department and what it can do for you, request a *Business Services Directory* from:

Office of Public Affairs
U.S. Department of Commerce
Fourteenth St. and Constitution Ave. NW, Room 5610
Washington DC 20230
(202) 219-3605

TTY (hearing impaired): (202) 482-4670
(This TTY number is not specifically for OBL, but by calling this number you will be directed to the appropriate person.)

A QUICK GUIDE TO COMMON TERMS

As you use this resource guide and talk with representatives of the programs that interest you, you may begin to feel overwhelmed with abbreviations, acronyms, and jargon. Here's a brief glossary of some of the terms you're most likely to encounter.

MBDA: Minority Business Development Agency. Sponsored by the U.S. Department of Commerce, the MBDA provides training, technical assistance, and procurement assistance to minority business owners.

MBE: Minority business enterprise.

NAWBO: National Association of Women Business Owners. NAWBO is an influential national membership organization open to all women business owners.

OSDBU: Office of Small and Disadvantaged Business Utilization. OSDBU has offices in all major federal agencies and departments to help small businesses sell their goods and services to the federal government.

OWBO: Office of Women's Business Ownership. OWBO, sponsored by the SBA, develops programs specifically designed to meet the needs of women business owners.

procurement: The procedure by which purchasing agents (in the public and private sectors) obtain the goods and services needed to run their organizations. Contracts are awarded to qualified businesses based on a competitive bidding process.

SBA: Small Business Administration. The SBA is the only federal agency whose sole responsibility is to foster small business development in the United States.

SBDC: Small Business Development Center. This is an SBA-sponsored site for training, technical assistance, and business counseling.

SCORE: Senior Corps of Retired Executives. This group is made up of volunteers who provide free business counseling.

small business: The federal government defines a small business as a business that is not dominant in its field and is independently owned and operated. In general, any business with fewer than five hundred employees is defined as small, although other standards, such as annual gross revenues, can also apply.

WBE: Women's Business Enterprise. The federal government defines a WBE as a business enterprise that is at least 51 percent owned, controlled, and run by women (or a woman).

Business Women Talk

The women business owners interviewed for this book are a diverse group, and their businesses—representing a range of sizes and industries—reflect that diversity. These are women who started businesses for a myriad of reasons, from a desire for flexibility during years of raising a family to a need to break out of a stifling job. And they bring widely varying skills and knowledge to the task of building their businesses.

But they have elements in common, too—ways of thinking, acting, and interacting—that play an important role in the success of these entrepreneurs. These elements can serve as guiding principles for all women business owners and women who are planning to start businesses.

- A business is more than just a way to make a living. Your business should be one that lets you do something you love and believe in. When women entrepreneurs talk about their businesses, they talk about their visions, not their bank accounts.

- A strong desire to succeed and a willingness to learn are as important as—and sometimes more important than—expertise in a particular field.

- People are important. Relationships with employees, vendors, and customers have to be valued and cultivated. They don't develop by accident.

- Quality services and products are critical to success, as is careful analysis of what the client or consumer really wants.

- Fear is a constant companion, but it doesn't prevent these women from making choices and moving ahead.

- Entrepreneurs don't always get things right the first time, but mistakes and failures are used as sources of new insight and new strategies.

- Persistence and ingenuity prevail when obstacles and challenges arise.

- Successful entrepreneurs use resources and ask for help when necessary. A spirit of cooperation may be at the root of many women's business successes. These women ask for help and help others when asked. All of the women interviewed here sought out help and relationships that would support them on their business-building journeys. If you read these interviews before the other chapters, you will see that every business-woman interviewed has used at least one, and often many, of the resources described in this book.

To give you an idea of the range of possibilities open to women in business, two of the women interviewed represent small, relatively young businesses, and the other four* represent established enterprises. The four owners of the larger, more established businesses were interviewed twice, one year apart, to provide insight into the effect of growth and longevity on a woman business owner's life.

SHANNON LORING, *Proprietor, Idleylde Park Lodge and Restaurant (Idleylde Park, Oregon)*

Shannon Loring, the second recipient in Oregon of a specialized SBA loan (the women's prequalification loan program), is a Chicago native and California transplant. She was just passing through Oregon to visit her daughter when she felt the pull of the vacant Idleylde Lodge. A seasoned restaurateur, she recognized the potential in the eight-thousand-square-foot 1920s dance pavilion that sat vacant across the street from the North Umpqua River—a river that draws sports fishing enthusiasts from around the world.

---

* Parts of these interviews were first conducted for the SBA's Office of Women's Business Ownership through a U S West-funded research project.

Eighteen months before, Shannon and her husband, Sandy, having recently sold their farm in Sonoma County, had left their home of ten years to travel. They weren't sure where their next permanent home would be or how they would make their living once they found it, but they knew work was still in the picture.

When Shannon and Sandy first saw the lodge, it was a down-at-the-heels building with a checkered history of tried-and-failed businesses. But where others might have seen a building past its prime, Shannon (whose background includes psychology as well as restaurant management) saw a community gathering place where residents could meet informally, hold special events, and dine on fresh, local food. Within six months of opening, the inn had become that gathering place, serving seventy dinners a night on weekends and offering a room for teens to play pool and munch free popcorn. In other rooms, local residents could hold meetings, weddings, and special events.

Q: Let's talk a little about how you got your start. I know this isn't your first venture in the restaurant business.

A: No. My first bar and restaurant business, just outside Sonoma, was a pub. I'd always wanted to have a pub, like an Irish pub, where people come for companionship, not necessarily to drink. Where families come, where the kids are welcome, where people come together—especially in this splintered society we have. It was an amazing success. We served the same kind of food we have here, but a little less bland. It was all home-done, though. People came. It was wonderful.

Q: What happened to that business?

A: Personal things. My first husband and I separated. He was a woodworker and worked at home, so he kept track of all the kids. When we separated, I had to become either a bar and restaurant owner or a mother. So I became a mother and managed other people's bars and restaurants.

Q: Why do you say you had to be either a mother or a bar and restaurant owner?

A: I had three children and I was there fourteen hours a day. Someone has to raise the children, and I mean literally. And for women to assume that they can do both—sometimes that is not the case. Now if you have a business that closes at five o'clock, that's perfect. But the restaurant business? Really! I mean, you'd be foolish to assume you could do this in an eight-hour period. If you open for breakfast and you serve dinner, then you are going to be there.

Q: So you started out running your own bar and restaurant and then got even more experience managing them for other people.

A: Yes. I managed the bar in this wonderful old hotel in Sonoma for seven years. I told these people I could increase their revenue 50 percent, and they said, "You can't put any more people in the bar at night." But I did it by doing a day bar. We had nonalcoholic drinks, and we just had a wonderful time.

Q: It's interesting that you did it with nonalcoholic drinks. That sounds like some of your psychology background coming through. You created a place where people could come to talk.

A: Yes, and that was what I was interested in. I was in graduate school at the time, and it seemed like the thing that was missing in the community—a gathering place. So we offer a gathering here also. So many people up and down this river have drug and alcohol problems, but it's loneliness. They sit in little trailers or RVs, and it's pouring down rain. So we have free coffee and popcorn. The kids come in and wait for the school bus in the morning, and they're welcome to come in after school to play pool. Sandy and I don't drink. It's been eight years since we had anything to drink, but I still believe in bars—in the concept of pubs. I talked to this young man from the OLCC [Oregon Liquor Control Commission] about this room, and he said, "You can have the room, just don't put a bar in it."

Q: This is the room off the lobby?

A: Yes. There are toys, a playpen, a high chair, a pool table. It's a place the kids can hang out. I hope it catches on.

Q: Do you charge the kids to play pool?

A: No, no. I don't charge them for parties either. The Lion's Club also comes here twice a month for breakfast meetings, but I don't charge them anything extra either, the way lots of hotels and restaurants do for meetings.

Q: So they have their meetings here for just the cost of their breakfasts, and that creates goodwill, so they bring their families here also. It really seems as if this place is so much more than just a restaurant and lodge.

A: We want the lodge to be a community asset, a place where people are comfortable. So I tell anybody who calls up that they can use the lodge, that it's their lodge, but it can't interfere with the business, because the rest of the community is using the lodge, too. So on a Saturday night, when we have seventy people for dinner, we can't do a wedding. I won't close for a party, so we work parties in. Last Saturday, we had a wedding in the main part of the lodge, right by the fireplace, but we had it at two o'clock in the afternoon, and they were out by five-thirty.

Q: Did you cater the wedding?

A: I would have, but they were happy to order right off the normal menu.

Q: So you didn't charge for the room, but you had a big group for lunch?

A: Yes. That's when it works the best. When there is mutual benefit. They were thrilled not to have to pay the usual $250 rent on top of that, like when people charge to use the building. I've never understood that. They're selling all this stuff to customers. I always feel good about good spirits. This permeates the wood. All the cars out in the parking lot, the kids running around—people see this as they drive by.

Q: You clearly have a vision about the kind of place you want this to be, and you've put in a lot of hard work to make it real. I'd like to talk about some of the resources you've used to do that. I originally contacted you because you had received a women's pre-qualification loan. Let's talk about that specific resource first. It really let you get your doors open.

A: Absolutely. I just read an article about the SBA. They're underwriting loans for the restaurant business more and more. They haven't done that so much before, but they're really putting themselves out, not only for the restaurant business—which has a 50 percent failure rate—but also for women and other minorities. This is a new program. We have a twenty-five-year loan. Most restaurant business loans are for five years maximum. In the restaurant business, you usually don't even break even for three years, so you can see that with a five-year business loan, many women or minorities wouldn't even be able to get started.

Q: One reason the SBA started this type of loan is that many women don't have the collateral or the credit needed to get a conventional loan. In the past, most women have gone into service businesses where it's possible to succeed without a lot of capital or assets. Now, though, women are starting businesses in all kinds of industries, and they need capital. This type of loan is an effort by the SBA to do something about the problems women encounter if they don't have a lot of collateral or an independent credit history.

A: Yes, and in our case the loan is for twenty-five years, and they underwrote it for the entire value of the property. But I had to write a huge business plan to prove to them that I knew about the restaurant business. We also had to have some money of our own and invest it in the business.

Q: But not as a part of purchasing the property?

A: No. Not at all. The purchase price was covered by the SBA loan. But we did have to invest in the business ourselves. We actually started working on the building before the loan came through. It took four or five months to get the loan, and the people who owned the lodge were desperate to unload it. They had just had to take it back from a previous buyer.

Q: So they were stuck with payments they didn't want. That turned out to be a good situation. You came in at just the right moment.

A: Yes. I think of the parable of the Red Sea, how life is just like that: it parts in front of you, and you go on. When you're standing on the shore, you say, "How could you ever do that?" Well, you just take one step at a time, and now all of a sudden, you're in the middle. And then you work to get to the other side, but at least by then you can see it. And for women, I think you just have to do that. Hold your nose, close your eyes, and keep going.

Q: So many women business owners I talk with say the same kind of thing—that if they had thought too much about what they were doing, they might never have taken the first step. I want to back up, though, to something you said about the paperwork required for your loan. Even though one of the features of this particular loan was reduced paperwork, you still had to write a good business plan. A lot of women I've interviewed who have been successful at getting loans have said that women who don't get loans often think it's because they are women, but many times it's because they don't have a good business plan.

A: Women need to keep trying, even if the business plan is wrong the first time. The business plan I did was exemplary. Terry Swagerty at the Small Business Development Center [SBDC] kept saying that I didn't have to do it that way. He had given me a workbook where you just fill out the pages. Well, I don't do well with workbooks because they don't go behind the knowledge that's necessary to answer the questions. Anybody could fill out the book. So to really understand what would be involved in the business, we went to the library. We spent hours in the library. We got information about local ordinances, payroll, workers' comp. We called up the highway department, and we did a car count of traffic on the road. There's a formula: 5 percent will stop and eat. But you can imagine how much conjecture there is. I mean, who knows why people stop to eat? Maybe you can do twice as much. But there are formulas you can use to project business, and the SBA wanted three years of projected business by the week.

Q: It sounds as if you used a lot of resources to help you get the loan. Going to the SBDC opened up the possibility of the women's prequalification loan and put the business plan workbook in your hands, but how did you end up there?

A: An area real estate agent sent us to a woman banker extraordinaire. On her own, this banker has helped many women get loans. And she and I just went for each other. She's a younger woman, but she's struggling, just like I did, to finish college. I graduated from college when I was forty-two. Anyway . . . she sent us to Terry Swagerty [at the SBDC].

Q: So you really have taken advantage of a lot of these resources?

A: Well, yes. That was a personal one, and I think she could see that I would work really hard. But yes, there are a lot of resources out there. If people just go for it. It sounds so simple, doesn't it? But really, there's terror built into every moment of this thing. It's not like with thirty years of restaurant experience, I didn't put every penny I'd ever worked for into this thing. I was terrified. I'm terrified sitting here wondering if we're going to get through the winter. It's built in. Everyone has to realize, it's never certain—especially the restaurant business. And that's part of the excitement of it.

Q: Lots of women I interview use that word—*terror*. But across the board is a never-say-die attitude. And it's reflected in the kinds of things I know you've done. Like getting down on your hands and knees to pull up carpet and adhesive—when everyone said it couldn't be done—because you wanted your restaurant to have its original wood floors.

A: If you can get those qualities . . . instead of a college education. All these things. I look back at my brashness when I was twenty-seven years old and opened up my first restaurant—I look back on that and I think I must have been out of my mind. But from that experience I've learned. Everyone has to be out of their minds.

Q: Are you talking about the restaurant business?

A: Any business the first time you do it. You can go to college. All this business planning I did, for instance. You know what you can do with it, what it's going to be worth out here in the middle of nowhere. It's mostly courage and conviction and all those things that everybody has. If you want to start a business, you can relate it to something you've already done. Like sticking it out in a difficult marriage, raising children, or maybe [working] three jobs to help send the kids to school—whatever. If you have that kind of conviction, you can do it.

Q: This whole business, right from the beginning, has been a reflection of your conviction that this inn could be successful, even with its history. Let's talk about some of the challenges you faced and what you've done to overcome them.

A: Well, I have a philosophy that when things feel out of control, I'll find something that I can control and look at that. Eleven years ago, I quit smoking just because my life was in such chaos. That was the one thing I could come up with that I could have some positive control over. And that same philosophy can be applied to the everyday chaos in the restaurant business. You focus on one thing. There are more women who make order out of the chaos of raising children alone. But sometimes I do get overwhelmed, and when that happens, I go upstairs, and I cannot move. I cannot even function. And then I come back downstairs with new resolve. And that's the kind of thing you have to do.

Q: All people who run their own businesses face that stress, but everyone handles it differently. One woman I interviewed goes out to comedy bars to help herself cope with the chaos and stress. Everybody does something! What about some specific things that have happened to you, though? You mentioned a problem that you had getting insurance.

A: Oh, yes. We had to have fire insurance to get the loan, and liquor liability insurance before we could open our doors to serve beer and wine. And the more money you borrow, the more insurance you have to have. In Oregon, the farther you are from a fire station, the more your fire insurance will cost. When I heard all this information, I bought the first policy that came along because I was told that we were a number nine fire hazard [on a scale of one to ten] because we are so far from a fire station. According to this agent, there were only a few companies that would insure us at all. That first policy was $15,800, more money than I'd made a whole year when I was raising my kids. We couldn't pay the premiums every six months. I told the insurance man that we would have to pay monthly. And he said, "Well, we'll just use a finance company."

Q: So it would cost you even more?

A: Yes. But we bought the insurance anyway, and we opened for business. And every month, it got harder to come up with that $1,300. The fifth month, I said to Sandy, "We can't do this anymore." So I didn't pay it. Well, I got a note from the finance company that said, "You let your insurance lapse and you signed a contract with us for one year. You owe us $6,000."

Q: Had you signed a contract with the finance company?

A: I'm sure we did. I'm sure in that insurance office that day, I did. We had just so many days to close, and we bought five kinds of insurance that day. When I look back on it now, it makes me feel stupid.

Q: Because you didn't get other bids?

A: Yes. I believed this man who told me that we were lucky to even get this insurance. After that, I started looking around. Tell people not to take the first thing someone says to them at face value. I had an underwriter come out to our business. He looked all around. He looked around the outside of the building, and he checked the men's and women's bathrooms. Then he talked to me for a long time, and he said, "The bathrooms are immaculate; someone's planted all those gardens around the building." And he based his insurance on how much we cared about the building. He could see that I would be just as careful about the building whether I had fire insurance or not. So this man underwrote us for our new insurance policy, which is $5,600 a year.

Q: You got it for one-third the cost of the first policy. So you ended up OK. The underwriter noticed the same thing I did: a lot of care has gone into this place. There's a good feeling when you walk in, and people are welcoming.

A: Part of the fun of a restaurant is that everyone working there becomes this little group. It's like a theater production, and you're all in it together. You've got to have every player back there behind the curtain, ready to go. You can't cut down on the actors.

Q: Your husband was in theater, wasn't he?

A: Yes, he went to Boston University in theater arts, and he was a production manager. In the restaurant business, every night is opening night. I don't know right now what the winter will bring. Perhaps Roseburg [residents] will drive up every weekend and keep us going. All indications are that that's going to happen.

Q: It sure looked like it last night.

A: Tonight there will be even more people. Last Saturday, people had half-hour waits.

Q: Is this word-of-mouth?

A: Yes. We've had hardly any advertising, because I don't have any money to do a brochure or anything else. One thing working for us was the fact that the lodge was such a jewel, people were waiting to see what would happen to it. Now the word—"Guess what? The lodge is open"—is going up and down the river. And because we are personable and family oriented, people are relieved. The last owners sold artichoke hearts and crab. They didn't want the local people eating hamburgers and french fries.

Q: Your menu is certainly a lot more interesting than french fries and hamburgers.

A: We've tried hard to see what the community wants, instead of just opening our business. The community will decide what your menu will be. You can have your own standards, but you have to meet them within the framework of what the community wants. If the community wants pork, you can take all the fat off after you cook it and serve it the best way you know how. A lot of things I make, they didn't know what they were. Like my tomato-basil sauce. People don't have to know what it is to love it. The community loves the lodge—they were ready for it to open. In that respect, we were very fortunate. But at the same time, our menu reflects what they want. Everyone told us: "No fresh fish up here. No one will eat it."

Q: Why? Because there is so much fresh fish around?

A: I'm not really sure. It's certainly easier to throw something frozen in the deep-fat fryer, and that sold pretty well. But one day I was shopping and I saw some salmon, and I wanted to try something new. So I bought just five pounds. Like *that,* it was gone. I said, "These people are hungry for fresh fish." And now we buy enough for probably forty to forty-five orders of salmon steak a week.

Q: Based on your experience starting this business and running other businesses, what words of advice or encouragement do you have for women who are thinking about starting their own businesses?

A: Well, my background is in psychology as well as restaurant management, so I tend to deal metaphorically with courage, with being your own boss. In nature, everyone has a job to do, and certainly it's unnatural for women to be the fathers and mothers both. But since they're doing it so much now, I think they're learning skills that make it easier for them to own their own businesses.

Q: Certainly more now than in other periods.

A: Yes. And I would also say that a successful business has to be something you care about, something you have some personal conviction about. That's my advice. I'm sure there are people who can open up a newspaper and invest in stock without being personally involved. But my advice to women who want to start their own businesses is to choose something that they have some conviction about. And it seems less important that they know *how* to cook or whatever than that they *care* about what they're doing. If they love to read, they might have a bookstore. But they need to sit and reflect on what those convictions might be.

BARBARA LUKAVSKY, *President, Lusan Inc. (Madrid, Iowa) and Merle Norman Cosmetics Studios (Des Moines, Iowa)*

Barbara Lukavsky was the 1994 recipient of the Iowa Women's Business Advocate of the Year award. She runs a beauty products empire that includes telemarketing, publishing, manufacturing, and retail businesses. Barbara started out in 1978 as part-owner of a Merle Norman Cosmetics Studio. Within two years, she bought out her partner. Then she went on to buy more Merle Norman studios, to purchase and revitalize a failing cosmetics manufacturing company, and to become the American licensing agent for Elite Publishing, a specialty beauty salon publisher. In addition, Barbara is a motivational speaker in the beauty and cosmetics field and actively advocates for and encourages women's business ownership.

Q: In my background reading before this interview, I found out that, at the time you bought your first Merle Norman studio, you did not even use makeup. That's an interesting twist. How is it that you ended up in the beauty industry?

A: When I got my start in business in 1978, women weren't really going into business on their own a great deal, so you had to choose carefully the kinds of things you wanted to do. I didn't really have the kind of career that I could turn into a business. I had been an X-ray technician. So I researched the market.

Q: You deliberately went out to identify a business that would interest you?

A: Well, yes. But before I started the studio, I had already left the medical field and gone to work for a headhunter and then, later, for a manufacturer. I started new divisions in both these companies, and all along I was aware that I was building up these new divisions for these men. I was going to the print shop at eleven o'clock at night, and they were calling in to see how the business was going.

Q: You were making them rich.

A: Yes, and all the while I'm thinking: "Wait a minute. I want to do this for *me*." But the opportunities for women were not quite as great as they are now. Things were more limited to maybe something in the service business or retail. And I knew I didn't want to be in service, because in service you *are* your product. I wanted something where I was not the product, something that would sell even if I wasn't there to sell it. My sister had been using Merle Norman and kept talking to me about it, so I went and looked at some of the studios and decided it was a good company.

Q: So you identified the characteristics of the type of business you wanted to own and then went out and found something that fit those characteristics?

A: Yes. And this is something I talk about when I do public speaking, especially with women. When you think about getting into a business, you have to realize that this is something you might be doing for the rest of your life. You need to associate yourself with things you like and enjoy. I know a woman who started up a fitness center even though she hated to sweat. And she lost the business.

But in my case, once I had identified Merle Norman, I didn't have the financial resources to get started. So I went to a gentleman I knew and offered him a partnership for putting up the initial capital. At that time, I didn't know any women with the net worth or credit that he had. So it was really that gentleman who gave me the opportunity.

Q: But you bought him out within two years and then went on to start more businesses in the beauty industry. How have you financed your expansion?

A: I have good relationships with my bankers, and not at just one bank. I think it is important to see a bank as a seller of a commodity. I tell my banker that he sells money and I sell lipstick. You have to have three things to get money: character, collateral, and credit. When I first started out, I didn't have the second two. Now I do. My inventory is collateral. I've had my banker tell me that my net worth couldn't carry any more debt, and that I would have to get more creative in what I was doing. But I take the attitude that I am a benefit to my banker. He would be hard-pressed to replace me with another customer who has borrowed what I have and who has the positive record.

Q: Let's talk about that idea of getting creative. You found out when you were working for other people that you had a knack for getting things started. That certainly takes a lot of creativity.

A: Doing that for other people was really an opportunity for me to learn something about myself. I found out that I'm an implementer. I like to put the deals together. I don't want to strategize a lot. I just want to do it. I think entrepreneurial companies have a lot of people who are like that. They start up, they're undercapitalized, they run around and bump into walls and learn the hard way. And then they get to a point where they're growing and they have to bring management in. To keep that blend of the administrative and "just do it" is one of the biggest challenges for a fledgling company.

Q: Again and again in my interviews, women say, "I really didn't have a big game plan. If I'd known exactly what I had to do, I might have been too scared." And then most of them quickly add, "Now, I don't recommend that other women do it that way, but that's what I did." The fact is, if they had had the whole game plan laid out, they might not have done anything.

A: I really do think that's true. You need to have a bit of a passion, and sometimes that passion blinds you just a little. You can never know everything that is going to happen. I had lawyers telling me way back not to start my first Merle Norman studio. Bankers told me I was too leveraged. But you see, I always knew what was inside of me. At one time, I even went back to work for an old boss on commission during the day because payroll was so tight. Then I worked evenings and weekends at the studio.

Q: So that let you keep the business until it turned the corner. What are some other significant challenges you've faced?

A: Well, the toughest thing is the start-up phase and the cash flow. Being so heavily leveraged, trying to come up with creative ways to position your product in the marketplace and still eat—that's a lot of stress. And that's when I see companies go under. So those kinds of issues are tough, and the personal sacrifices. I've been fortunate because my husband understands what it takes to be successful. It's not an eight-to-five thing. You can tell people this, but they don't really understand it until they get there. I remember one year on my husband's birthday, there was an important business luncheon for him where I was supposed to have coffee with all the corporate wives. But I was in one of my retail stores with no phones, ruined inventory, and my whole staff crying, helping shovel out disintegrated ceiling tile because we had been flooded. And not only that, I had to borrow against my life insurance to get it back open and running.

Q: Obviously, it hasn't been easy for you to get where you are now. What kind of advice do you have for women who are thinking about starting their own businesses?

A: Well, in terms of sacrifices, it really helps if you have a good support system. What is your family situation? Will your friends understand? You might need a new support mechanism. And find something that feels like it can be part of you, because it *will* be a part of you. It will go everywhere with you. It's like having children. The business will have a pulse and a personality.

And always look for new ideas and resources. That's why I'm on a lot of corporate boards. I get a lot of resource information by working with these business minds. Their decimal points are bigger than mine, but the problem-solving process is the same. So I would say do your homework, and then also go back inside and listen to only the voices you can hear. Only you know what you can do. I would never give you blind encouragement, but I would never say no to your idea, either. Other people out there can't know how much you have to give, how high a price you're willing to pay.

One Year Later

Our follow-up interview with Barbara focuses on the changes in corporate structure that will allow her to tap global markets *and* prepare for a future in which she can adopt a slower pace.

Q: Since I spoke with you last year, your business has undergone a major reorganization. Fill me in on what has happened and why you're making the changes.

A: Yes, my business life has changed. We recently opened an office in Boston, and I have an administrator/vice president on location there. I also have a business partner in London who is a part of all this. I've rolled my two former companies together and brought in the man who has been my vendor in London for the past ten years, and he's now gaining an ownership position. So those are all the kinds of things that women in leadership roles in companies have to be abreast of.

Q: With the success you had already achieved, some people might wonder why you did all this.

A: A business is a living, breathing thing. I say it's like a piece of art—it's a work in progress. It's a continual stretch of who you are. If it doesn't change or get a little better, it's going to slide backward.

Q: What have all these changes meant for your day-to-day working life? Are you traveling more, spending more time away from the head office?

A: Yes, yes. So there's a dichotomy that goes on. You spend a lot of years working, and you need to see the vision of the company, and you need to caretake the people in the company. And to do that, you need to continually grow. But as you move through this, you realize that it's more on your plate, and that's not something you're always that excited about. I have a home in Scottsdale, and I would like to think that my life could start slowing down, and I could begin to move westward, instead of traveling to an eastern office location. If these changes we've put in place are successful, these key people will certainly relieve me of some of the things on my plate.

Q: So you have a strategy that is requiring more from you right now, even though you might like to slow down right now . . .

A: Right. I need to get people in place and good market share so that I can hand off the baton. That means having this associate of mine in London become a partner now so that we have a whole-world market. He takes care of the European market, and I the American market.

Q: And it also sounds as if you've selected—or are grooming—some people in this country to take over some key roles.

A: Yes, the person in Boston, and then also an individual on-site here who does the national stuff and works with the new person in Boston.

Q: How do you select people for these key roles?

A: I think it's important that people with you understand your philosophy and attitude about life and how you function. I believe that long-term people buy into your philosophy and attitudes. And people who are at odds with your philosophy and attitudes make another choice about their lives. It's important in smaller businesses that key people understand your philosophy. And I don't mean just a mission statement. I just mean knowing who the individual is and what the heck he or she is about.

Q: So it's a very personal process and, in a sense, self-selective. The people you have to pick from are there because they support how you do business.

A: Yes. You have to develop your people along with everything else. It takes a *lot* of energy.

Q: All this energy you put in: how do you recoup?

A: Well, I just went through a period of trade shows and public speaking and travel. I had a trip planned to Scottsdale, but it wasn't for two weeks, and I told my husband I had to go now. And he said, "But your ticket isn't for two weeks." And I said, "I know, but I have to go now." And I did, because there comes a point where you know that it's: "Save me now. Save the rest when I have saved myself."

LORRAINE MILLER, *President, Cactus & Tropical, Inc. (Salt Lake City, Utah)*

Lorraine Miller, recipient of the 1994 Utah State Small Business Person of the Year award and the National Small Business Person of the Year award, had no business background or experience working with plants when she decided to open a plant store one day in 1975. But, with $4,000 from savings and lots of interest in plants, Lorraine has grown her small start to over one million dollars in annual sales, fifteen employees, four greenhouses, and a steady annual growth rate of about 20 percent.

Q: No business background, undercapitalized for the kind of venture you were starting, and no working experience with plants . . . What motivated you to start your own business?

A: I think the reason I did it is important for entrepreneurs to hear. I was working as a lab technician at the university medical center, and I kept asking my boss what the different blips on the screen meant or what the reports based on our work meant. And he just told me that I would never understand it and to get my woolly head out of the way.

Q: Just do your job?

A: Right! And my response was that I didn't want somebody else deciding how smart I was going to be. I'm not going to let someone else make that choice for me of how much I'm going to learn. I was feeling very suppressed. And so I decided I was going to be my own boss. Otherwise I wouldn't have jumped in my car and said, "I'm going to go find my own place." I think a lot of people who start their own businesses want to decide for themselves how their lives will go. They want to control their own destinies.

Q: How did you choose the idea of running a plant store?

A: Well, the decision to be my own boss came first. Once I had definitely made that decision, then I asked myself what the business would be. And plants was one of the things that went through my mind. That was something I liked.

Q: Did you do a lot of gardening as a hobby?

A: No, I just knew that this was something I liked.

Q: So you did everything. You started a business and learned the field at the same time?

A: That's right. I've been in business now for twenty years, and I'm very satisfied with my decision. I've found owning my own business to be the most creative thing I could have done. It's let me self-actualize and continue to learn and grow in areas I think are important.

Q: Let's talk a little about that. Tell me about the opportunities for growth that you've had.

A: Well, one is other people. Learning to work with so many different kinds of people— my staff, my suppliers, my customers—and making sure that all those relationships are good ones. I'm talking about integrity, the way we treat one another, and building self-esteem in other people.

Q: Sitting in front of a microscope eight hours a day might not have given you opportunities to practice those kinds of relationships.

A: Well, doing it in my own business, I can do it the way I choose. For example, in a bureaucratic situation, you can't do too much about the fact that there is a pecking order. But in my business, I was my first delivery person, so I know what my delivery people go through everyday. And that makes me so much better at understanding what they're feeling, and it lets me know how I can help them if they're having problems.

Q: This is a theme that comes up again and again in my conversations with women business owners. The people aspect of running your own business seems to count for a lot. What are some other areas of growth?

A: When you own your own business, you have to be able to do everything. You have to be an accountant or a bookkeeper. You have to be an advertising agency. You have to know marketing and merchandising. You have to be a personnel or human resource manager. You have to be a janitor. And of course, you have to know your product and customer service.

I have a lot of opportunities to expand my skills. And they give you opportunities to think about things in new ways. My goal now is to expand to ten million dollars in annual sales. That is a quantum leap in my thinking. When I started out I said, "If I can just do twenty dollars a day, I'll be OK." Now I'm doing over $1.5 million a year. But my next transition requires a whole new way of thinking.

Q: Setting goals and going through transitions seems to be a theme for you and your business. Have you gotten help along the way?

A: The first thing I did was get a SCORE [Senior Corps of Retired Executives] counselor. She was tough, but she taught me. She came out to my business once a week for almost a year, and I learned to use a spreadsheet and keep my financial records. And I've used SCORE in other situations also. I've also gotten two SBA loans. But I only got those loans after I had been in business a long time. I got my first SBA loan in 1987. Another thing, though, that really helped when I was first starting out, was that I belonged to the National Association of Women Business Owners [NAWBO]. It was a strong source of support and camaraderie for me. It would have been awful in the beginning without that support.

Q: Let's talk a little about some of the things you've gone through that have been difficult. What have some of your biggest challenges been?

A: I feel like I've been challenged from the day I started. I built my greenhouse in subzero weather. But my most significant challenges have been financial, getting the money I needed. And planning and zoning. I'm building a greenhouse right now, but I had to fight. The zoning allows a used car lot, but not growing plants. And learning to be a good boss has been a challenge—learning how to take care of people and the money too. It's important to me that my employees are in a happy situation where they can learn and continue to grow.

Q: You keep coming back to the people aspect of what you do. If a woman came to you and said she was thinking of starting a business, what kind of advice or encouragement would you give her?

A: Well, first I would say, "Get going. Go, girl!" And then I would tell her to really think about what she was doing and to be authentic. To walk her talk. And to be tenacious and persistent. Like sometimes when I've needed a new permit, I've actually waited until one person went to lunch and then I've gone back to the counter and gotten the permit from someone else. You can't let anybody tell you no, that it can't be done. Stay until you hear yes. That is really critical to success. And I would tell her to have some ways to deal with things when times are difficult. For me, it's going to nature and sitting quietly by a stream. But whatever it is, you need some way that works for you.

One Year Later

Our follow-up interview with Lorraine focuses on her strategy to grow her company to more than ten million dollars in annual sales.

Q: When I spoke with you last year, you had set a goal for yourself to expand your business substantially. How are you progressing toward that goal?

A: What I've been doing is getting myself ready at the starting gate. I've dropped my wholesale emphasis. At one point I was almost totally wholesale, unless someone just happened to wander in the door. Wholesale is such hard work and at such low profit. I'm in a tough business. Live plants are perishable products that need constant care in terms of watering and insect control and disease control. The temperature of the greenhouse has to be constantly monitored. So I'm getting my nursery ready for handling stronger retail sales, and I have been working *very* hard to expand my commercial horticultural service.

Q: What is that?

A: Well, right now we take care of the plants in over two hundred buildings in town, all the way from doctors' offices to Salt Lake's biggest shopping mall. I have about thirteen people who do nothing but come and get a professional watering machine, and they go to these buildings and spend their days watering, cleaning, clipping, removing leaves, dusting, fertilizing—whatever needs to be done. My program offers a guarantee: if something becomes unhealthy, I replace it at my cost.

Q: So you're very motivated to keep the plants healthy and good-looking.

A: The main part of my fee is actually what I call liability insurance, because they know they will always have good-looking plants. And, partly because of my award [1994 Utah Small Business Person of the Year], I've been able to get the local colleges and university to offer a degree in horticulture. So now I'm able to find good people for the horticultural work. I've been working very hard to increase the self-esteem of the service technicians and to elevate the whole profession of horticultural services so we don't seem like janitors, so I can pay better wages and attract more reliable people. I guarantee millions of dollars of plants in the valley, and if all my people said, "Hey, let's go skiing today," I'd be in serious trouble. There's been a disregard for horticulture, which is really a multibillion-dollar industry in this country if you include florists, golf courses, nurseries, sprinkler systems, and so on. And I've tried to change the image, so it's really enhanced my position here.

Q: So you've influenced policy and gotten new programs started. When I spoke with you last, did you have the horticulture business?

A: I did, but when I analyzed my business, looked at it in terms of dollars, I saw that the wholesale was requiring all my labor and making my lowest profit margin. My horticulture was making a good profit margin, so I've been focusing on that.

Q: So you are making a strategic move there.

A: Exactly! And in the same way, I'm getting horticulture service in a lot of wealthy people's homes. And they want not only the big palms, but the potted orchid arrangements and the topiary, so I need to direct my services more toward floral arrangement and European gardens and things like that. What I want to be able to do is have fewer employees who are paid more and are more skilled for this work.

Q: Will changes in service require modifications to your physical plant?

A: Last year I bought a corner property that had been a gas station. It was winter, and the ground was frozen, so I could do nothing on it then. But this year I had my first season with an expanded outdoor garden center that was visible from a busy intersection.

Q: So that is a retail market you're capturing?

A: Yes. Because of that corner lot, my retail sales in May were $270,000. That's double what they were a year ago. And right now the lot is full of Christmas trees. They're gorgeous, and I've got them on consignment. So what otherwise would be an empty lot—since there are no petunias out there—is full of beautiful evergreens. And people have to come in through my greenhouses and look at the orchids to get to the tree lot. And I built a little breezeway that joined my gift shop to the other side of the greenhouses.

Q: So you set it all up so people have to wander through quite a bit of your facility to get from one place to another.

A: I've tried to create a wander. And in the greenhouses, where you would normally have benches lined up in rows, I've created wandering paths and little vignettes of plant arrangements to give people ideas of how they can use plants in their homes: putting plants in really neat containers, having ivy growing down the sides, using different kinds of mosses.

Q: The way you describe it makes me want to visit. You have to have a lot of vision to create the kind of place you're describing.

A: One of the things in my mission statement is: "Create a beautiful place." I love it when people say to me, "This is better than going to any museum," or, "This is better than any botanical garden I've ever visited." I'm in this for the long haul. I want to really build up a reputation for quality.

MARY KAY MARMO, *Owner, West Beverly Cosmetics* (*Chicago, Illinois*)

Mary Kay Marmo, the recipient of a microloan from the Women's Business Development Center (WBDC) and a graduate of its JumpStart program, started her own business so she would have the flexibility to spend time with her children while building a business that could make a long-term financial contribution to the family.

With the clear goal of balancing work and family responsibilities, Mary Kay avoids the overhead and responsibilities of a shop by offering her West Beverly Cosmetics line and her nail sculpting, makeup, and skin care services at a select salon and at home makeover parties.

Mary Kay started out in 1987 by enrolling in cosmetology training and, soon after, in business training through the WBDC. Now, with a growing clientele and her microloan paid off, Mary Kay's planning has also paid off. Positioned to control the growth and direction of her business, she can devote as much time as necessary to raising her children, knowing that her business is there, ready to grow when the time is right.

Q: Let's talk a little about how you got your start. Did you have a background in this area and then decide to go into business for yourself?

A: It's kind of funny because right out of high school I went to secretarial school, and I worked downtown as a legal secretary for, oh, about five years. Then I worked for an attorney on the South Side. So nothing that I did was remotely like what I do now. But as it all turns out, I use those skills constantly now.

Q: Let me guess what those might be—writing skills, organizational skills, typing skills, all that stuff?

A: Yes, right. But I was getting married, and I wanted to do something so that I could stay home with kids and still have a job. I took a one-day class in how to do nails, and that's how it all started. I did nails for everyone I knew in the whole entire world.

Q: It sounds as if you were pretty enterprising. Were you working independently and just telling people you would do nails?

A: Well, the way it started was that I had to practice. I did it for free. I did my mom, my sister, my friends—I did everybody's nails for free. And then I decided I was good enough to go into a nail salon. Really, I barely knew what I was doing, but I had decided this was what I really wanted to do.

Q: This is common, what you're telling me. Many women go into fields based on chutzpah as much as anything else.

A: Well, I always look at it: no guts, no glory. I always thought, "Either, I'm going to do this or I'm not." And the woman I worked with was wonderful. She taught me all the other skills I needed to become a manicurist. I worked with her for about a year. I was expecting my second daughter. I already had my first daughter, so I was working on Saturdays and maybe one night a week. But I was also going to the Midwest Beauty Show, and I was learning more about makeup. And in the meantime, people were starting to come to my house for me to do their makeup. They were calling me and asking, "Mary Kay, could you do my makeup for this wedding?" And I'd tell them to come on over. But I was working out of a shoebox!

Q: Were you charging them for that?

A: No, I wasn't doing that yet. It was just a come-on-over kind of thing. But it was fine. And then all of a sudden, I was labeled as being able to do makeup. Then my mother-in-law saw something in one of my books from the Midwest Beauty Show about having your own line of cosmetics, and she said, "Oh, Mary Kay, you should do this."

Q: Now, when you say your *own line*—that's something I was intrigued by when I saw your brochure. Do you have things packaged with your name on them?

A: That's exactly what it is. There are about six distributors in the United States, and you buy from them. It's all labeling; it's all marketing. So I started taking classes with the company that supplies my cosmetics. They hold many kinds of classes—marketing classes and classes in how to use their products.

Q: So they not only supply packaging support, but also help you learn how to sell. That's a pretty smart move on the distributors' part.

A: Exactly! They teach you how to use the products and how to market them. So it was great. I took all their training. Then I started to work with a photography studio in my neighborhood. I grew up here in West Beverly, and a guy I grew up next door to came up with the name West Beverly Cosmetics. The people here are very proud of the area. They love West Beverly, so I'm going to go with that. I love living here, and I know I'm going to stay here. I started doing home parties in the neighborhood.

Q: How did you get those organized? Did you start with friends, kind of a Tupperware idea?

A: Yes. I'd ask friends to get some of their friends together, and we'd have a makeup party.

Q: But you were charging by then?

A: Oh yeah. I was using my packaged products, but I was moving slowly. I was also in a salon on my own by this time, doing nails. And I was also doing makeup in the salon, and I was very confident. I started working with the WBDC downtown. By then I was saying, "OK, I need to get serious about this, because I really want this to work."

Q: You took the JumpStart program?

A: Yes. Three years before, I had taken a Getting Started business workshop, and I thought, "I would love to take this whole seminar." But it cost five hundred dollars, and there was just no way. My husband was finishing college, getting his master's degree, and I was having a baby. So I put the idea on the back burner until one day when I saw in the newspaper that they were giving out scholarships for the program I wanted. They were interviewing people, and I qualified. I was very serious about it, and my husband was extremely supportive. Two nights a week I had to hop on the train and go uptown to take classes, plus the homework. It was a twelve-week program, very intensive, and I had to write a business plan.

Q: It was a tough program, and you had to juggle things, but the result was that your business plan helped you get a microloan.

A: Oh, it was worth it. I knew it was going to be worth it. I knew that if I took all the right steps, worked through the whole process the way they wanted me to—I knew they knew more than I did—things would work. These women *know* how to run businesses, so I'm going to take every step they tell me to.

Q: And it worked.

A: And it worked. After I wrote the business plan, they had a nice graduation ceremony. Then I was really ready to get some money. I knew all I needed was five thousand dollars, and I told myself, "It's not a lot of money," but I was still afraid to get it. I wasn't sure things were going to work. I did have to keep revising my business plan.

Q: So they continued to work with you even after you graduated?

A: Yes. I took a lot of counseling. I could work with any of the marketing directors, anyone I wanted to. I could go to their library—it's all part of the JumpStart program. They knew I was working toward getting the microloan. I went downtown constantly, and they kept revising my business plan, but they were right. I had to have all my cash-flow statements, and I had to do projections for five years, but it was worth it. A year after I graduated, I got into the microloan program.

Q: You say you "got into the microloan program." Did you receive a loan at that time?

A: No. They opened up a savings account with me, and I put the amount of the loan payment in there every month.

Q: So this was a collateral account you were building up?

A: Yes. They just wanted to see that I could put so much in that account on my own, so they'd know I could pay back the loan. That process was good training for me, because it taught me that the business loan has to be paid every month, and I'll work to do it. I'll figure a way.

Q: This is a very interesting approach. Before you even tried to get the microloan, they were training you to put that money in the bank every month just as if you were paying off a loan.

A: Exactly! They said, "Let's get you set up and organized so you know exactly what it's going to be like." And they threw every punch at me. How much are you going to make every month? How much are you going to spend on your marketing? So when I signed for the microloan, I knew I could pay it back. It wasn't very much money, but I was starting a business within a business, so I didn't need very much money. It was a big jump for me, though. My kids were little, and I was very afraid to take the money.

Q: You've used a lot of resources to make sure you were doing things the smart way—classes with your distributor and working with the WBDC. But I'm interested to know about some of the challenges or setbacks you've faced and what you've done to overcome them.

A: Quite a few setbacks, actually. The salon I was in was having a hard time, so I left for a couple of months. And when I did that, I had to figure out how to make the payments for my loan. That was very stressful. I had some home parties and was able to sell my products, then I went back to the salon, but things are still not good there. And my business depends on their business running well, so I've made the decision to go to a different salon.

Q: So you have another salon all lined up?

A: Yes. It's a bigger salon, and this is a big jump for me. They have fifteen stylists. I'm a little bit afraid. I'll be doing much more.

Q: So, by overcoming this particular setback, you're actually setting yourself up with a bigger challenge.

A: Exactly. I was very afraid to make the move, and I thought, "Well, it is a setback, but it is pushing me to take another, bigger step." But I know I'll handle it. It's a very established salon, and the woman who owns it obviously knows what she's doing, or she wouldn't have so many people working for her.

Q: Sometimes things that look like problems end up revealing new possibilities. What about other challenges or setbacks?

A: Well, the first salon not working out caused me a lot of stress, but there was an earlier setback. When I first ordered all of my main supplies, I had ordered a display case, and it wasn't ready on time. That set me back a couple of months. So I had to get inventive there, because I didn't have a counter display to put in the salon. That's when I did a couple of parties in my home. I had all the stock, and I had to get started.

Q: By this time, did you have the microloan?

A: Yes. I had to make my loan payment. I had all my start-up costs, so not having the display case kind of threw me for a loop. I learned some valuable lessons there. I had paid the man before I received the case, and he was really dragging his heels.

Q: So he wasn't very motivated to finish it up for you?

A: Right. If I had had the check, he might have worked a little quicker to get his money, but I paid him beforehand. That was a very big mistake. I'll never do that again, but it's all learning. I've learned so much from that.

Q: You have learned a lot, even if it wasn't always easy. With all that you've done and learned, what kinds of advice or encouragement would you give other women who are interested in owning their own businesses?

A: I think what I would tell most women is this: if you have a vision or a dream about a business, you can do it. There are ways to do it. That is *the* most important thing. I knew that I could do this somehow, and I had to figure it out. I wanted it—I wanted it so badly that I knew I could do it. If a woman believes there is a remote chance she can do a business, she can. I've started a business and raised a family at the same time, and that was a challenge. Use *every* resource that's available—women's organizations, small business organizations. They're there to help.

Q: This is important for women to hear, because if they're going through a discouraging phase, they might say, "I can't do this." Most of the time, if they get out there and get some professional guidance, they *can* do it.

A: Exactly. And I knew that was the key when I started this whole thing. I said, "I know I'm not going to be able to do this on my own. I'm not going to be able to walk into a bank. They're going to laugh me right out." You need support from other people who are doing this. I have something in common with other women who are struggling and trying to make it. The business world was a man's world, and to enter it as a woman is lonely if you don't have support. But if you have those people who are telling you that you can do it, then you say to yourself, "I *can* do this."

MARY ANN PADILLA, *President, Sunny Side, Inc./Temp Side (Denver, Colorado)*

Mary Ann Padilla's first job was picking beans in the fields of Brighton. Now, more than forty years later, as president of her own employment company and temporary placement service, she puts other people to work and has her own full-time staff of sixteen. She was a recipient of the 1987 Avon Women of Enterprise award (for women who have overcome hardships or handicaps to build their businesses) and the U.S. Hispanic Chamber of Commerce Business Woman of the Year award. Mary Ann Padilla started her own employment firm when she had trouble finding a job during a downturn in Colorado's economy. With a small loan from her brother, an office furnished with a card table, and a background as a recruiter, Mary Ann used her knowledge of how human resource departments work to build a company that now employs more than a thousand temporary workers weekly.

Q: You were working as a recruiter for another firm before you went out on your own. What made you decide to leave the firm you had been working for?

A: I had been working for the same company for about ten years, and I was in a situation where I thought it would be better for me to leave and take another job. But I couldn't find another job. I didn't have the skills. I couldn't type and all the other stuff you need.

Q: But as a recruiter, you were involved in some high-level activities—assessment, evaluation, things like that.

A: Yes, but I couldn't go to another recruiter at the time because we were in a recession. Nobody needed another recruiter. They'd look at me and say, "You're crazy. You left your job?" So I decided to start my own business. I'm not afraid to work, and I think there is dignity in all work. I will do whatever I have to do to support myself. I was brought up to believe that you didn't depend on other people, particularly the welfare system. So you just do it.

Q: I like that: "Just do it." I have heard that same line from many other women business owners.

A: You know, I talk with so many people who tell me how lucky I am. They say that one day they want to start their own businesses. But you know that 99 percent of them won't, because they won't "just do it."

Q: And it's not just luck.

A: Oh, no. It's a lot of work. Sometimes you sit there and ask yourself, "Why did I do this?" But when I started out, I just needed a job.

Q: Once you made that decision—to start a personnel service—how did you find people to fill positions and develop relationships with organizations who needed employees?

A: Well, first I sat in an empty office on the floor, because I didn't have any furniture. Then I called the human resource departments of large companies, and I said, "Hi, this is Ann Padilla, and I want to know if I can help you recruit somebody for your company." People were wonderful. They gave me the openings and I put ads in the paper to find people to fill the positions. And applicants came to my office. I had to ask them to please excuse the office. (Well, I did have a card table by then.) But I placed a person, then another one, and it grew from there. I was a broker, and I knew which companies were looking, because I had just been looking for a job for two months. I had kept track of all the openings when I was out looking and why I didn't get the jobs.

Q: Then you went out and found somebody to do the jobs you couldn't do. That was pretty savvy.

A: Really it was just plain old common sense. One thing led to another, and within three months, I was so busy that I needed to hire someone else, although I really didn't want to. I had intended to do this until a "real job" came along. But within six months, I had to hire another person, and it's grown from there. Then in 1985 I started the temporary placement service, because of the recession here in the early 1980s. We had so many people wanting a job. They needed to pay the rent. Now the temporary placement accounts for about 90 percent of our business. At the time, I knew nothing about the temporary business. All my competitors were working for or had worked for large, national companies that specialized in temporary placements.

Q: What do you think allowed you to grow so much in an arena where you were competing against large companies with more resources and experience?

A: I had already established a rapport with a number of companies, and they wanted the quality of service we were able to provide. They knew me and I knew them. The nationals have regional managers who are constantly changing. They're not part of the community. We've made a major emphasis on being a part of the community, belonging to the chamber of commerce, those kinds of things.

Q: Let's talk about that a little, participating in groups and taking advantage of some of the resources available to you as a business owner.

A: Well, the chamber—that's where I learned the business. I took courses that were reasonably priced over at the chamber of commerce—how to start your own business, finances, how to hire, how to put an office together, compensation. I've learned all of that from the different organizations that offer training. I started at my local chamber, and eventually I moved over and worked with the National Association of Women Business Owners [NAWBO]. And that was wonderful, because I was with peers, and we could share our experiences. It was like having your own board of directors. I'm still very supportive of it, because I think other women should have the same opportunities.

Q: Even with support and good training, every business owner is going to have to deal with some difficult situations. What were some of the challenges you faced as you developed your business?

A: The biggest challenge was competition. When you're small, they don't think of you as a legitimate business—a ma-and-pa operation. It's very difficult to get credibility and therefore difficult to get the business you need to keep going. Another thing that was very frustrating for me in the 1980s was that large corporations had been directed to get bids from woman- and minority-owned companies. So they would give me contracts to bid on, and I would do all the work on the proposal, but they had no intention of using my service. It was discouraging, but once I learned what was happening, I went back to the one-on-one and concentrated on delivering the service they needed.

Q: With all that you've learned and the experiences you've had, what advice or encouragement would you give a woman who told you she wanted to start a business of her own?

A: I've done a lot of that. I like to work with other women who are interested in starting their own businesses. But I only work with the ones I think are realistic and willing to do the work that needs to be done. They need to be realistic about their goals and realistic about their expenses. Don't fool yourself. I think a lot of people have the tendency to look at things from where they'd like to be, instead of from where they're at. If you're going to go ahead, then I think you have to take care of yourself. To be successful, you have to focus your full attention on the business, and it's going to take a lot out of you physically and mentally. Sometimes we forget the most obvious things, like eating well and getting some exercise. At this point in my life, I'm beginning to do so many interesting things that this business has afforded me the opportunity to do. I sit on boards. I do a lot of community work. But for the first ten years, I didn't know anyone or do anything except focus on my business. It took my full attention. And you've got to recognize that that is what is required.

One Year Later

In our follow-up interview, Mary Ann shares some insights into what it takes to be successful in business, insights gained through her own experience and her work on corporate boards.

Q: When we spoke last, you described how, after ten years of focusing almost exclusively on your business, you were enjoying a period when you could spend more time at other activities.

A: I'm in a fortunate position where my business has done well and my employees are wonderful. They can run the business without my being there all the time. I have been able to spend some time recouping, just giving some rest to my body. We forget to do that. I think part of that happens because, as a business owner, I was always so busy running the business and doing my community things. I don't have children, but I have a husband who needs some nurturing every once in a while. So I chose to spend that time recouping, because my business didn't demand the time it used to in the beginning. And now I've chosen to spend that time doing community service, a lot of work with women's organizations, the chamber of commerce, and nonprofits. I also sit on three boards of for-profit companies.

Q: What sorts of things have you learned in that role?

A: Sitting on a board where you're responsible for setting policy of a major corporation but not managing the business is so interesting. We're concerned about the stockholders, as an investor and owner in the company. One of the companies just bought out a smaller company, so we went through an acquisition and public offering to finance the acquisition. Those are things that I could never have learned in college or in my own business because it's too small. So it's been absolutely fascinating. Watching what happens in that process, and the education that goes with it, are opportunities I couldn't have had any other way. Owning a small business, and being successful in a small business, gave me those opportunities.

Q: That's an interesting facet of being successful in business. It can open up the possibility of learning about aspects of the world that you might never have had access to otherwise.

A: That's exactly right. Never did I think I would know what I know now—or even be exposed to what I know about banking, finance, investments, and acquisitions. It's been a wonderful learning experience. And I think my contribution has been that I could look at the overall picture. When you're a small business owner, you don't look at just marketing. You look at how marketing is going to affect your accounts receivable. You look at how that's going to affect cash flow—the whole picture.

Q: That is an interesting point, because sometimes the specialists, like the finance people in a large company, can't get a bird's-eye view of how the whole business is running. You have to do that when you're running a small business.

A: Yes, and I have found that this is a tremendous asset on the boards I sit on. The other people, even if they aren't owners, also have the overall picture. They're CEOs and presidents. Sometimes we—small business owners—go into a business because we know the product very well, and we don't realize that in order to make the business successful, we have to look at the overall picture all the time, not just some of the time. Every decision you make is going to affect the overall business. I have a friend who has been in business now for ten years, and she just went out of business. I could have told her she was headed that way, even though her company had prospered and done very well.

Q: What tipped you off that things were headed in that direction?

A: She was giving her employees quarterly bonuses and pay raises. My attitude is, the company may be doing fine today, but what happens at the end of the year? I don't give out bonuses until the end of the year when we have the full picture.

Q: The year-end information is like the bird's-eye view. It gives you that big picture.

A: Yes. And I've also seen companies that had been in business more than five years go out of business because they didn't change with the environment. You've got to be flexible enough to change. For example, I think we're still in business today because we were able to make the change from recruiting to temporary placements in the mid-1980s when the economy changed.

Q: So when you talk about the "big picture," that includes what's going on inside your company *and* the environment around your company.

A: Right. You have to look at both. If you don't, you're going to be closing your doors sooner than you expected. A lot of people aren't visionaries, but you've got to be realistic enough to know that about yourself and hire someone who can help you. Hire that expertise, whether it is a consultant, a partner, a general manager, or someone else.

CAROL RAE, *President, Magnum Diamond Corporation (Rapid City, Iowa)*

Carol Rae, recipient of the 1993 South Dakota State Small Business Person of the Year award, took her first step into business ownership as a business and marketing consultant. With a background as director of marketing for a small airline, she made a natural transition to developing business strategies for other small companies. In 1984, she founded her own small manufacturing firm, MedVal Technologies, specializing in orthopedic finger splints. When the founders of Magnum Diamond Corporation, an ophthalmic surgical instruments start-up, asked her to consult on their business development strategy, she so impressed them that they recruited her to serve as president of the fledgling company. She agreed to serve for three months to help during the early start-up phase. Six years later, with more than sixty-five employees, more than ten million dollars in annual sales, and a buyout by a distributor, Carol is still there.

Q: Let's go back to the very beginning. Indirectly, you became president of Magnum Diamond because your expertise as director of marketing for an airline allowed you to work as an independent business consultant. How did you get started in marketing and business development to begin with?

A: Well, that's what is so interesting, because it doesn't fit any kind of career path, training pattern, or anything else. I was a teacher. In order to be a good teacher, you have to be able to sell those little darlings on wanting to learn and wanting to participate. So that thought process for presenting information is probably a sales skill we learn in doing our jobs, and then we translate that into other things. That's probably why you find a lot of teachers in sales. Another reason is that teachers are underpaid, overworked, and under-appreciated, so a lot of them choose to leave teaching and get out where they can be more effective. Teaching can be very frustrating, because you're bound by a number of things that reduce you to less than you set out to be as far as effectiveness is concerned.

Q: Yes. With so many forces at work influencing education today, it would be hard to be in that kind of position. But how did you come to realize that you could transfer your skills to a marketing arena?

A: My first job after teaching was as director of marketing for a small airline in Arizona. That more or less evolved into an interest in small-company marketing needs and promoting that as a service. Most small companies do not have the wherewithal to have full-time, in-house marketing, but they're willing to bring somebody in to help design a program. That's what really launched me into my consulting business.

Q: So that's how you got involved with Magnum Diamond. Do you continue to do any consulting with other companies now?

A: No, I don't. I miss it, though. It's very interesting to see how people evolve an idea and how their attitudes seem to play into the success factor of whether they take that great idea and make something happen with it—or not. But I haven't the time now to divert my attention away from what we're doing. Magnum Diamond has continued to grow and be very challenging because we're in a dynamic industry.

Q: Let's talk about that. The company did grow rapidly. What are some of the biggest challenges you've faced, and what were some of the things you did to deal effectively with those challenges?

A: Initially, capitalization was one of the most significant challenges. Making payroll! And the second biggest challenge was probably selecting or identifying the distribution network and whom we would associate with in that. In our case, we ended up going into an exclusive distribution agreement. That proved to be a very good decision in that the distributor was also a young company, so we got a lot of their attention.

Q: Let's talk first about capital. As a technology company with rapid growth, where did you go for the financing you needed?

A: We got two SBA loans, and we were very fortunate to have a state fund called a Revolving Economic Development Initiative [REDI] fund. We were able to get funds from that. It's fabulous, and it works. South Dakota has many value-added opportunities for business that enable small business start-up. People need to realize, however, that this kind of opportunity is just like going to a bank. You need to wade through all the paperwork and give them the kind of information they're looking for. They're looking for principal source of repayment, stability of the individuals—that sort of thing. What appears to be a difficult process becomes much easier when you understand what it is they want.

Q: It's important for people to understand that banks and other lenders *want* to lend money, as long as they're pretty sure they'll get it back. And businesses need to convince them they will. Let's jump to the other challenge you mentioned—product distribution. The company you selected eventually bought you out. They must have believed in your product and learned to sell it well. What do you think accounted for their success with your product?

A: Well, we did get a lot of attention from them, and we were—and still are—very proactive in authoring some of the marketing approaches and educational programs used to market our products.

Q: When you say "educational programs," are you talking about training medical professionals in how to use your products?

A: Right. Basically, the idea is recurrent training for surgeons as they learn new surgical techniques. We offer educational courses, which include a didactic or theory portion, and then a wet lab where the doctors actually perform the surgery on animal eyes. Then we follow up with an in-service, where we work with the entire medical staff and the doctor to familiarize them with the equipment. Another part of the training is an internship for the physician, where he or she will spend a minimum of a day in surgery with one of our selected surgeons. Everything is education, education, education.

Q: Education is the basis for the high level of customer service you provide?

A: I think the wave of the future in everything is going to be recurrent training, because technology and information are moving so rapidly. In order to be current, people have to continue the educational process forever. And in our particular business, a huge responsibility goes with producing the product, and that is managing the risk associated with the use of that product. We have to have concern for the safety and effectiveness of the instruments so that patients get the best care.

Q: You've gone from consulting with a number of small companies to fostering and managing the growth of a start-up that went from no revenue to more than ten million dollars in less than six years. With that kind of track record, what kinds of advice or encouragement would you give women who are considering business ownership?

A: My first question would be: "What is the worst that can happen?" Once you clear the air and answer that question, then start shooting for the sky. If it meant losing your home, and your children going without food and clothing and perhaps their future education, then I would say, "That's probably not a good idea." I think you need to calculate your risks, know what the downside is, and then go from there.

Q: So if you analyze the risks and don't stand to lose those important things you mentioned, then . . .

A: Go for it! We hear all the time how small business is the engine of the economy. And I think that, more and more, it's women who are driving the engine. Women have found out that they are survivors. They have often been the ones to keep the homes together, to educate the children, and so on. And, in that process, they discovered their strength and their power to make something happen.

One Year Later

Our follow-up interview with Carol focuses on her changing role as the result of a corporate merger and her role as cofounder of another start-up company specializing in multimedia product development.

Q: The company that originally bought out Magnum Diamond has gone through some restructuring since we last talked. What have the changes meant for you?

A: As a result of mergers and acquisitions, all the satellite operations have been downsized, eliminated, or moved so that all their operations will be centralized in California, including Magnum Diamond.

Q: Does that mean you will be going there?

A: No. I will stay here, but I will have a new focus on the external affairs of the company. I believe they thought I had been very actively involved politically, and it was probably time, as a corporation, for them to have someone focusing on governmental and legislative issues that affect the business. My new title is Vice President of External Affairs.

Q: So your role is as a conduit of information into the company about what is happening politically that might affect operations, and also of information back out to policy makers about how their decisions might affect your business.

A: Yes. It's really a chance for me to stretch and grow and do something different. It's put me in touch with some interesting people. I sit on the board of the U.S. Chamber of Commerce. The business community is just coming alive in terms of its voice in Washington. It's really been a tremendous education for me. My mentor for all of this has been a woman at Varian Corporation. In the process of trying to identify opportunities to be effective and get information, I met her through the Medical Device Manufacturers Coalition. She has the same job for her company, but on a worldwide basis.

Q: So she's been a role model for you in a new field. My impression from speaking with you last year was that you always learn whatever new skills are required.

A: Well, you know, there isn't a book. Your best resources for this are other people. That's one thing that's been really neat. I've met so many wonderful people. In that process, you learn what to do as well as what not to do.

Q: What are some of the things that you've learned about that don't work? Sometimes that information can be as helpful as the successes.

A: One thing I've learned is that, the bigger the organization, the more muddled the communication, and the greater the opportunity for some people not to be held accountable. It's very frustrating because, when you come from a small business where everybody wears many, many hats, and you're all focused on the whole operation, people tend to be more accountable. They're aware of the challenges and problems and opportunities across the whole business, whereas, in bigger companies, where people get isolated in their specialties, they get tunnel vision. In some cases, they can go down a path for a long time before there's a check, and it may be past the point of no return. The damage may already be done.

Q: So you see a difference in the cultures and an effect on productivity?

A: Yes. But from the public policy side of things, I believe that what was once a huge difference between large and small businesses is changing. Many of the same problems are plaguing both. The large corporations are beyond the days of fluff, and they're having to be very bottom-line oriented, very practical. Those are becoming more of the operational issues, as they are for small businesses.

Q: Speaking of small businesses, do you still own MedVal Technologies?

A: Yes. That's my own little business. I've had it since 1984 and it just trots along. And I've started another one. I'm financially involved and more of a consultant.

Q: You don't like to sit back at all, do you? What is the business?

A: The name of the company is Integrated Media and Marketing. It is an electronic media production company. We're producing a lot of educational presentations, videos, CD-ROM, electronic catalogs—that sort of thing.

Q: What sorts of clients do you work with?

A: We have a major project going on right now with Disney. And we work with a lot of manufacturers. We set the company up as a sort of a virtual company that has all these resources for producing marketing tools, plus we have a team of marketing strategists. Everybody comes to this from a marketing background, so we go in and look at a company that needs to introduce a new product line or change the way they market their current line. We go in as their marketing partner. We put a program together, and we implement it. Then, through our Internet and e-mail order-entry system, we can process orders for them.

Q: Are the manufacturers you work for start-ups or down the road more?

A: Down the road. We're looking for established companies, not necessarily troubled, but that need to be updated. For example, we're working with one company with revenues of thirty million dollars and the potential to grow 30 percent in the next eighteen months. We want the established companies. We're not going in as a problem-solver to start the engine. We like to see the train gone, and just give it a bunch of new tracks. Sometimes we just go in and provide a service, but we're looking for more joint-venture opportunities.

Q: Sometimes the entrepreneurial types don't enjoy staying in a company when it gets very large or when there's a buyout. Their companies outgrow them, but that doesn't need to be the end. Here you are doing it all at one time.

A: My bias would always be to work in a smaller organization, rather than a larger one, simply because I think the opportunity for creativity is greater in a smaller organization. But with the new corporate structure, right now I have both. There is no job description. I'm creating it as I go.

Information Sources

Business success is often an information game. Knowing what to do, whom to contact, and how to locate the information you need all play critical roles in making sound business decisions. This chapter provides general resources to help you find out almost anything you'd need to know in the business arena. Included are:

- State and federal offices that can either provide information themselves or refer you to appropriate offices or individuals

- Private and government books and publications on just about any business issue you can imagine

- Private organizations offering business resource and referral services

In addition to the listings in this chapter, the membership organizations in Chapter 6 are excellent sources of information targeted to individual needs and interests.

The material in this chapter is organized in three categories: federal, state, and private resources. Only brief references to sponsoring federal agencies are included so that you don't get bogged down in unnecessary details. For more information on federal agencies, see "A Guide to Federal Agencies" on page xiii.

Listings with the symbol **EW** are exclusively for women.

FEDERAL RESOURCES

Office of Women's Business Ownership (OWBO) **EW**

- Information specifically for and about women business owners
- Sponsored by: SBA

This office serves as the SBA's clearinghouse and office of advocacy on issues related to women's business ownership. OWBO staff testify before Congress, disseminate data, collect resource information, and work closely with private- and public-sector organizations across the country to help policy makers and business-service providers better understand and serve the growing population of women business owners. OWBO also works closely with other SBA agencies to develop and deliver programs designed to meet specific needs of women business owners across the country. (See page 89 for more information about these programs.)

For more information about OWBO and its activities, contact:

Office of Women's Business Ownership
Small Business Administration
409 Third St. SW, 6th Floor
Washington DC 20416
(202) 205-6673
http://sbaonline.sba.gov/womeninbusiness

National Women's Business Council (NWBC) **EW**

- A special council that studies issues related to women's business ownership
- Sponsored by: U.S. Government

The NWBC was established by the Women's Business Ownership Act of 1988 to study the status of women business owners. In 1994, the council was reorganized as an independent advisory council of the federal government and charged to study women's business ownership issues and advise federal agencies and policy makers on appropriate actions and programs. The council works closely with OWBO, the SBA, the Interagency Committee on Women's Business Enterprise (see below), the president, and Congress to:

- study and advise on women's access to business capital and credit

- assist in developing accurate ways to count and document the number and types of women's business enterprises

- formulate and monitor plans allowing all federal agencies to contribute to the growth of women-owned businesses

- advise the Interagency Committee on Women's Business Enterprise on the development of a comprehensive plan to foster public- and private-sector support for women-owned businesses

In 1995, NWBC cosponsored the National Research Agenda Strategy Conference, which examined current research and discussed areas of needed research. Access to capital, the effect of targeted training and technical assistance, the role of the government in supporting women-owned businesses, and a host of other topics were identified for a new national research agenda. Reports on the council's findings on a wide range of topics are available.

The council is also a member of the National Coalition of Women's Business Organizations. The coalition's mission is to strengthen women's economic position across the country through collaboration among organizations, researchers, and policy makers. (Many of the groups listed in Chapter 6 are members of the coalition.)

For information about the NWBC, its reports, and the coalition's activities, contact:

National Women's Business Council
409 Third St. SW, Suite 5850
Washington DC 20416
(202) 205-3850

The Interagency Committee on Women's Business Enterprise EW

- Representatives from federal agencies studying the needs of women business owners

High-level officials from ten federal agencies work to ensure that federal policies foster the establishment and growth of women's business enterprises. Areas of study include government contracting, access to capital, training and technical assistance, and data collection. The committee reports its findings and policy recommendations to the House and Senate Small Business Committee and the president. For more information about the agency and its activities, contact OWBO or the NWBC.

SBA Publications and Videotapes

■ Low-cost publications available by mail on starting and running a business

■ Sponsored by: SBA

The ABCs of Borrowing, Understanding Cash Flow, Small Business Decision-Making, and *Managing Employee Benefits* are just a few of the titles you can order from the SBA for one dollar or less. Also available are videotapes about exporting, business planning, and business promotion.

How to Proceed

To request an order form and a brochure on available publications, call the SBA Office of Initiatives at (202) 205-6666. Orders and mail requests for the brochure can be sent to:

> SBA **Publications**
> P.O. Box 46521
> Denver CO 80201-0030

SBA Answer Desk

■ Toll-free recorded information about SBA programs

■ Sponsored by: SBA

This is a toll-free telephone line to the SBA office in Washington, D.C. You can call and listen to any of several short, recorded messages describing various SBA programs.

Messages available include:

■ starting your own business

■ financing your business

■ counseling and training

- SBA services and local assistance

- minority business information

- veterans' affairs

- women's business ownership

- international trade

- procurement assistance

Have a pencil and paper handy to jot down the numbers of the prerecorded tapes you're interested in.

How to Proceed

Call (800) 8-ASK-SBA (827-5722) to select from the library of audiotapes.

The TTY number (hearing-impaired) is (202) 205-7333.

SBA OnLine

- An on-line computer database of SBA services, programs, and representatives

- Sponsored by: SBA

If you have a computer and a modem, the SBA's on-line computer bulletin board can be an excellent source of up-to-date information on current programs, seminars, local resources, and other government services.

Using an easy-to-follow series of menus, you can access information and download files on every aspect of the SBA, including application forms for financial and procurement services. And there's a special area for details on programs, seminars, agencies, and human resources in your area.

The best way to use this service is to browse through the menus and explore what's available. You have up to two hours per call, so don't feel rushed. Or you can download a list of all the files available on the system and view it or print it out using your word processor. The filename is SBAFILES.TXT, and it takes just a couple of minutes to download.

Because the 800 service was so heavily used during its first year, a 900 number has been added. You can still view and download all files related to the SBA and the government from the 800 service, but some of the computer software must now be downloaded from the 900 number. Calling this number gives you access to IBM and Macintosh software libraries containing more than 100 programs. You'll find everything from software for writing a business plan to spreadsheet templates and tax-preparation programs. It's well worth looking through.

The 900 number also gives you access to a mail service and other government bulletin boards, including the National Technical Information Service, which shares results of government-sponsored research.

How to Proceed

Call (800) 697-4636 for all baud rates. On your first call, you'll be asked to enter your name, city, and state. You'll also need to choose a password (and remember it). You can call twenty-four hours a day. If you have trouble logging on or need to speak with someone about technical issues, call (202) 205-6400. You can also access SBA OnLine through its web site at *http://sbaonline.sba.gov.*

The toll number is (900) 463-4636. The cost is $.30 for the first minute and $.10 for each additional minute, so a half-hour session is only $3.20, which isn't bad. On-line services such as CompuServe normally charge between $8 and $16 per hour for similar downloading time.

Business Information Centers (BICs)

- Business information available in centers around the country

- Sponsored by: SBA

Located in district offices around the country, Business Information Centers (BICs) offer the latest high-tech resources in market research, business training, and counseling. (For more information about the full range of services offered, see page 95.) Made available through a partnership with private industry, BICs offer access to:

- market research databases

- on-line information exchange and research

- interactive business-training media

- planning and spreadsheet software

- video, print, and CD-ROM libraries

How to Proceed

There are currently twenty-five BICs located around the country. For the location of the one nearest you, see page 213.

U.S. Department of Commerce Information Resources

- A federal source of information and data to help your business grow

- Sponsored by: U.S. Department of Commerce

The Department of Commerce is a gold mine of information on topics of interest to business owners—international trade, patents and trademarks, economic analysis, census data, technology transfer, and more. The department makes its information available in a number of ways.

A good place to start is with the department's automated phone information system and its *Business Services Directory*. The automated phone system uses voice prompts to let you get detailed information on the topics mentioned in the preceding paragraph (or you can also speak with an operator by staying on the line). The services directory is packed with information on federal agencies, including addresses and phone numbers. This free booklet is available from the department's public affairs office, whose staff can also help you with specific questions and refer you to appropriate offices and personnel.

How to Proceed

To use the Department of Commerce's automated phone system, call (202) 482-2000. You may select topics in response to voice prompts or stay on the line to speak with a staff person.

For a copy of the *Business Services Directory* or help with specialized questions, call the public affairs office at (202) 219-3605.

You can also request a copy of the directory by writing:

Department of Commerce
Office of Public Affairs
Fourteenth St. and Constitution Ave. NW, Room 5610
Washington DC 20230
(202) 219-3605
TTY: (202) 482-4670

Once you've started to use data and resources from the Department of Commerce, the next good stop is their National Technology Information Service (NTIS). This service makes available thousands of publications and information products including reports, software, and databases on international trade, health care, the environment, and a host of other topics. Print and on-line catalogs of available products, fax and on-line ordering, and electronic access to government reports make NTIS a valuable and accessible resource.

How to Proceed

To order a print catalog, which serves as a handy reference guide to all NTIS phone, fax, and modem lines, contact:

> **National Technology Information Service**
> Customer Service Department
> U.S. Department of Commerce
> 5285 Port Royal Rd.
> Springfield VA 22161
> (703) 487-4660

For access to NTIS information on-line, tap into the FedWorld Information Network at *http://www.fedworld.gov* or (704) 321-FEDW (3339).

Federal Information Centers

- More help in dealing with the federal bureaucracy
- Sponsored by: U.S. Government

Federal Information Centers were set up to help citizens with questions about the federal government to get off the referral merry-go-round. Specially trained and selected staff will answer your questions directly or find the appropriate person for the job. When you first hear the voice prompts, it may sound as if the only information they have is on topics such as social security and federal job listings. But stay on the line until you hear the prompt to speak with an information specialist—these people can help!

How to Proceed

Toll-free calls can be made from anywhere in the country using (800) 688-9889. If the 800 number does not work, call (301) 722-9000 for help. For TTY (hearing-impaired), call (800) 326-2996.

U.S. Government Printing Office (GPO)

■ Tap into a gold mine of print and electronic information for business owners

■ Sponsored by: U.S. Government

The GPO offers books, periodicals, pamphlets, and electronic information sources on business and other topics related to small business owners' needs. Review the information that follows for specific areas that interest you. In addition to offices in Washington, D.C., there are more than twenty government bookstores located around the country. These stores are open to the public for direct purchases, or their staff can order GPO publications for you if the store does not stock what you want. For the locations and phone numbers of these stores, see page 223.

The store in your area can provide you with a packet of catalogs and a description of all their services. The following information provides an overview of services and products offered by this agency.

How to Proceed

For information specifically on business topics, request the *Catalog of Publications and Subscriptions for Business*. Pamphlets, books, CD-ROMs, and newsletters are available on topics such as procurement, international trade, accounting, health and safety, federal regulations, and more. To receive this specialized catalog, contact:

U.S. Government Printing Office
Free Business Catalog
Mail Stop SM
Washington DC 20402

The printing office publishes more than 15,000 books, pamphlets, posters, and other publications on topics ranging from labor relations to census data. To receive information about these publications, request a book catalog and a subject bibliography index from:

U.S. Government Printing Office
Superintendent of Documents
Washington DC 20402
(202) 512-1800

Subscriptions to regularly updated publications such as *Business America: The Magazine of International Trade* can be purchased through the GPO on general business topics as well as specific industries such as agriculture, construction, or waste management. To request a subscriptions catalog, contact:

U.S. Government Printing Office
Mail Stop SSMB
Washington DC 20402
(202) 512-1800

The GPO also offers access to government information and publication ordering through an electronic bulletin board. For more information about the GPO's Electronic Information Dissemination Services, call (202) 512-1526 or fax (202) 512-1262.

U.S. Fax Watch is a new service offered by the GPO. Fax Watch uses the GPO's automated fax information system to send specific bibliographies, catalogs, and ordering information directly to your fax machine. From a Touch-Tone phone or fax machine, dial (202) 512-1716 and then follow the voice prompts.

Government Access and Information Network (GAIN)

■ Interactive fax system that provides federal facts fast

Would you like to get an up-to-date list of federal contract opportunities for services or products your company can supply? Or find out about current federal loans or grants you might be eligible for? Now, thanks to GAIN, you can.

GAIN, run by a private company (DynamicFAX in Rockford, Illinois), is an electronic database and interactive fax system that leads you through the federal information maze to help you find just the information you're looking for. This interactive fax system targeting small business—including minority- and women-owned businesses—provides instant information about federal contracts, loans, grants, and technical assistance. Then, when you've found what you want, the system transmits it directly to your fax machine (or any fax you designate). It's fast, current, and easy to use.

How to Proceed

To tap into the GAIN system, dial (800) 876-4246 and follow the voice prompts. You'll have to punch in a credit card number, and your faxed documents will be billed to your credit card.

STATE RESOURCES

Each state has different resources available to help its business community. The first three in our listing—first-stop offices, economic development agencies, and women's commissions—are particularly good places for women to start identifying local and regional resources. The SBA women's business ownership representative in your district office (see page 192) can also be helpful; these representatives work closely with federal, state, and private economic-development and business-assistance organizations.

First-Stop Offices EW

- The place to start in your state

- Offices set up specifically to help women business owners

- Sponsored by: State governments

Because state programs (and their names) vary, the term *first-stop office* refers to the fact that these are the best places to start to find out about procurement, certification, conferences, training, special programs, and financing in your state. Some of the offices provide services, and some do not, but all provide referral services to appropriate agencies. Not all states have first-stop offices; if yours doesn't, contact the other offices described in the chapter (state economic development departments and state women's commissions).

To give you an idea of the types of activities or resources you can expect to find, a profile of one first-stop office follows.

PROFILE

The Office of Minority, Women, and Emerging Small Business (Oregon)

This first-stop office in Oregon is a state-funded agency set up to help women business owners in several ways. It operates as a referral and resource agency, providing a packet of information about agencies a woman needs to contact when starting a business (such as the Secretary of

State's Corporation Division to register a trade name) and another packet of information about looking for business financing. In addition to providing these packets and general referral services, the office refers women to sources of business counseling in their area.

The office runs the state's Women's Business Enterprise (WBE) certification program, which allows women business owners to take advantage of a variety of contracting opportunities. In conjunction with the certification program, the office publishes a directory of WBE-certified businesses. This directory is used by private and public purchasing agents to identify companies that can fulfill their organizations' needs for services and products. The office sponsors workshops and training to help women become certified.

How to Proceed

Contact the first-stop office listed for your state (see page 225).

State Departments of Economic Development

- Offices whose sole function is to improve a state's economy, in part by providing referral, resources, and direct assistance to the business community

- Sponsored by: State governments

The exact title and specific functions of these offices vary from state to state. Some are called Department of Commerce or the Governor's Economic Council. Some provide direct assistance such as training and financing, and some work only with established companies, referring start-ups to other agencies. Others may provide only a business information hotline to steer callers to appropriate sources of information or assistance. But all are set up to help business in some way. The following profile gives you an idea of how one state agency is organized and the services it offers.

PROFILE

The Business Assistance Center (Washington)

The Business Assistance Center (BAC), sponsored by the Washington State Community, Trade, and Economic Development Department, provides help to start-up and expanding businesses through its Minority and Women's Business Development Program, Business Finance Group, Small Business Ombudsman, and a statewide, toll-free hotline.

The hotline is used as a point of entry for business owners or people considering business ownership. Hotline staff evaluate callers' needs and refer them to appropriate specialists at the BAC or another state agency, the SBA or another federal agency, or a private business service provider. If a caller is referred to a specialist in the BAC, individualized assistance is provided. For example, if a caller is referred to the Business Finance Group, the finance specialist there will provide support—from identifying an appropriate source of capital to helping prepare a loan application.

The BAC also compiles and publishes information about government (state, federal, and local) and private business assistance programs. The BAC's 250-plus-page book is available free of charge to state residents.

How to Proceed

Contact the economic development agency in your state (see page 234), and request an information packet about available services, or ask to speak with a business development specialist.

State Women's Commissions EW

■ Offices charged with improving the status of women in their respective states

Most states have commissions that work to improve the educational, economic, and social status of women. The specific responsibilities and activities of these commissions are targeted to specific state's needs and therefore vary widely. In general, though, these commissions collect data on women and advise the governor and other policy makers on the implications of such data. They also function as clearinghouses on women's issues and information. Some commissions publish a newsletter and informational materials, develop training programs, and sponsor conferences. As business ownership becomes more common among women, more state commissions have focused resources on women. Most commissions also work to maintain an up-to-date listing of state and local women's organizations.

How to Proceed

Contact the commission in your state to determine what kinds of services it may offer prospective or current women business owners. For a state-by-state listing, see page 240.

The National Association of Commissions for Women can refer you to a commission in your state or provide you with current contact information if the listing in Chapter 7 has changed. Some states also have municipal or regional commissions (not included in our listing), and the association can direct you to those also. Contact the association at:

> **The National Association of Commissions for Women (NACW)**
> c/o The D.C. Commission for Women
> Room N-354 Reeves Center
> 2000 Fourteenth St. NW
> Washington DC 20009
> (202) 628-5030

National Association of Women's Business Advocates EW (NAWBA)

- A network of government representatives and independent businesswomen working to improve opportunities for women in business

This association is made up of advocates across the country who work at the state level to advocate for women business owners and assist states in implementing useful programs for the women's business community. The advocates meet semiannually to share information about successful programs and activities. Described as a state-to-state mentoring program, NAWBA is helping ensure that more and more states recognize and support their women business owners by:

- fostering national recognition of the contribution women-owned businesses make to the economy

- developing systems that will help public and private business-assistance programs share resources

- identifying important issues related to women's business ownership and work to educate the public about them

- helping states develop and implement programs to foster the establishment and growth of women-owned businesses

Advocates are knowledgeable about programs, legislation, and policies that affect businesswomen at the state and national levels.

NAWBA also publishes a useful and attractive calendar with information about women's organizations and events across the country.

How to Proceed

For general information about NAWBA, to order a calendar, or to see if there is a women's business advocate in your state who can steer you toward useful resources or bring you up to date on policy and legislation that may affect you, contact:

> **Mollie Cole**
> **National Association of Women's Business Advocates**
> c/o Illinois SBDC Office of Women's Business Development
> 100 W. Randolph, Suite 3-400
> Chicago IL 60601
> (312) 814-7176

Women's Business Resource Program

- Up-to-date information on whom to contact about business resource programs in your state

- Sponsored by: Ohio Department of Development

The Women's Business Resource Program has compiled a state-by-state electronic database of business resource programs and offices. Anyone can call in and get names, addresses, and phone numbers of people and programs to contact in their state.

Information is not restricted to programs that assist women business owners, so you will get a good cross-section of business assistance opportunities in your state (including those designed for women only). Their printed directory provides information about the key contact office in each state responsible for coordinating women's business issues.

How to Proceed

For more information about the program, or to request information about your state's programs, contact:

> **Women's Business Resource Program**
> Ohio Department of Development
> 77 S. High St., 28th Floor
> Columbus OH 43266-0413
> (800) 848-1300
> (614) 466-4945

State Executive Directory Annual

- A directory of state-by-state listings of government offices and agencies
- Published by Carroll Publishing Co.

This directory provides state-by-state listings of all governmental offices and agencies, including those involved in business development. To locate appropriate agencies, check your state's headings for Department of Commerce and Department of Economic Development. Each state is organized differently, with different agencies and activities, but under these two headings you will find such agencies as Office of Business Development, Women in Business, and Community and Business Development.

How to Proceed

Most public libraries have this book in the reference section. If yours doesn't, ask the reference librarian if it is available on interlibrary loan. Also, tell the librarian what kind of information you're looking for, because he or she will probably know of some other ways to locate it for you.

You may also contact the publisher directly at:

Carroll Publishing Co.
1058 Thomas Jefferson St. NW
Washington DC 20007
(202) 333-8620

State Blue Books

- State directories that cover offices, agencies, and programs involved in business assistance

- Published by: Individual state governments

Almost every state publishes a directory of its government offices, agencies, and programs. These directories may have different titles in different states, but they will provide you with information similar to that found in the *State Executive Directory Annual* (see preceding entry), except that the information will be more detailed with respect to special state and local programs.

How to Proceed

Ask your local reference librarian for the title of this publication in your state.

The States and Small Business: A Directory of Programs and Activities

- State-by-state listings of small-business-related offices, programs, and legislation

- Published by: U.S. Government Printing Office

This book provides information about each state's legislative activities, business offices, and programs affecting small-business development. There is also information about state loan programs, procurement and regulatory assistance, special programs for targeted groups (e.g., minorities) and industries (e.g., high-tech), and trade and export assistance. The latest edition of this book was published in 1993, so some of the listings may be outdated. However, the book is updated periodically, so call for information about the most current edition.

How to Proceed

The directory may be available in your local library, or you can order it from:

> **Superintendent of Documents**
> U.S. Government Printing Office
> Mail Stop SM
> Washington DC 20402

To place a credit card order, call (202) 783-3238, or fax your order to (202) 512-2250. The publication number is S/N 045-000-00266-7.

PRIVATE RESOURCES

Each year, new organizations, Web sites, and publications emerge to document, research, and disseminate information about the growing role of women in the economic life of our country. From organizations that study women's economic life and influence policy with their research results, to resources designed to tap into the dynamic market created by women's economic independence, a wealth of interesting private resources is available. This section covers two types of resources:

1. Organizations: groups that study women (and publish reports about them) and groups that offer a forum for exchange among women

2. Publications: books and magazines for women that specifically address business-ownership issues

The Business Women's Network (BWN) **EW**

- A group that studies the professional and economic life of women

This group identifies issues influencing women's success in the business and professional arena and seeks corporate sponsors to help cover the costs of research and publication of research results. One of the group's first efforts was *The Business Women's Network Directory*, which includes in-depth descriptions of national, regional, and local women's groups. Updated annually, this comprehensive directory is valuable for identifying groups in your area, networking nationally, and planning marketing programs directed to women. The *BWN Update,* a bimonthly newsletter, includes a national calendar of events sponsored by women's organizations and updates on resources available around the country. Other BWN publications cover topics from accessing capital to women and technology. Women can also call the network's office for individual referrals to organizations in their area or referrals on specific business-related topics.

How to Proceed

For more information about the network and its activities and publications, contact:

> **The Business Women's Network**
> 1120 Connecticut Ave. NW, Suite 400
> Washington DC 20036
> (800) 48-WOMEN (96636)
> (202) 466-8212

National Education Center for Women in Business (NECWB) **EW**

■ Leading-edge information on women business owners

NECWB, a women's entrepreneurial training, research, and resource center, makes information about entrepreneurship for women available in a number of ways. (See page 107 for information about the center's training activities.) The center conducts ongoing research that examines issues of women and entrepreneurship, and it is currently coordinating a multiphase research project on the management styles of women in business. Results from the study will be used to educate corporations about how they can benefit from women's natural management styles and provide the groundwork for planning business-school curricula that will attract women applicants.

The center's free newsletter, *The Source,* provides general information about women in business and keeps readers updated on the center's seminars, research, and other activities.

The center also publishes books, reports, videos, and workbooks on women's business ownership issues. Some current titles include *Women Entrepreneurs in Action* (video), *The Woman Entrepreneur* (research report), *Women and Family Business* (article reprints), and *The ABCs of Business for Children.* These products and others are available through the NECWB Store catalog.

How to Proceed

For information about NECWB activities and resources, contact the center at:

> **The National Education Center for Women in Business**
> Seton Hill College
> Seton Hill Drive
> Greensburg PA 15601-1599
> (800) 632-9248
> (412) 830-4625

National Foundation for Women Business Owners **EW** (NFWBO)

■ Gathers and disseminates data on women business owners

NFWBO initially teamed up with Cognetics, Inc., to develop the first comprehensive database of information on women's business ownership in this country. The database contains the results of surveys of the membership of the National Association of Women Business Owners (NAWBO) and surveys of women business owners across the nation. With it, the foundation can make available a wide range of valuable information on women-owned businesses. In conjunction with NAWBO, NFWBO also offers specialized training programs for women business owners (for more information, see page 108). The project's first publication, *Women-Owned Businesses: The New Economic Force,* is an informative, lively, and inspiring mix of statistics and profiles of successful businesswomen. *Women-Owned Businesses: Breaking the Boundaries,* a follow-up report with the same interesting mix of data and profiles, chronicles the increasing momentum of women-owned businesses.

NFWBO also prepares frequent press releases reporting on the status of their research on women business owners. Members of NAWBO receive these press releases—on topics as far-ranging as women-owned home businesses to women's leadership styles—as part of their membership benefits. (See page 164 for information about NAWBO.)

How to Proceed

Contact NFWBO at the address below to order a specific publication, request a list of current publications, or find out how to receive press releases if you are not a NAWBO member.

National Foundation for Women Business Owners
1100 Wayne Ave., Suite 830
Silver Spring MD 20919-5603
(301) 495-4975

Catalyst EW

■ Studies issues related to women and work

Catalyst is an independent, not-for-profit organization that studies issues affecting women in the work environment. Their mission is to effect positive change for women through research, communication, and advisory services. While Catalyst's focus is on women's success and achievement in the corporate environment, many of their findings and papers are useful and interesting for business owners.

Publications cover a broad range of topics, including flexible work schedules, female management styles, and child-care criteria. Catalyst has also pioneered a successful corporate mentoring program, which serves as an excellent model for anyone interested in establishing or improving mentoring opportunities for women.

How to Proceed

For more information about Catalyst and to receive a current publication list, contact:

Catalyst
250 Park Ave. South
New York NY 10003-1459
(212) 777-8900

Women's Policy Inc. **EW**

■ A group that monitors congressional activities related to women and families

This nonprofit group keeps you up-to-date on its monitoring activities with periodic reports and a quarterly newsletter, *Women's Policy Quarterly.*

How to Proceed

For more information about the group and subscription costs, contact:

> Women's Policy Inc.
> 409 Twelfth St. SW, #705
> Washington DC 20024
> (202) 554-2323

National Council for Research on Women **EW**

■ A coalition of research centers and professional organizations that disseminate information about women

The council serves as a clearinghouse for information on women's issues and works to increase the influence of research on policy makers. Information is disseminated through newsletters, reports, and directories published by the council. Members receive the council's newsletters, *Issues Quarterly* and *Women's Research Network News.* Other publications (covering social, economic, educational, and work issues) are available to nonmembers. Publications of particular interest to women business owners include *A Women's Mailing List Directory, Directory of Women's Media,* and *Directory of National Women's Organizations.*

How to Proceed

For membership information or a publications list, contact the council at:

> National Council for Research on Women
> 530 Broadway, 10th Floor
> New York NY 10012-3920
> (212) 274-0730

Center for Policy Alternatives ▊EW▊

■ A research organization focusing on issues affecting women entrepreneurs

The Center for Policy Alternatives is a nonprofit organization with a network of more than six thousand policy makers and activists working to build an inclusive, just economy. As part of that mission, the center has made women's business ownership a central focus of its research efforts, studying policies and programs that have spurred and hindered the establishment and growth of women-owned businesses. Research results and other topics are covered in the center's publications, which include a series on women and the economy.

How to Proceed

For more information about the center's activities and publications, contact:

Center for Policy Alternatives
1875 Connecticut Ave. NW, Suite 710
Washington DC 20009
(800) 935-0699
(202) 387-6030

About Women, Inc. ▊EW▊

■ A research firm providing data about women

If you offer a service or product specifically for women, or if you want to find out what kinds of products and services women are looking for, this organization's publication may be for you. *About Marketing to Women* is a monthly newsletter that publishes market research data on women in an understandable, concise format. Each month, staff members review approximately ninety research studies, gather reports from all major market research firms (Gallup, Neilsen, and others), and review articles from an on-line database of more than 650 publications. From eating habits to reading habits, and just about everything in between, this newsletter can provide you with critical information for designing an effective program to market to women.

How to Proceed

For more information about the newsletter and About Women, Inc., contact:

About Women, Inc.
33 Broad St.
Boston MA 02109
(617) 723-4337

How to Market to Women EW

■ The complete book on understanding and reaching the woman's market

How to Market to Women (1994, 306 pages, $19.95), based on the premise that women are a driving force in today's marketplace, explores how to reach women consumers by identifying target markets, understanding buying patterns, and selecting appropriate media. Case studies, demographic profiles, statistics, marketing checklists, and sample ads are included.

How to Proceed

This book may be available in the reference section of your library. To order it directly from the publisher, contact Gale Research at:

Gale Research Inc.
835 Penobscot Blvd.
Detroit MI 48226-0748
(800) 877-GALE (4253)

Women's Information Directory EW

■ The *Women's Information Directory* (1993, 763 pages, $75) includes information about more than six thousand organizations, agencies, institutions, and publications that address women's needs, including business-related issues. Full contact information for federal, state, regional, and local listings is included.

How to Proceed

An expensive reference book, the *Women's Information Directory* is probably not something most individuals will want to purchase unless it will be used for developing a marketing campaign. If it is not available at your local library, it can be requested through interlibrary loan. To purchase the book, contact:

Gale Research Inc.
835 Penobscot Blvd.
Detroit MI 48226-0748
(800) 877-GALE (4253)

National Association of Women's Yellow Pages   EW

■ A woman-to-woman advertising network

The *Women's Yellow Pages* is a directory (modeled after the phone book) of women business owners in a particular state or area. Business owners pay to advertise, and businesses and individuals purchase the directory as a reference publication. This is an excellent way for women to get the word out about their products and services and to learn about other woman-owned businesses they might want to patronize.

For women interested in becoming Yellow Pages publishers, there is help through the national office. An initiation fee provides a new publisher training opportunities, attendance at the national conference, and use of the national logo.

How to Proceed

To find out if there is a directory in your area, see page 245. For general information and to investigate the possibility of starting a *Women's Yellow Pages* in your area, contact:

National Association of Women's Yellow Pages
c/o Women in Business Yellow Pages
7358 Lincoln Ave., Suite 150
Chicago IL 60646
(708) 679-7800

The Women's Information Resource Exchange (WIRE) **EW**

■ An on-line service for and about women

This is an on-line computer service just for women that includes conferences on health and fitness, political issues, careers, finance, parenting, and more. It also includes a forum for women business owners called the Business Roundtable. Designed to be user-friendly, the service has a point-and-click interface, phone support, and a Big Sister program for new subscribers. In addition to the many forums available, the service holds an open on-line discussion for all subscribers every Wednesday evening. WIRE can be accessed from CompuServe, The Microsoft Network, and its own Web site, where you will find information about women's events and groups.

How to Proceed

Contact WIRE for a brochure or a start-up kit that includes software, access information, and a user manual. The 800 number is an automated system, but you can speak with a staff person if you stay on the line for all the voice prompts.

> WIRE **Networks Incorporated**
> 1820 Gateway, Suite 150
> San Mateo CA 94404
> (800) 210-9999
> *http://www.women.com*

Some Selected Web Sites for Women **EW**

WWBizNet

http://www.womweb.com

■ An on-line information resource brought to you by *Working Woman* magazine, *Ms.*, and *Working Mother* helps you keep current and find fun, useful resources for women

BizWomen

http://www.bizwomen.com

■ This is an on-line information exchange forum for women entrepreneurs

Women Online Forum

http://www.netmedia.com/kelsey

■ Sponsored by The Kelsey Group, this site offers information on women's conferences and related issues

Women@Work

http://www.nafe.com

■ Sponsored by the National Association of Female Executives (see page 164), this site can be visited by anyone interested in finding out about the organization and other topics of interest to women

Books for and About Women in Business **EW**

■ A get-started list of good reading material

Vision, inspiration, and a large supply of nuts and bolts to help with the success of daily operations are all yours for the reading. Books on marketing, management, financing, and communication, along with stories of other women's successes, challenges, and failures can go a long way toward keeping you inventive, effective, and motivated.

To limit our listing to current information, we have included only those books published after 1986 that were written specifically for or about women. This list, though not comprehensive, provides a good starting point for the woman business owner looking for information, encouragement, and ideas. And the bibliographies in the books listed here may also prove valuable in locating other general business books and books on specialized topics.

How to Proceed

Many of these books are available in libraries and bookstores. If not, contact the publisher to order directly or find out where the book is carried in your area.

Body and Soul: Profits with Principles, The Amazing Success Story of Anita Roddick

Anita Roddick
Crown Publishing Group (Random House), 1991, 256 pages, $22
(800) 726-0600

An inspiring success story that proves a business can succeed without following the old maxims, this book shows how business practices can foster social change and environmental responsibility.

Competitive Frontiers: Women Managers in a Global Economy

Nancy Adler and Dafna Izraeli, eds.
Blackwell Publishers, 1994, 460 pages, $29.95
(800) 488-2665

Competitive Frontiers brings together the writings of top academics and practitioners on the subject of women and their role as managers in countries around the globe.

Diary of a Small Business Owner: Day by Day, Dollar by Dollar, How I Built a Profitable Business

Anita F. Brattina
Amacom, 1995, 224 pages, $21.95
(800) 262-9699

This personal account of one woman's ten-year journey—and struggle—to build a business with annual revenues of a million dollars reveals the highs and lows that almost all business owners face. Practical tips on hiring, firing, management, marketing, and every aspect of small business management complement this highly personal tale that should be required reading for any woman contemplating business ownership.

Dive Right In—The Sharks Won't Bite: The Entrepreneurial Woman's Guide to Success

Jane Wesman
Upstart Publishing (A division of Dearborn Financial Publishing), 1995,
208 pages, $19.95
(800) 638-0375

Drawing on her own experience and the experience of many other women entrepreneurs, the author introduces the practical aspects of business ownership with a frank discussion of the attitudes and fortitude required for success. She then goes on to offer practical, action-oriented strategies for solving the myriad of daily and long-term challenges that business owners face, from hiring good employees and selling your service or product to locating professionals such as accountants, lawyers, and consultants. Quizzes, checklists, and resource listings are also included.

Doing Business with Japanese Men: A Woman's Handbook

Christalyn Brannen and Tracey Wilen
Stonebridge Press, 1993, 176 pages, $9.95
(800) 947-7271

This book of cultural literacy offers women a complete guide to doing business with Japanese men, whether on travel to Japan or from a home office. Etiquette issues, dress and makeup considerations, concerns when traveling in Japan on business, and strategies for how to answer personal questions and establish your authority are all covered. The book includes interviews and anecdotes from women who work daily with Japanese men. This publisher also offers *Asia for Women on Business*.

Enterprising Women: Lessons from the 100 Greatest Women Entrepreneurs of Our Day

David Silver
Amacom, 1994, 224 pages, $21
(800) 262-9699

This book profiles 100 women business owners who grew their companies to over ten million dollars in annual sales despite obstacles and scarce capital. Included is a description of the factors that contributed to their success.

Entrepreneurial Women, Book 2: Twenty-One More Success Stories

Colleen Perri
Possibilities Press, 1989, 144 pages, $12.95
(414) 652-6516

This book profiles twenty-one women who have found their niches, from shepherd to court reporter. The featured women discuss practical aspects of being in business for themselves, from start-up to zoning issues. They also frankly discuss the struggles, disappointments, and problems of entrepreneurship.

The Entrepreneurial Women's Guide to Owning a Business

Entrepreneur, 1992, 300 pages, $74.50
(800) 421-2300

A comprehensive guide that addresses the basics for prospective and current business owners. Covers all phases of business start-up—analyzing your readiness, researching your business idea, writing a business plan, getting capital, going to market, and more.

Exceptional Entrepreneurial Women: Strategies for Success

Russel Taylor
Greenwood Publishing, 1988, 160 pages, $12.95
(203) 226-3571

An analysis of how and why fifteen prominent women entrepreneurs successfully grew their companies to over ten million dollars in annual sales. Based on in-depth interviews, the book examines issues facing women business owners. It covers special problems, strategies for success, and common traits.

The Female Advantage

Sally Helgesen
Doubleday, 1990, 288 pages, $14.95
(800) 323-9872

An in-depth examination of leadership styles based on studies of women in leadership roles, this book includes case studies of four successful women leaders.

The Female Entrepreneur

Connie Sitterly
Crisp Publications, 1994, 200 pages, $15.95
(800) 442-7477

Designed to address the unique challenges women face as entrepreneurs, this book helps women analyze what it takes to be successful in business by looking at risks, rewards, and other key aspects of business ownership.

For Women: Managing Your Own Business, a Resource & Information Handbook

Diane Publishing, 1993, 230 pages, $20
(610) 499-7415

This book is a clear and comprehensive guide to issues involved in starting and running your own business. The book begins with a discussion of personal issues to consider when planning for business ownership. It covers key topics on business management, including business planning, accounting, marketing, legal issues, personnel management, and more. Practical and informative, the book also includes some worksheets and a glossary of business terms.

From the Other Side of the Bed

Katy Danco
The Center for Family Business, 1991, 163 pages, $9.95
(216) 442-0800

Written by a woman who has worked with thousands of women involved in family-owned businesses, this book offers insight into business and personal needs of women in family enterprises.

Hardball for Women: Winning at the Game of Business

Pat Heim (with Susan Golant)
Lowell House, 1992, 224 pages, $21.95
(310) 552-7555

This book examines the unwritten rules of business in a culture where men learn to play the game early on. Offering practical strategies for overcoming the disadvantages of a late start, the book is designed to help women become successful players in business. A series of situations and solutions in the authors' companion book, *The Hardball for Women Playbook,* provides an opportunity to practice applying the ideas in a no-risk environment.

Hers: The Wise Woman's Guide to Starting a Business on $2,000 or Less

Carol Milano
Allworth Press, 1991, 208 pages, $12.95
(212) 777-8395

This practical book covers the nuts and bolts of starting a good business on a shoestring. It includes information about how to decide what business to go into, how to decide if entrepreneurship is for you, how to research the viability of your idea, and how to get to the point where you're ready to open. Profiles of women who have done it on a shoestring add interest and credibility to the approach.

How to Succeed On Your Own

Karin Abarbanel
Henry Holt & Co., 1994, 320 pages, $12.95
(212) 886-9200

This book details what to expect when you make the move from employee to entrepreneur, covering emotional, psychological, and social aspects of the change. Included is a unique discussion of the stages women go through in their relationship to money, providing practical suggestions for moving through those stages until money is perceived and used as a tool for business growth and development.

Inc. Your Dreams: For Any Woman Who Is Thinking About Her Own Business

Rebecca Maddox
Viking Press, 1995, 262 pages, $22.95
(800) 331-4624

This book, based on the premise that a business should be an expression of what you love to do, combines the nuts and bolts of business start-up with the central issue of analyzing whether business ownership is for you. Starting with a story of her own progress toward entrepreneurship, the author presents an honest portrayal of the challenges of business ownership, making the point that not everyone is cut out to be self-employed. The rest of the book is presented as a journey of discovery, from Chapter 1 "Getting Ready for the Trip," through "Lifescaping," and finally to "The Road Ahead," where practical guidance is provided. Valuable for any woman who is reassessing her work and life, *Inc. Your Dreams* is more than just a how-to book.

The International Businesswomen of the 1990s: A Guide to Success in the Global Marketplace

Marlene Rossman
Greenwood Publishing, 1990, 192 pages, $19.95
(203) 226-3571

This book examines how women's socialization as cooperative team players opens a world of business opportunity in the changing global economy.

Keys for Women Starting and Owning a Business

Carole Sinclair
Barron, 1991, 160 pages, $4.95
(516) 434-3311

This book looks at special issues of being a woman in business, including financing, discrimination, special opportunities for women, working effectively with men, and building supportive relationships with other women.

Leadership Skills for Women

Marilyn Manning and Patricia Haddock
Crisp Publications, 1995, 88 pages, $9.95
(800) 442-7477

Part of this publisher's "50-Minute Series," this book offers concise information designed to help women develop leadership skills in the business environment. For entrepreneurs and managers, it covers issues such as productivity, collaboration, communication skills, and other related topics. Differences in leadership styles between men and women are also discussed.

Mary Kay's You Can Have It All: Practical Advice for Doing Well by Doing Good

Mary Kay Ash
Prima Publishing, 1995, 258 pages, $32.95
(916) 632-4400

The founder of Mary Kay Cosmetics describes how she started her company with five thousand dollars in savings while raising three children as a single mother. This book is filled with inspiring stories about Ash and other women. It weaves practical advice and savvy business strategy into an account of how Ash turned her initial investment and hard work into a multibillion-dollar international company.

No More Frogs to Kiss

Joline Godfrey
Harper Business, 1995, 189 pages, $12
(800) 242-7737

From the author of *Our Wildest Dreams: Making Money, Having Fun, Doing Good* (see page 78), this book offers fun and practical activities for parents and teachers who want to encourage entrepreneurship in young girls.

A Nurse Entrepreneur: Building the Bridge of Opportunity

> Carolyn S. Zagury, MS, RN, CPC
> Vista, 1993, 136 pages, $21.95
> (908) 229-4545

Changes in the health-care field mean new opportunities for enterprising nurses—both men and women. This book is a practical guide designed to help you evaluate your potential as a health-care entrepreneur and then lead you step-by-step through all aspects of business start-up and development. Topics covered include assessing the viability of your idea, writing a business plan, managing the business, marketing the business, and building relationships that will promote business longevity.

On Our Own Terms: Portraits of Women Business Leaders

> Karen J. Olsen, with photos by Liane Enkelis
> Berrett-Kohler, 1994, 168 pages, $19.95
> (800) 929-2929

The women profiled in this book are not all business owners, but their stories all offer inspiration and practical advice for any woman struggling to find her personal style in the business world while balancing work and personal life. The portraits offer an in-depth view of how each of the fourteen women forged her own path to success, including the challenges, sacrifices, and successes along the way.

On Your Own: A Woman's Guide to Building a Business

> Laurie Zuckerman
> Upstart Publishing (A division of Dearborn Financial Publishing), 1990,
> 320 pages, $19.95
> (800) 638-0375

This is a comprehensive discussion of personal and business issues involved in business ownership, including how to set up a support network, develop (and use) a business plan, analyze your market, and manage your finances.

101 Great Home Businesses for Women: Everything You Need to Know About Getting Started on the Road to Success

> Priscilla Huff
> Prima Publishing, 1995, 368 pages, $14.95
> (916) 632-4400

A successful home-based businesswoman shares her knowledge about how to select the right business and get up and running. Resource listings are included as well as information about 101 kinds of businesses that can be successfully operated from home.

Our Wildest Dreams: Making Money, Having Fun, Doing Good

> Joline Godfrey
> HarperCollins, 1992, 272 pages, $12.95
> (800) 242-7737

Here's an informative, inspiring account of one woman entrepreneur's developing awareness of how women business owners are perceived and treated in our society. It includes success stories, resources, and a wealth of good ideas about what needs to happen to improve the status of women business owners.

The Smart Woman's Guide to Starting a Business

> Vickie Montgomery
> Career Press, 1994, 216 pages, $14.95
> (800) 227-3371

This book covers every key topic women need to understand to successfully start, manage, and grow a business. Using a down-to-earth, problem-solving style, this book answers questions and provides advice on everything—start-up, marketing, daily operations, managing growth, and more.

Strategies for Small Business

Jane Applegate
Plume (Penguin Group), 1995, 251 pages, $12.95
(800) 253-6476

Written by a woman business owner and an advocate of women's business ownership, this book is directed to both men and women business owners. But along with the straightforward discussion of almost every topic of value to all business owners (from financing and international trade to management and market strategies) this book includes several women's resource listings. Many women's business assistance programs are mentioned throughout the chapters.

Success Strategies for Women in Business

Jean Ramsey-Wilkes
Kendall-Hunt, 1993, 224 pages, $19.95
(800) 228-0810

For women business owners and women working in the corporate environment, this book begins with a discussion of gender politics and then goes on to cover key issues related to effective self-management. From career development and communicating in the workplace to juggling career and personal life and goal-setting, *Success Strategies* offers analysis and practical solutions to the challenges women encounter in the business environment.

The Web of Inclusion

Sally Helgesen
Currency Doubleday, 1995, 320 pages, $24.95
(800) 323-9872

From the author of *The Female Advantage,* this book uses five case studies to illustrate how and why an inclusive web paradigm of cooperation, collaboration, and flexibility—the natural style women bring to relationships—works so well in our emerging information-based economy.

What Mona Lisa Knew: A Women's Guide to Getting Ahead in Business by Lightening Up

Barbara Mackoff
Lowell House, 1991, 151 pages, $9.95
(310) 552-7555

Mackoff's book is a compelling look at why being too serious can keep you from getting ahead. Sprinkled with accounts of the author's own experience, anecdotes about other women, and research data, this book offers practical strategies for making the power of humor work for you. It covers how humor can be used to more effectively manage others, work with men, and cultivate a happy home life.

When the Canary Stops Singing: Women's Perspective on Transforming Business

Pat Barrentine, ed.
Berrett-Kohler, 1994, 280 pages, $24.95
(800) 929-2929

In this selection of writings by women entrepreneurs, consultants, and executives, women write of the need to reinvent the business culture to create a humane workplace where individuals *and* organizations can thrive. The essays offer perspectives on issues as far-ranging as how intuition is used to build business success and how men's and women's styles can interact harmoniously.

Woman to Woman: Street Smarts for Women Entrepreneurs

Geraldine Larkin
Prentice Hall, 1993, 265 pages, $14.95
(800) 947-7700

Woman to Woman is a fast track for entrepreneurs who want to do it right the first time around. Written by a seasoned entrepreneur and women's business trainer, this book lets you learn from the author's frank discussion of her own mistakes and the mistakes of her clients. Covering all the practical aspects of business—from inception and financing to marketing and management—it also includes chapters on family involvement in business, retirement planning, and how to live a happy, healthy, and successful life.

Woman's Guide to Starting a Business

Claudia Jessup and Genie Chipps
Henry Holt & Co., 1991, 432 pages, $14.95
(800) 488-5233

This four-part guide to getting started, surviving, and thriving as a business owner includes a blueprint for effective planning, a start-up guide, profiles of successful women entrepreneurs, and a resource section.

A Woman's Guide to Starting a Small Business

Mary Lester
Pilot Books, 1989, 32 pages, $3.95
(516) 422-2225

This is a guide to developing a low-overhead service business, with a twenty-point beginner's checklist.

Women Entrepreneurs: 33 Personal Stories of Success

Linda Pinson and Jerry Jinnett
Upstart Publishing (A division of Dearborn Financial Publishing), 1993,
244 pages, $19.95
(800) 638-0375

A diverse group of women business owners tell their stories about getting started, overcoming hardship, and serving as role models for others. History and statistics about women in business, as well as a resource directory, are included. These authors have several other excellent books published by Upstart on home-based businesses, marketing, business plan development, and others. If you call to request a catalog from Upstart, it will include information about their other titles.

Women Entrepreneurs, Networking and Sweet Potato Pie: Creating Capital in the 21st Century

Delores Ratcliff
Corrita Communications, 1994, 143 pages, $16.95
(213) 624-8639

This resource guide for women business owners includes home-based business planning ideas, a business plan outline, marketing information, and management and survival tips.

Women in Business: Perspectives on Women Entrepreneurs

Sheila Allen and Carole Truman, eds.
International Thomson, Publishing, 1993, 221 pages, $23.95
(800) 842-3636

This book brings together leading researchers' interpretations of data on women entrepreneurs, discussing the relationships between women's styles on and off the job and how business and family life affect each other.

Work of Her Own: A Woman's Guide to Success Off the Career Track

Susan Wittig Albert, Ph.D.
Putnam Publishing Group, 1994, 179 pages, $12.95
(800) 847-5515

If you are looking for inspiring stories about women who gave up successful careers to find more meaning in life, these thoughtful, practical accounts will provide you with guidance and courage. Not all of the women profiled went into business for themselves, but the portraits offer insight and practical advice about women in transition.

Magazines for Women and Entrepreneurs

■ Regular installments of ideas, information, and inspiration

When you're busy just trying to make it through each day or week, getting a regular dose of new ideas can do a lot to boost your morale, energy, and effectiveness.

Some of the best magazines specifically aimed at businesswomen are available as membership benefits from associations listed in Chapter 6. Because these association magazines are not available on the newsstand or by subscription, we have not included them in this list. Most associations will send you a sample copy of a publication when you request membership information.

How to Proceed

Many of the magazines listed here are available in libraries or at newsstands. For subscription information, call or write the publisher.

Black Entrepreneur

Earl G. Graves Publishing Co., Inc.
130 Fifth Ave.
New York NY 10011
(800) 727-7777
Annual subscription: 12 issues, $16.95

Using real companies and people as examples, this magazine covers a wide range of business topics—money management, marketing strategies, daily operations, hiring, and more. Regular departments such as "MoneyWise," "TechWatch," and "PowerPlay" offer quick tips and overviews on the issues.

Entrepreneur

125 Armstrong Rd.
Des Plaines IL 60018
(800) 421-2300
Annual subscription: 12 issues, $19.97

Entrepreneur provides information on all aspects of starting and running a business. Pro-files, resource listings, in-depth articles, and quick tips address topics from technology and marketing to business financing—and everything in between. Topics and resources of interest to women business owners are frequently included.

Home Office Computing

> P.O. Box 53561
> Boulder CO 80322
> (800) 288-7812
> Annual subscription: 12 issues, $19.97

This magazine covers diverse issues of interest to home-based business owners. *HOC* focuses on hardware and software selection, but many other topics are covered—time man-agement, efficient home office setup, stress management, where to find capital for home-based businesses, and more.

INC.

> The Goldhirst Group
> 38 Commercial Wharf
> Boston MA 02110
> (800) 234-0999
> Annual subscription: 12 issues, $19

INC. offers practical information selected to help business owners solve the short- and long-term challenges of starting, running, and growing a business. Regular features include in-depth profiles of businesses and their owners, along with discussions of tech-nology, marketing, financing, and a host of other topics. One issue each year profiles top women-owned businesses.

Nation's Business

U.S. Chamber of Commerce
1615 H St. NW
Washington DC 20062-2000
(800) 727-5869
Annual subscription: 12 issues, $22

Published by the U.S. Chamber of Commerce, this magazine covers political, legislative, technical, and management issues related to all phases of business ownership. Frequent profiles of businesses, both large and small, provide insight into the day-to-day and long-term concerns of people running their own businesses. Data, resources, and articles about women in business are frequent. Readers can also send in questions to get answers from experts.

Winning Strategies

P.O. Box 118007
Chicago IL 60611
(800) 664-2121
Annual subscription: 6 issues, $25

Winning Strategies is targeted to the financial and business interests of women, offering practical advice about starting a business, investments, and financial management. Women writers for the magazine function as mentors, providing personal profiles, accounts of other women's experience, encouragement, and lots of practical ideas and suggestions.

Women's Business Exclusive **EW**

3528 Torrance Blvd., Suite 101
Torrance CA 90503-4803
(310) 540-9398
Annual subscription: 6 issues, $39

If you want to keep up on public policy, new resources for women entrepreneurs in the public and private sector, and events for and about women in business, this eight-page, bimonthly newsletter is a gold mine. In addition to quick takes on what's going on around the country, the magazine includes in-depth profiles, interviews, and articles that focus on key issues such as procurement, affirmative action, financing, and training. This company also publishes *Minority Business Entrepreneur*, which covers topics of interest to minority-owned business owners.

Working Woman **EW**

> P.O. Box 3274
> Harlan IA 51593
> (800) 234-9675
> Annual subscription: 12 issues, $11.97

Working Woman is *the* newsstand magazine for women entrepreneurs. For more and more women, going to work each day means going to their own businesses, and this magazine has followed and supported this trend. In-depth articles, tips, and resources are useful to employees and the self-employed alike, but special features focusing on women's business ownership issues and a "Dear Abby" column by small-business writer Jane Applegate offer specific, practical ideas for the self-employed. One issue a year features successful women entrepreneurs.

Training, Technical Assistance, and Counseling

ree, low-cost, and specially designed training, counseling, and technical assistance abound for women entrepreneurs. The material in this chapter is organized into three categories: federal resources, state resources, and private resources. Listings with the symbol **EW** describe programs or resources that are specifically for women. This section will help you find sources of:

- One-on-one counseling—everything from one-time sessions to long-term associations

- Training—classes, seminars, and workshops

- Technical assistance—focusing on specific areas of business such as financing, computer setup, accounting, marketing, and staffing

Other listed resources, while not for women only, offer excellent opportunities that you should not overlook.

Only brief references to sponsoring federal agencies are included so that you don't get bogged down in unnecessary details. For more information on such agencies, see "A Guide to Federal Agencies," on page xiii.

The definitions of common terms on page xvi may also be helpful as you read this chapter.

FEDERAL RESOURCES

Women's Network for Entrepreneurial Training (WNET) Mentorship Program **EW**

- A year-long program that matches successful businesswomen with owners of growing businesses

- Sponsored by: SBA's Office of Women's Business Ownership (OWBO)

Wouldn't it be wonderful to have a successful, experienced businesswoman available for free advice and problem-solving every month for a year? OWBO has just such a program. WNET matches successful women entrepreneurs with owners of growing businesses in a yearlong association.

The businesswoman, called a mentor, will meet with you approximately four hours each month for a year to give you advice and suggestions on just about any aspect of running your business. She serves as a coach, sounding board, guide, counselor, and critic, providing you with a wealth of expertise, experience, and savvy. There is no charge to participate in the program, but you must:

- have been in business at least one year

- be ready to expand

- demonstrate strong entrepreneurial skills

- show potential for continued success

- be willing to spend approximately four hours a month with your mentor

- demonstrate a willingness to put into practice the advice you receive

To qualify as a volunteer mentor, a woman must:

- have founded her own company

- have been in business for at least five years

- be willing to commit four hours a month for one year

WNET with a Twist, a regularly scheduled group problem-solving and brainstorming session with experienced and novice entrepreneurs, provides another way for women to participate in mentoring experiences.

How to Proceed

For information about WNET, contact your SBA women's business ownership representative. (See page 192 to locate a representative in your area.)

Specialized Training Programs EW

- Training in the areas of financing, procurement, and international trade presented in a series of regional seminars
- Sponsored by: SBA's Office of Women's Business Ownership (OWBO)

If you want to find out what it really takes to get a business loan, or how to take the plunge into international trade, OWBO's specialized training programs will interest you. Training sessions are customized by OWBO field representatives to meet specific local needs by using local sponsors and experts.

The training sessions usually last one day, and fees vary (but are usually low). If a program is presented only by the SBA, it is often free. Current topics include:

- Access to Capital
- Meet the Lender
- Selling to the Federal Government
- Women Going International (international trade)

How to Proceed

To receive information about upcoming conferences in your area, contact your local women's business ownership representative (see page 192) or, if you have access to the Internet, check SBA OnLine (page 47) for dates and locations of upcoming seminars.

Women's Business Development Centers EW

■ Demonstration sites around the country that offer in-depth training and assistance

■ Sponsored by: SBA's Office of Women's Business Ownership (OWBO)

Thanks to OWBO, there are now more than fifty women's demonstration sites across the country.

These demonstration sites, set up to provide long-term local training and counseling, are private organizations with people qualified to help women find capital, develop a business plan, set up financial management systems, design marketing programs, and successfully manage a host of issues critical to business success.

These sites offer longer-term and more in-depth learning opportunities than OWBO's specialized training conferences. Services, training, and costs vary from one demonstration site to another.

To give you an idea of the types of opportunities available at these training centers, we have profiled one site, the Women's Business Development Center (WBDC) in Chicago, which is the parent organization of three demonstration sites in Illinois. (Keep in mind that each training site addresses local needs, so specific programs will vary.)

PROFILE

Chicago's Women's Business Development Center
(WBDC)

WBDC is a place to which prospective, emerging, and established women business owners can go to get comprehensive business training, personalized counseling, and assistance for specific technical issues facing their businesses. The center offers the Fast Track Workshop Series and the JumpStart Business Certificate Program for women planning to go into business or in the early stages of business development. Individualized counseling is available for established business owners who need assistance in specific areas including marketing, financing, management, and just about any task facing the small business owner. In addition, WBDC coordinates a mentorship program that allows owners to receive guidance, encouragement, and management expertise from experienced women business owners. Women's Business Enterprise (WBE) certification is available, and, in conjunction with the certification program, the center offers specific workshops on how to win contracts in the public and private sectors. The center runs its own microloan program for center graduates and provides loan guarantees to help women obtain bank financing.

Each year, the center also sponsors an Entrepreneurial Women's Conference and a Women's Business Buyers Mart that features successful businesswomen as speakers, offers women an opportunity to meet government and corporate purchasing agents, and provides a venue for women to exhibit their products and services.

How to Proceed

To find a demonstration site in your area, check the state-by-state listing on page 198. If there is not a site near you, periodically check with OWBO headquarters to find out if a new site is being added in your area. OWBO can be contacted at:

Office of Women's Business Ownership
Small Business Administration
409 Third St. SW, 6th Floor
Washington DC 20416
(202) 205-6673

American Indian Women's Business Assistance Project: A Specialized Demonstration Project EW

- Targets Native American women for business start-up and expansion

- Sponsored by the National Center for Indian Enterprise Development and the SBA's Office of Women's Business Ownership

This innovative new project helps Native American women with pre-business strategy development, actual start-up, and one-on-one technical assistance once an enterprise is up and running. The program includes opportunities for women to meet successful Native American women business owners and certifies participants so they are eligible to bid on government contracts as minority- and women-owned enterprises. The program is currently available in the Southwest, Pacific, and Northwest regions.

How to Proceed

For more information about the programs and to receive an application to participate, contact:

> **National Center for Indian Enterprise Development**
> **American Indian Women's Business Assistance Project—Northwest Region**
> 100 W. Harrison
> S. Tower, Suite 530
> Seattle WA 98119
> (206) 285-2870

> **National Center for Indian Enterprise Development**
> **American Indian Women's Business Assistance Project—Pacific Region**
> 9650 Flair Dr., Suite 303
> El Monte CA 91731-3008
> (818) 442-3701

> **National Center for Indian Enterprise Development**
> **American Indian Women's Business Assistance Project—Southwest Region**
> 953 E. Juanita Ave.
> Mesa AZ 85204
> (602) 545-1298

SCORE Women's Business Counselors EW

■ Free counseling from retired women executives

■ Sponsored by: Senior Corps of Retired Executives (SCORE)

SCORE provides free one-on-one counseling by a corps of volunteers nationwide. (The name is somewhat misleading. Although most of the volunteers are retired, more than 20 percent of them are employed full-time.) SCORE runs a program open to all business owners, but there is also a cadre of retired women executives called Women's Business Ownership Coordinators, who specialize in advising women business owners. SCORE tries to match a client's specific needs with a counselor experienced in a comparable line of business. (The coordinators also work to recruit women counselors because they know that many women business owners enjoy working with women.) Your counselor will help you identify and solve basic management problems as well as advise you on other business decisions. The counseling takes place either at your office or at a SCORE chapter office.

How to Proceed

To find a SCORE Women's Business Counselor in your area, contact the women's business coordinator for your region from the list on page 211. These counselors change frequently; for the latest information, contact the national SCORE coordinator, the women's SBA representative for your region from the list on page 192, or the Washington, D.C., office of the SBA's Office of Women's Business Ownership at (202) 205-6673.

To receive general SCORE counseling from any one of their counselors (not necessarily a woman), you can find local offices listed under SCORE in the white pages of your telephone book.

To receive more general information about SCORE services or to identify a SCORE counselor in your area, contact:

National SCORE Office
409 Third St. SW, Suite 5900
Washington DC 20416
(202) 205-6762

Small Business Institutes (SBIs)

- Free consulting services for serving as a case study for qualified business students

- Sponsored by: SBA

Small Business Institutes provide free business consulting with a twist: the consultants are graduate and undergraduate business students who work under expert faculty guidance to help you solve management problems. This program gives students real-world experience with specific business problems such as computerizing an accounting system, developing a personnel policy, starting a market study, or designing a production plan.

The emphasis of the program is to help you find practical, realistic, and affordable solutions to real problems or challenges facing your company. At the conclusion of the project, the student will provide you with an oral presentation and a written report detailing a course of action.

According to SBA figures, more than 150,000 businesses and 370,000 students from more than five-hundred colleges and universities have benefited from the SBI program. To find out if there is an institute in your area, contact your regional SBA office (see page 189).

Small Business Development Centers (SBDCs)

- A comprehensive program of counseling, workshops, classes, and seminars at seven hundred centers around the country

- Sponsored by: SBA

SBDCs, sponsored by the SBA and an educational or state or local government agency, offer one-stop shopping for business owners who need help. Any business owner—or prospective owner—can go to one of the nearly seven hundred centers around the country and get involved in pre-business workshops, one-on-one business counseling, classes and seminars on business start-up, financing, management, and marketing. Some SBDCs have long-term training programs for businesses in which a group of business owners go through a comprehensive program together that can last up to a year. People who have been through this program swear by it.

Counseling services are free. Fees may be charged for seminars, classes, workshops, and specialized training programs.

How to Proceed

To locate an SBDC in your area, contact the SBDC director's office in your state (see page 205).

Business Information Centers (BICs)

- Business resources and counseling at specialized information centers around the country

- Sponsored by: SBA

Need the latest market research data in your industry? Wish you had a computerized tutorial for that spreadsheet program you can't get the hang of? Need to talk with someone about a difficult personnel problem? Odds are, you'll be able to find that—and a lot more—at a Business Information Center (BIC).

BICs offer a combination of high-tech business resources and one-on-one counseling from SCORE executives to help business owners increase their productivity and competitiveness. If you don't live close enough to a center to visit personally, assistance from on-line databases and phone counselors is available. Face-to-face counseling may also be available to you even if you can't make it in to a center. The Seattle BIC, for example, sends SCORE counselors out on circuit rides to make their services more widely available.

Made possible through a partnership with private industry, BICs offer access to:

- market research databases

- on-line information

- interactive business training media

- planning and spreadsheet software

- video, print, and CD-ROM libraries

How to Proceed

There are currently twenty-five regional BICs. To locate the one closest to you, see page 213.

Assistance for Economically Disadvantaged Minorities: The 7(j) Program

- Long-term technical assistance for economically disadvantaged minorities and socially and economically disadvantaged individuals

- Sponsored by: SBA

If you are one of the 400,000 or so minority women that the federal government estimates are also business owners, or if you are socially and economically disadvantaged, you may be eligible for up to nine years of free or low-cost technical assistance in accounting, marketing, proposal preparation, or other areas specific to your industry.

This technical assistance is provided through the 7(j) Management and Technical Assistance Program, a special program for what the SBA designates as 8(a) businesses—businesses that can't compete effectively against others in their field because the owners don't have access to the same capital and credit opportunities as their competitors.

The first step in taking advantage of the 7(j) program is to find out if you qualify as an 8(a) business. If you are African American, Hispanic, Native American, or of Asian descent, you are halfway there. These ethnic and racial minorities (and others designated periodically) are automatically considered socially disadvantaged. If you can also show economic disadvantage (and here the SBA considers both personal and business financial information in making a determination) you can become certified as an 8(a) firm. If you do not belong to a group automatically considered socially disadvantaged, you may still qualify as an 8(a) firm if you can show a pattern of both economic and social disadvantage.

To apply for 8(a) certification, you must fill out a detailed application and return it to an SBA office. Applications are considered on a case-by-case basis. If approved, you will be eligible for 7(j) assistance and other types of help through the SBA.

If you become 8(a) certified, contact the Business Opportunity Specialist in your district office's Minority Small Business Office to discuss your specific technical assistance needs. Also, if you have been in business in your area of specialization for at least one year and can provide a business service in accounting, marketing, or certain other areas, consider applying to the program to become a contracted provider to 7(j) firms. Most 7(j) providers are selected through a competitive process.

How to Proceed

For information about 7(j) or 8(a) certification, contact your regional SBA office (see page 189).

To receive information about becoming a provider and to be put on the SBA's Solicitation Mailing List, contact:

Director, Division of Management and Technical Assistance
Office of Procurement and Grants Management
U.S. Small Business Administration
409 Third St. SW, 5th Floor
Washington DC 20416
(202) 205-6621

Training and Technical Assistance for Minorities

- A national network of offices that provide technical assistance to all minority business owners

- Sponsored by: U.S. Department of Commerce Minority Business Development Agency (MBDA)

According to federal government figures, nearly 400,000 women business owners are also members of minority groups. If you're one of these women, you are eligible for some specialized business assistance through the MBDA.

The MBDA was set up by the Department of Commerce to foster the establishment and growth of minority-owned businesses. (The MBDA's definition of minority includes African Americans, Hispanic Americans, Native Americans, Asian Americans, and Hasidic Jews.)

MBDA Services

The MBDA has six regional offices that oversee Minority Business Development Centers (MBDCs) in their areas. The MBDCs—about one hundred nationwide—are independent businesses or organizations (for-profit and nonprofit private businesses, educational institutions, state and local agencies, or Native American tribes) that receive partial funding from the MBDA to provide low-cost technical assistance to the minority business community. Each MBDC is staffed with business specialists who have expertise in:

- business planning
- marketing
- financing
- management counseling
- bid estimation and bonding assistance for construction projects
- procurement
- franchising
- international trade

To give you an idea what you can expect, following is a profile of MBDC Impact Business Consultants.

PROFILE

Impact Business Consultants

Impact offers a free initial consultation to discuss the nature of your business and the areas in which you need assistance. Based on that first meeting, a contract is drawn up specifying the work to be accomplished together.

Impact charges a low hourly fee for their consulting services. Contracts can be for accomplishing specific tasks or providing ongoing consulting services as needed. Because MBDCs are private organizations, each one will work (and charge) a little differently.

Minority Enterprise Development Week (MED Week)

In observance of MED Week each September or October, the MBDA, in partnership with the SBA, sponsors activities across the country and in Washington, D.C., to promote and acknowledge minority business ownership. Workshops, seminars, procurement trade fairs, recognition awards, networking events, and other activities highlight MED Week celebrations.

How to Proceed

To locate the MBDC nearest you, call your regional MBDA office (see page 218). MBDC locations change frequently, so we have not included a listing for them.

For general information about the MBDA, contact:

Minority Business Development Agency
U.S. Department of Commerce
Public Affairs, Room 6707
Washington DC 20230
(202) 482-5196

For more information about MED Week, contact:

MBDA/MED **Week, Room H-6708**
U.S. Department of Commerce
Fourteenth St. and Constitution Ave. NW
Washington DC 20230
(202) 482-5916

The Women's Bureau (U.S. Department of Labor) EW

- A federal office set up specifically to study issues of women and work and to improve the status of working women, including self-employed women

- Sponsored by: U.S. Department of Labor

In addition to regional programs designed to meet women's local employment needs, the bureau studies women and work and disseminates information to the media, policy makers, and the public. In recent years, the bureau has started a working woman count and a commission on family leave and has provided information and resources on sexual harassment, pregnancy, child care, and other work-related topics.

The bureau also offers a variety of free fact sheets about women and work, as well as other publications, including a series of lively four-color posters called "Women's Work Counts," which must be purchased through the Government Printing Office (see page 51).

Although the Women's Bureau does not offer standardized programs and services across the country (as does the SBA's Office of Women's Business Ownership), it is included here because it and its regional offices offer some excellent resources for women entrepreneurs.

The bureau helps create opportunities for women by setting up demonstration programs, sponsoring educational events, and providing information about those events to policy makers in order to influence their decisions about laws and programs for women. In 1995, the bureau sent representatives to the Fourth Annual Conference on Women in Beijing and preceded that event with regional conferences across the United States.

The workhorses of the bureau are the ten regional offices in charge of delivering products and programs to meet local needs. Keeping in mind that activities vary by region, the following list of projects from several offices will give you an idea what to expect:

- development of a directory of blue-collar women-owned businesses
- development of a women's small business referral resource
- sponsorship of a Hispanic women's conference
- sponsorship of a women-in-trades fair
- sponsorship of a displaced homemakers conference

In other regions, there have been demonstration projects to help welfare recipients start micro-businesses and to extend unemployment benefits to women who wanted to go into business for themselves.

Each region also has discretionary funds to support small projects (such as the development of the previously mentioned women-in-trades directory) that will improve the status of women in the region. Individuals, groups, businesses, and nonprofit organizations are all eligible to approach their regional office with project ideas.

How to Proceed

To find out more about the bureau's activities in your area, contact the regional office that serves your state (see 221).

For general information about the bureau, to receive bureau publications, or to participate in any of the national programs such as Working Women Count, contact:

The Women's Bureau
U.S. Department of Labor
Room S 3317
200 Constitution Ave. NW
Washington DC 20210
(800) 827-5335 (clearinghouse and voice messages)
(202) 219-4486 (automated information-request system)

STATE RESOURCES

Because this directory has a national focus, we have not included detailed information on each state. Instead, we are providing key contacts and information resources to help you begin tapping into your state and local programs. The best places to start to find out about these programs are first-stop offices and state economic development departments.

First-stop offices are described in more detail in Chapter 2 (see page 53). For a state-by-state listing of first-stop offices, see page 225.

State economic development departments also are described in more detail in Chapter 2 (see page 54). For a state-by-state listing of economic development departments, see page 234.

Local and regional chapters of membership organizations (see Chapter 6) are another valuable source of information on activities and events in your local area. Also, if you have not reviewed the sections in this chapter on federal and private sources of training, counseling, and technical assistance, don't pass them by. You might be surprised to find out how many valuable federal and private programs are available in your area.

PRIVATE RESOURCES

As more women start their own businesses, and more appreciation develops for the unique challenges they face (as well as the special contribution they can make to how we do business in this country and abroad), more programs targeted to women will undoubtedly spring up. The resources in this section include nonprofit and for-profit private organizations and companies that offer entrepreneurial and business learning opportunities on a national or regional basis. In addition to these listings, check:

- *Chapter 6 for a listing of business associations.* Most offer educational and professional development opportunities. Even if you do not want to join a particular group, you can often attend interesting workshops and seminars by asking to be put on the group's conference mailing list.

- *The SBA-sponsored women's business development centers.* These sites (described on page 90) are private organizations that receive partial funding through the SBA. The programs they offer are targeted to local needs, so check to see if there is a site in your area.

- *The first-stop office in your state* (see page 225). These agencies will have information about local and regional organizations that offer women's entrepreneurial training and counseling.

American Women's Economic Development Corp. (AWED) **EW**

- Entrepreneurial training with phone counseling outreach

AWED offers fee-based personalized training, counseling, and support services for women entrepreneurs in key areas of business operation (finance, accounting, marketing, design, planning, public relations, etc.). Telephone counseling and a telephone hotline make AWED resources available to women outside the areas served by their sites. AWED coordinates the national membership organization, American Women in Enterprise (see page 162).

How to Proceed

For more information about AWED in general, contact the New York office at:

> AWED
> 71 Vanderbilt Ave., Suite 320
> New York NY 10169
> (212) 692-1900

Other centers are located in Washington, D.C. (202/857-0091), Connecticut (203/326-7914), Long Beach, California (310/983-3747), and Irvine, California (714/474-2933).

An Income of Her Own **EW**

- Entrepreneurial education opportunities for teens and mothers

Founded by Joline Godfrey, author of the bestselling book *Our Wildest Dreams* (see page 78), this organization offers a variety of activities and opportunities to foster entrepreneurship in young women, including:

- a national business plan competition
- summer camps to explore the excitement of entrepreneurship, including mother/daughter camps
- membership benefits, including a newsletter and profiles of many successful women entrepreneurs
- entrepreneurship awareness conferences and videos about how to foster teen entrepreneurship in your community
- game and activity packets for girls interested in exploring business ownership

How to Proceed

The organization has an automated, toll-free telephone system that plays short tapes you can select with a Touch-Tone phone. Try calling the 800 number first for an overview, then call the direct line if you need to speak to someone in person.

An Income of Her Own
1804 W. Burbank Blvd.
Burbank CA 91506
(800) 350-2978
(818) 842-3040

Institute for Professional Business Women **EW**

■ Low-cost seminars on topics of special interest to women

The Institute offers reasonably priced seminars at locations around the country (or at your business location by special arrangement) targeted to the needs of professional and business women. The seminars can be used for Continuing Education Units (CEUs). The Institute's seminars offer busy women a way to continue learning and meet other professional women at the same time. They run from 9:00 A.M. to 4:00 P.M., and most cost $49 to $99 (although some intensive seminars may cost $195). The seminar's price includes a participant workbook.

How to Proceed

Call or fax a request to be added to the Institute's mailing list:

Institute for Professional Business Women
(A Division of Pryor Resources, Inc.)
P.O. Box 2951
Shawnee Mission KS 66201
(800) 255-6139

National Businesswomen's Leadership Association **EW**

■ Low-cost seminars for women in business

This association, affiliated with the Rockhurst College Continuing Education Center, offers seminars around the country designed to meet the special needs of women leaders and managers. Taught by experts in their fields, these one-day seminars offer busy women a tool for professional development and an opportunity to meet other women in business and management. Seminars range in price from $49 to $125 and include a participant workbook.

How to Proceed

Call to order a catalog of seminars and to be added to the mailing list:

National Businesswomen's Leadership Association
6901 W. Sixty-third St.
Shawnee Mission KS 66201-1349
(800) 258-7246

National Chamber of Commerce for Women ▪EW

- Low-cost training, technical assistance, and counseling for chamber members

The chamber is a membership organization that makes a variety of resources and services available to working and self-employed women for an annual fee of $96. Members participate in committees developed by the chamber to meet member needs. Committees include:

- *The Business Owner's Advisory Task Force,* for women who own and run businesses located in commercial office space, retail stores, and manufacturing facilities

- *The Home-Based Committee,* for women who run businesses out of their homes or who work as independent contractors or freelancers

- *The Productivity Improvement Network,* which analyzes issues of gender difference in work and management styles, productivity incentives, quality controls, employee diversity, and other productivity-related topics

- *The wow (World of Women's) Business Committee,* which provides assistance in the areas of micro-financing, imports and exports, international expansion, and letters of credit

Assistance is provided primarily by:

- Business Committee Counselors who have expertise in various fields and serve as free mentors for a period of time (If no counselor for your type of business is available in your geographic area, you will be provided with a telephone counselor.)

- access to the resources and expertise of the chamber's information banks

- free workshops on business, work, and self-employment issues (If you cannot attend the workshops, you will receive a free manual.)

- technical assistance on business plan development and finding financing

Other services and a low-cost, introductory membership are also available.

How to Proceed

Call or write the chamber for an overview kit:

> **National Chamber of Commerce for Women**
> 10 Waterside Plaza, Suite 6H
> New York NY 10010
> (212) 685-3454

Meredith College EW

- An MBA (Master's in Business Administration) program for women in management and administrative positions

- Meredith College, John E. Weems Graduate School

This graduate program for women is designed for professional women who want to integrate their business experience with current theory. This flexible program provides thirty-six hours of coursework designed to help participants improve decision-making skills, analyze problems from many perspectives (e.g., social, legal, economic), and explore new concepts in business development, including marketing, accounting, and economics.

How to Proceed

For more information about the program, contact:

> **John E. Weems Graduate School**
> **Meredith College**
> 3800 Hillsborough St.
> Raleigh NC 27607-5298
> (919) 829-8423

National Education Center for Women in Business EW

■ Intensive learning opportunities for professional service providers, women business owners, and young girls aspiring to entrepreneurship

The center offers four main programs for aspiring and active women entrepreneurs:

Strategy 2000: A two-day seminar addressing issues of women's business ownership as the turn of the century approaches, when it is anticipated that more than half the businesses in this country will be owned by women. The first day is for professional advisors (lawyers, accountants, etc.) to help them understand how to best serve women business owners. The Center will bring this program to any community across the country that finds sponsors and can assist in coordinating the event.

Camp Entrepreneur: Two camps for budding entrepreneurs are offered. One is a one-day camp for girls interested in exploring entrepreneurship, and the other is a six-day residential camp for girls growing up in a family business. Both camps offer hands-on experience in business development, including visits to businesses, use of computer simulations, budgeting, and other related areas.

Take Off: An intensive, personalized learning opportunity for successful business owners who are ready to take a growth step. Take Off is available in different locations around the country each year. Call for an annual schedule.

Campus Programs: The center offers classes, workshops, and conferences at the Seton Hill campus (and elsewhere in the western Pennsylvania area) on a variety of topics, including a special course for women who want to start a business or change the nature or structure of their existing business. Other topics include family business ownership, business ownership issues for women with disabilities, and women in high-tech businesses.

In addition to sponsoring conferences and workshops, the center conducts research on women entrepreneurs and publishes books, workbooks, videos, and a free newsletter. (For more information about these activities, see page 61.)

How to Proceed

For more information about the center's activities and dates and locations of programs and tours, contact:

> **National Education Center for Women in Business**
> Seton Hill College
> Seton Hill Dr.
> Greensburg PA 15601-1599
> (800) 632-9248
> (412) 830-4625

National Foundation for Women Business Owners (NFWBO) EW

- Intensive short-term and ongoing learning opportunities for both established and start-up business owners

- Sponsored by: NFWBO, a nonprofit education fund founded by the National Association of Women Business Owners (NAWBO)

This foundation offers entrepreneurial training for owners of start-up and young businesses, and leadership training programs for established women business owners. Its entrepreneurial training program, called EXCEL, combines intensive training sessions, ongoing mentoring, and personalized counseling by qualified NFWBO chapter members.

Costs for participation in the EXCEL program vary depending on which chapter is offering it. The program is currently available in a limited number of sites around the country, but NFWBO's goal is to expand and eventually make the program available on a national basis.

NFWBO's leadership training is an intensive residential program in which fifteen to twenty established women business owners attend a two-day seminar to fine-tune leadership skills, receive personalized guidance on key issues facing their companies, and participate in personalized coaching sessions in media presentations and negotiating. The program, set up to maximize interaction between participants and provide opportunities to interact with leaders in management thinking, gives attendees a chance to engage in problem-solving sessions related to specific issues facing their businesses. The curriculum changes yearly, thus offering new learning opportunities for women who want to return.

In addition to these specific training programs, NFWBO is working to identify sources of capital for women business owners and plans to develop work-force training and mentoring programs for the women's business community.

How to Proceed

Contact the national office for general information about NFWBO and its programs, and to find out if the EXCEL program is available in your area:

> **National Foundation for Women Business Owners**
> 1100 Wayne Ave., Suite 830
> Silver Spring MD 20910-5603
> (301) 495-4975

Simmons Graduate School of Management **EW**

■ An MBA (Master's in Business Administration) program for women that addresses their special needs and interests

Simmons offers an MBA program designed specifically for women. Founded by Margaret Hennig and Anne Jardim—coauthors of the 1974 bestseller *The Managerial Woman*—the program adds to the traditional MBA program with course offerings on organizational management and gender differences.

Simmons seeks out a diverse student body. Students range in age from twenty-four to fifty-five, have an average of ten years prior work experience, and reflect educational backgrounds varying from pre-bachelor to doctoral level. Rather than select applicants only on the basis of what they bring to their participation in an MBA program (as many business schools do), Simmons looks at what the outcome of a woman's participation might be.

The one-year MBA program offers an opportunity to receive training in a field traditionally dominated by men (in the classroom and in the boardroom) by mastering all traditional subjects, gaining confidence in a supportive environment, and learning specifically about gender issues that influence behavior and success in the business world.

How to Proceed

Contact the admissions office for an information packet:

> **Admissions Office**
> Simmons College
> 409 Commonwealth Ave.
> Boston MA 02215
> (617) 536-8390

Women's Collateral Funding **EW**

- Specialized training and consulting for women entrepreneurs

Women's Collateral Funding started out to provide unique financing options for women business owners (see pages 123 and 127) and moved into the business-assistance arena as it learned more about women's needs. Women's Collateral Network works with a range of experts and consultants to deliver customized assistance to its women clients in the areas of business planning, locating capital, loan package preparation, operations, and sales and marketing. Free one-hour initial consultations are available to some clients. Several centers are currently available to serve regional needs, and there are plans to expand nationally.

How to Proceed

For more information about the organization's programs and the locations of its current centers, contact:

> **Women's Collateral Funding**
> 1616 Walnut St., Suite 1010
> Philadelphia PA 19103

A Woman's Education and Leadership Forum (WELF) **EW**

- Low-cost seminars foster self-esteem and business savvy

WELF sponsors one-day conferences around the country on a variety of topics that help women acquire self-sufficiency, decision-making, and personal-success skills. Past conference workshops include *Self-Worth: Your Ultimate Power; Financial Management: Give Yourself*

Credit; How to Start and Manage Your Own Business; The Psychology of Winning; and a host of other topics specifically for women.

The organization's programs are based on a belief that self-esteem, self-confidence, and self-knowledge are as critical to success as are specific skills. WELF tailors its conferences to local interests and concerns by surveying local women and working with local women's organizations and agencies.

Corporate sponsorships and contributions help keep conference attendance costs to a minimum, usually in the $35–45 range.

How to Proceed

Call or write for an information packet and for locations of upcoming conferences:

> A Woman's Education and Leadership Forum
> 1390 Chainbridge Rd., Suite 960
> McClean VA 22101
> (703) 352-0551

Women's Information Bank (WIB) EW

■ Technical assistance referral for women entrepreneurs

WIB is an informal, international network of individuals who help educated women find business partners, start-up capital, and business incubator services. In addition to this technical business assistance, WIB coordinates the Thinking Women's Network, a network of female problem-solvers and authors around the world. It also maintains a library and placement services, conducts children's programs, and offers computerized database services.

WIB publishes the *Thinking Women* newsletter and helps women find travel partners, work and educational opportunities, and short-term housing and home exchanges in Washington and other major cities around the world.

How to Proceed

Contact WIB at:

> Women's Information Bank
> 3918 West St. NW
> Washington DC 20007
> (202) 338-8163

The Center for Family Business

■ Specialized help for women in family-owned enterprises

The Center for Family Business, founded and run by Leon and Katy Danco, has been described by *Business Week* magazine as the "country's leading consulting firm for family companies." The center offers seminars and publications to address the special needs of owners who have inherited a business or set up their own companies as family enterprises.

The center offers an annual seminar, *Managing Succession Without Conflict,* which addresses issues critical to the success of the family-owned enterprise. The seminar is designed for all family members, even those who may not be active in the business but whose lives are affected by the way the business operates.

Key managers who are not family members are also encouraged to attend to learn about the dynamics of successful family-owned businesses. The three-day seminar is held twice a year, once usually in Cleveland, Ohio, and once in Orlando, Florida.

For business owners unable to attend the seminar, the center makes available a number of books written by the Dancos. *Inside the Family Business* and *Beyond Survival* discuss the unique issues facing family businesses, including formulating effective strategies for successful management and succession. *From the Other Side of the Bed* (by Katy Danco) looks at life in the family business from the woman's perspective.

How to Proceed

Contact the center at:

> The Center for Family Business
> P.O. Box 24219
> Cleveland OH 44124
> (216) 442-0800

The Family Business Program

■ Seminars, workbooks, and family camp for owners of family-owned businesses

Founded by nationally recognized speaker, researcher, and consultant Pat Frishkoff, The Family Business Center offers seminars (primarily in the Pacific Northwest), workbooks, and a newsletter on family business ownership issues. Seminars cover communications, teamwork, succession, and ownership transition. A summer family camp is also offered. The program's workbooks, *The Succession Survival Kit* and *Preparing . . . Just in Case,* help families address issues of the transition process. The quarterly *Family Business Newsletter* includes case histories, articles, and national news about family business issues.

How to Proceed

Contact the program at:

> Family Business Program
> College of Business
> Oregon State University
> Bexell Hall, Room 201
> Corvallis OR 97331-2603
> (541) 737-3326

National Business Incubation Association (NBIA)

■ Support and technical assistance for start-ups

Business incubators are facilities set up to provide small start-up enterprises with affordable space, support services, and business development services, such as marketing, financing, and business management. The five-year success rate for businesses that locate in incubator facilities is much higher than for other small businesses (80 percent compared with 62 percent). There are more than five hundred incubators in the United States, and it is projected that this successful phenomenon will grow, making incubator facilities available in more and more communities. Specialized incubators for women and minorities are also springing up.

How to Proceed

To locate an incubator in your area, and to receive a free information sheet about incubators, contact the NBIA at:

> National Business Incubation Association
> One President St.
> Athens OH 45701
> (614) 593-4331

U.S. Chamber of Commerce Small Business Institute (SBI)

■ Self-study programs and business information

■ Sponsored by: U.S. Chamber of Commerce and Crisp Publications

The U.S. Chamber of Commerce and Crisp Publications have teamed up to offer self-study courses that business owners and employees can complete at their own pace. Courses on marketing, productivity, finance, sales, leadership, and a host of other topics are available through the SBI program. Courses are specifically designed to meet the needs of small business, with lots of practical information at a reasonable price (most courses are $20 or less). Certificates of achievement and Continuing Education Units (CEUs) are available for completing the courses.

How to Proceed

You can receive a description of the program and its courses by using the SBI's Fax Back system. Call (800) 851-8705. A voice prompt will ask you for a box number. Enter 600, and then follow the rest of the voice prompts. Within minutes, you'll have a description of the SBI and all the courses offered. If you have any problems using the Fax Back system, call the Quality Learning Services Division at (800) 835-4730.

Private Seminar Providers

■ A seminar smorgasbord at reasonable prices

The companies listed here deliver reasonably priced ($50 to $100 per day) seminars around the country on a variety of management and business issues. Typical topics include customer service, total quality management, team-building, communications skills, stress management, and employee relations. Some offer individual seminars for women.

How to Proceed

Call the individual organizations to be put on their mailing lists.

CareerTrack
3085 Center Green Dr.
Boulder CO 80301
(800) 334-6780

Clemson University
Office of Professional Development
P.O. Box 912
Clemson SC 29633-0912
(800) 258-1017

Dun & Bradstreet
Business Education Services
P.O. Box 5100
New York NY 10150-5100
(212) 692-6600

Fred Pryor Seminars
P.O. Box 2591
Shawnee Mission KS 66205
(800) 255-6139

Key Productivity Center
P.O. Box 410
Saranac Lake NY 12983-0410
(800) 821-3919

SkillPath Inc.
6900 Squibb Rd.
P.O. Box 2768
Mission KS 66201
(800) 873-7545

CHAPTER 4

Business Financing

Business financing presents a challenge to every new or growing business. Statistics suggest, though, that for women business owners, the challenge is especially great. Despite research by the National Foundation for Women Business Owners that shows women-owned businesses to be as creditworthy as the average U.S. business, and *more* likely than the average U.S. firm to remain in business for three or more years, women themselves identify access to capital as one of their biggest challenges.

More than half of all women business owners finance their businesses with personal resources—from credit cards and second mortgages to loans from family and friends—either because they have been turned down by conventional lenders or investors or because they opt to avoid those sources altogether.

Businesses that are undercapitalized often face failure—or at least failure to grow. But, despite limited access to capital, women-owned businesses are beating the odds and succeeding in record numbers. And that success has fostered a growing awareness and appreciation of the need to support these businesses—businesses that are making a significant contribution to the economy. As a result, specialized financing programs are becoming available for women in both the start-up and expansion stages of business ownership, and conventional lenders and investors are opening their doors wider.

When looking for business capital, it is important to understand the types of financing available and the advantages and disadvantages of each kind. The four most common types include:

Conventional loans: A specific amount of money is loaned by a private party, institution, or public entity, with fixed payments until the debt has been paid off.

Guaranteed loans: These are similar to conventional loans, but with a third party—usually an organization or institution—guaranteeing all or part of the loan. The guarantee sweetens the pot for the lender; if you default, the guarantor is responsible for paying off the loan.

Microloans: These are small loans of $25,000 or less (and sometimes as little as $500) with a fixed repayment and interest schedule. Microlenders usually provide loan recipients with technical assistance to help ensure business success. Microlending started in the developing world, where loans as small as $50 have helped women turn a craft or agricultural plot into a source of family income.

Venture capital: Unlike debt-based financing, this option offers a way to get capital by selling part of your business to an investor. In other words, the investor takes an equity position in your company, becoming a part-owner.

Loans have the advantage of predictability: you know what your monthly payments are and when they will end. The downside is that you must make regular payments, regardless of how well the business is doing. Venture capital, on the other hand, is not a loan. You don't have regular payments to make, but investors can wield influence over the companies in which they invest. This influence can be an advantage when the investor provides appropriate management and technical assistance, or it can be a disadvantage when assistance is inappropriate or the investor is dissatisfied with the return.

Understanding and selecting the right kind of financing is your first job. Your second is to convince the lender or investor that you are a good risk. This means having a realistic and well-thought-out business plan and providing all the financial data required. Recognize also that you are selling yourself. When successful women entrepreneurs review other women's business plans that did not attract capital or a loan, they often say the plans were not persuasive. If a man had gone to the bank with the same plan, he might well have had the same disappointment. At the same time, one woman's banker said he approved a larger loan for her than he would have for someone else with a similar track record because she radiated drive, confidence, and intelligence. The point here is: *be prepared.* Be prepared with your business plan and financial data, and be prepared to sell yourself. One of the best ways to prepare yourself is to participate in the training, counseling, and technical assistance programs described in Chapter 3.

In addition to the four capital sources just described, we suggest two alternatives that may meet some individuals' or businesses' needs:

Factoring: Factors are companies that buy accounts receivable at a slight discount, giving you cash and freeing you from the often time-consuming collection process.

Nonprofit entrepreneuring: A nonprofit organization can be run like a business—and the successful ones are—yet function to meet an educational, social, or philanthropic mission. As a nonprofit organization, grants may be available to help launch and sustain your venture.

Listings with this symbol **EW** describe programs exclusively for women.

FEDERAL RESOURCES

The federal government provides many opportunities for businesses, individuals, and organizations to receive funding for a wide range of projects. The purpose of this section, though, is not to tell you about every possible source of federal financing or funding. Rather, it is to steer you toward those programs designed specifically for entrepreneurs and business owners. For that reason, most of the information will be about Small Business Administration (SBA) programs. *The* federal agency charged with helping the small business community thrive, one of the SBA's most important activities is ensuring access to capital. Loan-guarantee programs, microloans, and venture capital funds are all available.

LOAN-GUARANTEE PROGRAMS

The Women's Prequalification Pilot Loan Program **EW**

- Nonprofit intermediaries help women prepare winning loan applications
- Sponsored by: SBA

This loan program was initiated in part because 1993 data showed that women, who own more than 30 percent of all businesses, received only 12 percent of SBA-guaranteed loans. The program is designed to increase a woman's odds of getting a business loan by decreasing required paperwork and increasing assistance before she submits a loan application to a bank. The applicant is teamed up with an expert from a nonprofit organization who helps her prepare the loan application. Then, unlike with most other loan guarantees, the SBA approves the application, signaling to lenders that the applicant's loan will definitely receive the SBA guarantee.

Loans in this program are limited to amounts of $250,000 or less and offer low interest rates and repayment schedules based on a woman's ability to repay and how the funds will be used.

How to Proceed

This pilot program, which may be expanded if successful, is available in sixteen locations across the country. Contact the SBA offices in the following list for more information.

Statewide availability:

Colorado
(303) 844-3461

Maine
(207) 622-8242

Massachusetts
(617) 565-5580

Montana
(406) 449-5381

New Mexico
(505) 766-1879

Utah
(801) 524-6831

Local availability:

Buffalo, New York
(716) 846-4517

Charlotte, North Carolina
(704) 344-6563

Chicago, Illinois
(312) 353-5429

Columbus, Ohio
(614) 469-6860

Louisville, Kentucky
(502) 582-5971

New Orleans, Louisiana
(504) 589-6685

Philadelphia, Pennsylvania
(215) 962-3804

Portland, Oregon
(541) 326-2682

St. Louis, Missouri
(314) 539-6600

San Francisco, California
(415) 744-8490

MORE LOAN-GUARANTEE PROGRAMS

- Loan guarantees for everything from long-term expansion and short-term capital needs to specialized export loans
- Sponsored by: SBA

Guaranteeing more than two billion dollars in loans annually, the SBA has worked hard in recent years to meet business owners' needs with new programs, streamlined application procedures, and a concerted effort to increase guarantees for women- and minority-owned businesses. Following is a summary of the SBA's main loan-guarantee programs:

- *LowDoc* is a program designed to reduce paperwork and speed response time.
- *CapLine* is a short-term revolving credit line or loan guarantee to help meet cyclic cash needs.
- *Export Working Capital* is designed to provide short-term working capital (up to $750,000, or 90 percent of the loan amount, whichever is less) for specific export projects.
- *The 7(a) program* is designed to provide start-up and expansion capital through loans from commercial lenders.
- *Specialized programs* meet specific needs with handicapped assistance loans and loans to help meet environmental requirements, for example.

Any bank can participate in an SBA loan guarantee. However, SBA-certified and preferred lenders work with the SBA on a regular basis and will understand the type of loan you are interested in. Working with a banker well versed in the requirements and application procedures will undoubtedly streamline the process.

How to Proceed

For more information about SBA loan-guarantee programs and to locate a preferred or certified lender, contact your SBA district office (see page 192).

Capital Access Program

■ A pilot program that targets specific types of businesses

■ Sponsored by: SBA and Citibank

The program is currently available on a two-year pilot basis in Washington, D.C., Las Vegas, Los Angeles, San Francisco, and Miami. Loans are available for amounts up to $250,000 for export and technical businesses and businesses creating new jobs.

How to Proceed

For more information and an application, call (800) 323-CITI (2484), ext. 2429.

MICROLOANS

MicroLoan Demonstration Program

■ Loans of $25,000 or less

■ Sponsored by: SBA

Initially introduced to meet the needs of women business owners who were typically not looking for large loans, the MicroLoan Program provides funds to selected nonprofit organizations that make loans directly to applicants. Although both men and women are eligible for the program, the majority of program participants are women. Counseling and management assistance, including development of a business plan, often accompany or precede the loan award.

How to Proceed

To locate an SBA microlender in your area, see page 249 in Chapter 7. If you do not find one, or the organization is no longer involved in the program, contact your local SBA district office (see page 192) or the SBA Office of Economic Development, Financial Assistance Division, in Washington, D.C., at (202) 205-6490.

VENTURE CAPITAL

Venture Capital from Small Business Investment Companies (SBICs)

- Private venture-capital firms licensed by the SBA to make equity investments and long-term loans

- Sponsored by: SBA

Venture-capital firms participating in the SBIC program are licensed and regulated by the SBA, thus providing business owners with the assurance that they are working with a reputable firm. The firms also receive partial funding by becoming licensed. An SBIC can either make an equity investment in your business (which means it becomes a financial partner) or make a long-term direct loan. Each firm makes its own investment and loan decisions and has its own set of requirements and application procedures.

A Specialized SBIC for Women-Owned Businesses **EW**

Women's Collateral Funding operates the Women's Worldwide Venture Fund™, a specialized SBIC for women-owned businesses with a ten-million-dollar-plus fund of its own that is supplemented by the SBA. This fund invests in women-owned or women-led companies in computer, communications, or health-care technologies industries in the mid-Atlantic region. For more information about the fund and its qualification criteria, contact:

> **Women's Collateral Funding**
> 1616 Walnut St., Suite 1010
> Philadelphia PA 19103
> (215) 722-1900

We have not included a state-by-state listing of SBICs in Chapter 7 because there are so many, and they change frequently. For a national listing of SBICs, call the SBA Office of Investment in Washington, D.C., at (202) 205-6520, and request the *Directory of Operating Small Business Investment Companies*. In addition to a state-by-state listing, this publication provides useful guidelines for business owners about approaching SBICs for venture capital. The Office of Investment also has its state-by-state listing on SBA OnLine (see page 47) and updates the list each month.

For more information about SBIC, you can also contact the National Association of Small Business Investment Companies (NASBIC). This association, whose members run SBICs, makes its membership directory available to nonmembers for $10. The directory includes information about the amounts invested and the preferred industries and locations each firm is interested in. Contact NASBIC at:

National Association of Small Business Investment Companies
1199 N. Fairfax St., Suite 200
Alexandria VA 22314
(703) 683-1601

STATE RESOURCES

Most states offer a variety of financial-incentive programs for business owners, from start-up loan guarantees and financing for high-tech companies to employee job-training grants. Job creation is usually the underlying goal of these programs. State agencies often work with nonprofit organizations and private and quasi-public entities (private nonprofits funded with state dollars earmarked for specific activities) to make capital available.

How to Proceed

Your state's economic development office (see page 234) is the best place to start to identify potential sources of state business financing. If your state also has a first-stop office (see page 225) involved in more than certification and contracting activities, also contact them. Your state's Commission for Women (see page 240) may also be able to refer you to appropriate resources. To give you an idea of the kinds of state financing programs available, a profile of one state's program follows.

PROFILE

The Governor's Office of Economic Development
(South Dakota)

The Governor's Office of Economic Development includes a Finance Division that offers a number of financing options. The Revolving Economic Development and Initiative (REDI) Fund, a low-interest, revolving loan fund, is available for existing businesses whose expansion will create jobs. In general, one job must be created for each five thousand dollars loaned. Venture capital is also available through the Venture Capital Investment Fund, which will match a business investment from private sources with one dollar for every two dollars of privately invested money.

For young, aspiring entrepreneurs, the Graduate Entrepreneur Loan Program (GELP) offers loans up to $50,000 to high-school or post-secondary graduates who need capital for land purchases, construction, equipment purchases, and other working capital needs. This program was started as an incentive to keep young South Dakota residents in the state. The Fast-Track Loan Guarantee program is also for young entrepreneurs, but targets high-school students who have not yet started a business. Loans of up to two thousand dollars are available. In addition to these programs, the state has established a network of Planning and Development Districts that work to foster economic development on a local level throughout the state. Revolving loan funds are available through many of these agencies.

PRIVATE RESOURCES

Only a few short years ago, there were very few private sources of capital earmarked for women business owners. That picture is changing, though. While women still face many obstacles in obtaining loans and investor capital from private sources, the information that follows represents the beginning of an encouraging trend.

CONVENTIONAL LOANS AND LOAN GUARANTEES

Capital Rose Perpetual Fund **EW**

■ A $40 million fund earmarked for economically viable, woman-owned businesses

■ Sponsored by: Capital Rose, Inc.

Capital Rose is currently raising money for a loan fund that will make loans of $50,000 to $1 million available to a mix of companies ranging from start-ups and established companies to franchises and management buyouts. Lending will begin when the fund reaches $10 million. The fund is not a bank, venture fund, or granting foundation and thus has the flexibility—and intention—to test innovative lending practices such as character-based lending. One such innovative program is a partnership with the National Federation of Business and Professional Women's Clubs (BPW) (see page 166) in which BPW members are raising money for the perpetual fund; the dollar amount raised will be earmarked for loans to BPW members. Although Capital Rose itself does not provide venture capital, in some specialized circumstances it can arrange access to capital for women looking for equity investments in the $500,000 to $1 million range. Capital Rose, Inc. was founded by Rebecca Maddox, author of *Inc. Your Dreams* (see page 75).

How to Proceed

For more information, contact:

> **Capital Rose, Inc.**
> 690 Sugartown Rd.
> Malvern PA 19355
> (610) 644-4212

Loan Fund for Entrepreneurs with a Two-Year Track Record ▉EW

- A loan fund created by the National Association of Women Business Owners (NAWBO) and Wells Fargo Bank for women who have been in business for two years

- Sponsored by: National Association of Women Business Owners (see page 164) and Wells Fargo Bank

This loan fund, started in 1995, is earmarked for women business owners through 1997. Applicants must have been in business for at least two years, have a good personal and business credit record, have a profitable business, and have not declared bankruptcy within the last ten years. The minimum loan is $5,000; loans between that amount and $25,000 can be applied for by phone. Loans over that amount require a written application, which can be mailed or faxed to Wells Fargo. This loan fund is available to all women business owners with a two-year track record, not just NAWBO members.

How to Proceed

For more information, call Wells Fargo at (800) 359-3557 (ext. 123) or NAWBO's national office at (310) 608-2590. Information is also available from NAWBO chapters across the country.

Women's Collateral Funding ▉EW

- Two innovative loan-guarantee programs

This company has developed two innovative approaches to increasing women business owners' access to capital. The Women's Collateral Funding *Women's Business Directory* ™ offers commercial lenders an incentive to lend to women applicants: bankers can't lose because loans are backed by funds that are generated by selling advertising in the directory and sales of the directory to corporations interested in buying services and products from women-owned businesses. The directory, offering advertisers an opportunity to tap into a targeted, growing market, also includes information about business-assistance resources and women's organizations in the area. The Women's Collateral Funding directory project is currently available in several locations, and there are plans to expand nationally.

The Delaware Valley Venture Collateral™ Access Fund provides a million-dollar collateral fund to lenders interested in working with women-owned firms. Although this program is regional, Women's Collateral Funding intends to develop the approach in other regions.

Women's Collateral Funding also offers business training, counseling, and consulting (see page 110).

How to Proceed

For more information about programs and locations, contact:

> **Women's Collateral Worldwide, Inc.**
> 1616 Walnut St., Suite 1010
> Philadelphia PA 19103
> (212) 722-1900

Membership Organizations EW

Many of the business organizations listed in Chapter 6 offer loans to members through partnerships with a variety of lenders, corporations, and nonprofit organizations. The partnership between Capital Rose and BPW described on page 126 is an example of this trend. The professional organizations do not sponsor loan programs as frequently, but they often provide educational and training scholarships. Keep these in mind as a way to raise your own skill level or foster development of your employees.

Business-Friendly Banks for Conventional Loans

- A report that saves time and frustration by identifying banks that want your business if you're looking for a loan from a commercial lender
- Sponsored by: SBA Office of Advocacy

More than 60 percent of business financing is in the form of commercial bank loans, but finding the right bank can be a time-consuming process of trial and error. To help borrowers in their selection process, the SBA Office of Advocacy studies the lending patterns of commercial banks across the country. Based on the dollar amount of a bank's small-business loans relative to its assets and deposits and the total number of business loans awarded, a bank is ranked on a scale of five to fifty. Final reports are available to the public.

How to Proceed

For a free copy of the report ranking banks in your state, contact:

> **Office of Advocacy**
> Small Business Administration
> 409 Third St. SW
> Washington DC 20416
> (202) 205-6928

Copies of the complete report (or regional portions) are available for a fee from:

> **National Technical Information Service**
> 5285 Port Royal Rd.
> Springfield VA 22161
> (703) 487-4650

Access to Capital: Money, Lenders, and Small Business Loans

- Free booklet offers insight into the lending process
- Sponsored by: Federal Reserve Bank of Chicago and The Women's Business Development Center

This booklet, written primarily to help lenders understand and cultivate the growing market of women borrowers, makes useful reading for potential loan applicants. The topics covered and recommendations presented are based on focus-group discussions with lenders and women business owners. Understanding the lenders' perspective is one of the best ways to prepare an effective application. Included are recommendations for women applying for business loans.

How to Proceed

For your free copy of the booklet, contact:

> **Federal Reserve Bank of Chicago**
> Public Information Center
> 230 S. LaSalle St.
> Chicago IL 60690-0834
> (312) 322-5111

MICROLOANS

Microloans are almost always provided through private, nonprofit companies or a local or regional affiliate of a larger nonprofit. Because microlending is based on the principle of meeting local community needs, loan types, sizes, and applicant eligibility requirements vary widely. On page 261 is a state-by-state listing of microlenders who lend exclusively to women or include women as a targeted group for their loan fund. This listing is not inclusive; many other microlenders across the country serve the unique needs of their local areas.

Here are some tips to help you identify other appropriate microlenders:

- Check the listing of SBA demonstration sites on page 198. Many of these sites have microloan funds available to women who participate in their programs.

- Contact your state economic development agency (see page 234). These agencies sometimes participate in microlending ventures with nonprofit organizations and can often provide referrals to microlenders in your state.

Directory of Microenterprise Programs

- A directory of microlenders published by the Aspen Institute's Self-Employment Learning Project

- Sponsored by: The Aspen Institute

Updated approximately every two years, the directory includes a listing and in-depth description of more than two hundred microlenders. Because there will be only a limited number of lenders included that serve your region or local area, consider suggesting the book to your local librarian as a worthwhile acquisition. At just $15, it would make a good addition to any collection. For more information, contact:

The Aspen Institute
Publications Office
P.O. Box 222
Queenstown MD 21658
(410) 820-5326

Credit Unions

■ Member-owned financial institutions that make loans to members

If you are an individual or sole proprietorship looking for a small loan to start or expand your business, your credit union may be one of your best bets. Some credit unions even focus specifically on providing capital for business and community development. The Self Help Credit Union in Chapel Hill, North Carolina, which has a specialized venture fund for women-owned businesses, is an exciting example of this trend. If you don't belong to a credit union, consider joining one. If you cannot identify a credit union in your community, contact the Credit Union National Association for a brochure about credit unions and a state-by-state listing of credit union leagues. The league in your state will be able to refer you to an appropriate credit union.

Credit Union National Association, Inc. (CUNA)
P.O. Box 431
Madison WI 53701-0431
(608) 231-4000

National Association of Community Development Loan Funds (NACDLF)

■ A group of lenders committed to fostering the growth of lower-income communities by extending credit often denied by other financial institutions

Although there are not NACDLF members in every state, and not all members participate in small-business lending programs, NACDLF will refer you to members in your area when possible. For more information, contact them at:

National Association of Community Development Loan Funds
924 Cherry St., 3rd Floor
Philadelphia PA 19107-2405
(215) 923-4754

Association of Enterprise Opportunity (AEO)

- A professional organization of more than five hundred individual and organizational members committed to helping low-income individuals and communities by fostering self-employment and small, small businesses—often called *microenterprises*

Members include lenders, community development groups, technical-assistance providers, policy makers, and many others. There is a special membership category for owners of small enterprises who pay a reduced membership fee. As a member, you will receive a membership directory, which will steer you toward programs and microlenders in your area. You will also be eligible to exhibit your products or services at annual membership meetings. For more information, contact:

Association of Enterprise Opportunity
320 N. Michigan Ave., Suite 804
Chicago IL 60601
(312) 357-0177

National Association of Development Organizations (NADO)

- An organization for economic development professionals who specialize in working in small cities and rural areas

The association will refer a caller to a member in her local area (when available) who can provide information about microloan opportunities. For more information, contact:

National Association of Development Organizations
444 N. Capitol St. NW, Suite 630
Washington DC 20001
(202) 624-7806

VENTURE CAPITAL FUNDS

Private investors and companies making equity investments in start-up or expanding businesses are often looking for fast results and high returns. Until recently, venture capitalists have had little interest in women-led businesses because those businesses did not grow at the same rate as companies led by men. But as more women start, purchase, or inherit businesses of all types—from high-tech and manufacturing to construction—the pattern of slow-growing woman-owned service businesses is changing, making them a more attractive investment. In addition, the recognition that the capital required for growth has often been denied to qualified women entrepreneurs has generated interest by socially responsible investors to seek out women's businesses. The companies in the list that follows either make investments nationally and regionally or intend to expand to meet national or regional needs.

Ark Capital Management

■ A venture fund targeting minority- and woman-owned businesses

The Ark Capital fund is operated by women and minority owners who know firsthand the challenges these groups face in finding business capital. To ensure high returns on investors' money, investment recipients also receive management assistance from a hand-picked team of experts who understand the company's industry and markets. The fund invests in small to medium-sized companies with potential for growth.

How to Proceed
For information about the fund and its selection criteria, contact:

>Ark Capital Management
>150 N. Wacker Dr., Suite 795
>Chicago IL 60606
>(312) 541-0330

Inroads Capital Partners

■ Fifty-million-dollar fund used to support midsized companies with ten million to one hundred million dollars in revenues

Inroads Capital Partners makes equity investments of $1 million to $5 million in mid- to latter-stage companies. It works with companies in all industries and throughout the United States but does not work with start-ups.

How to Proceed

For more information, contact:

> **Inroads Capital Partners**
> 1603 Orrington Ave., Suite 2050
> Evanston IL 60201
> (708) 864-2000

Investors' Circle

■ Matches investors with socially responsible entrepreneurs

Investors' Circle is a select network of investors interested in supporting the growth of women-owned businesses as part of an interest in socially responsible investing. Investors' Circle sponsors two Social Venture Fairs each year, where a select number of entrepreneurs can meet investors. The first Venture Fair, in August 1994, included ten women-owned companies selected from a prescreened pool of one hundred. The ten companies went on to raise more than two million dollars in equity investments. In addition, a woman entrepreneur can submit a two-page briefing about her business to be made available to members of Investors' Circle. Investors then contact a business owner directly if they are interested in learning more about the company.

How to Proceed

For information about Investors' Circle, its venture fairs, and its referral system, contact:

> **Investors' Circle**
> 31W007 North Ave., Suite 101
> West Chicago IL 60185
> (708) 876-1101

Women's Equity Fund **EW**

■ Equity investment and strategic consulting that increase the odds of success

Providing equity capital in amounts from five thousand to one hundred thousand dollars, this fund emphasizes a partnership with the companies it invests in by offering strategic advice in finance, marketing, product and service design, customer service, and other critical areas of management and operations. Companies in a wide range of industries are eligible for funding, including light manufacturing, professional services, and specialty retailing. High-profit companies with the potential for expansion or franchising are emphasized. Start-ups with large capital needs are generally avoided. Currently serving Colorado only, the fund plans to expand regionally and nationally over time.

How to Proceed

For information about the fund and to find out what the current service area is, contact:

Women's Equity Fund
P.O. Box 17143
Boulder CO 80308-7143
(303) 443-2626

MEMBERSHIP ORGANIZATIONS **EW**

Venture fund sponsorship by business organizations is beginning to catch on. Some of the organizations in Chapter 6 make venture capital available in a variety of ways. For example, the National Association of Female Executives (NAFE) sponsors a venture capital competition, and the National Women's Chamber of Commerce has a venture capital program providing capital and/or technical assistance by chamber committee members. The National Association of Women Business Owners (NAWBO) sponsors an "angel" network for NAWBO members who have not been successful in finding financing from other sources. The names of "angels" are entered into an electronic database, and applications that meet these angels' interests are forwarded directly to them. Currently, all angels are members of NAWBO, but the organization hopes to expand the network to include nonmember angels.

National Venture Capital Association

■ A professional association of leading venture capitalists across the country

This association, serving the professional needs of venture capital firms, provides information about its organization on request. Reviewing the material directed to venture capitalists is educational for any entrepreneur considering equity investments in her business. The types of investments venture capitalists are looking for, ethical practices, qualifications for investors, and a host of other topics are covered in the association's information packet. The association also makes its membership directory available to nonmembers.

How to Proceed

For more information, contact:

> National Venture Capital Association
> 1655 N. Fort Meyer Dr., Suite 700
> Arlington VA 22209
> (703) 351-5269

Venture Capital Clubs and Forums

■ Matchmaking groups and meetings help entrepreneurs find the right venture capitalists

Meetings, forums, and computerized matchmaking are springing up across the country to help hook up investors and entrepreneurs. Some clubs organize regular meetings where entrepreneurs can make presentations and then speak afterward with interested investors. Others collect information about investors' interests and entrepreneurs' needs and match up those with common goals. When joining a club or forum, ask if the investors are accredited and how they are screened.

How to Proceed

Because there is not a single clearinghouse for information about these clubs and forums, try the following:

■ Contact your local and state chambers of commerce. In some areas, chambers sponsor forums as part of their economic-development efforts.

■ Review copies of the magazines listed in Chapter 2 (see page 83) on a regular basis. Many list local and regional forums and matchmaking services.

■ Look for a copy of *Venture Capital Journal,* a monthly publication that lists forums across the country. This journal is very expensive (approximately $880 a year) for individuals who want to use it only to look up forums. If you have access to a university library with a business periodicals collection, it may be available there.

    For more information, contact the publisher, Venture Economics/Securities Data Publishing, at (800) 455-5844. This company also publishes a national directory of venture capitalists, *Pratt's Guide to Venture Capital Sources,* which is available for $225.

THE FACTORING ALTERNATIVE

Factoring (see page 118 for a definition) is becoming a more common practice. For established businesses, it can be a good, fast solution to a short-term cash crunch. Factoring can also be used on a permanent basis if the time spent at collections could be used more productively. The following resources will help you locate factors.

Edward's Directory of American Factors

■ An annually updated listing of nearly two hundred factoring companies across the United States

This book, which costs $199, may be available at your local library or through interlibrary loan. For more information, contact the publisher at:

    Edwards Research Group
    P.O. Box 9510
    Newton MA 02195
    (800) 936-1993

Commercial Finance Association

■ A trade association for the asset-based financial services industry

The Commercial Finance Association makes its membership roster available free of charge to start-ups and small businesses interested in locating a factor. (Their membership also includes lenders.) For more information or to request a roster, contact:

> Commercial Finance Association
> 225 W. Thirty-fourth St., Suite 1815
> New York NY 10122
> (212) 594-3490

Riviera Finance

■ A national factoring company with branches in many locations across the country

They have developed specialized programs for women and minorities in the past and are interested in working with women business owners. For more information and to locate the office closest to you, call Riviera headquarters at (800) 872-7484.

THE NONPROFIT ENTREPRENEUR

Studies have shown that women go into business as much to do something they believe is worthwhile as to make money. If your business idea lends itself to nonprofit status, and you would be satisfied to be a paid employee of the organization, explore this possibility. An Income of Her Own (see page 103) is an exciting example of a nonprofit organization that generates revenue from the sale of products and services, receives support from granting organizations, and forges innovative alliances with public and private entities.

Described here are some resources to help you explore the implications and potential of establishing a nonprofit organization, as well as some beginning sources to help you locate grants.

The Foundation Center

■ A foundation that helps educate the public about foundations and nonprofit entities and helps nonprofits locate funding sources

The Foundation Center acts as a clearinghouse on issues related to nonprofit funding. They publish many books on the topic of nonprofit ventures and directories of granting foundations and organizations. In addition, they help individuals and organizations identify appropriate funding sources through five national and regional centers and fifty cooperating libraries across the country. The foundation also publishes an excellent introductory book, *The Non-Profit Entrepreneur (Creating Ventures to Earn Income),* which describes what a nonprofit organization is, how it differs from a for-profit entity, and what the advantages and disadvantages of running one can be. Examples of interesting nonprofit ventures are included. (This book, last revised in 1988, is still available from The Foundation Center and remains one of the best overviews on the subject. Check your local library before ordering a copy.)

How to Proceed

For more information about the Foundation's services, publications, and locations, contact:

The Foundation Center
79 Fifth Ave.
New York NY 10003-3076
(800) 424-9836

Women's Funding Network **EW**

■ A network of nonprofit organizations that awards grants for projects about women

If your idea is designed to help improve the educational, economic, or social status of women or girls, contact the Women's Funding Network. This network is made up of granting foundations all across the country interested in supporting projects designed to help women. Each foundation has its own areas of interest and selection criteria for awarding grants. The Women's Sports Foundation, for example, is interested in projects that will improve women's (and girls') physical, mental, and emotional well-being through participation in sports and fitness activities. Others support projects in their local areas to fight physical and sexual abuse. For more information and to locate a network member in your area, contact:

> Women's Funding Network
> 1821 University Ave., Suite 409N
> St. Paul MN 55104-2803
> (612) 641-0742

Working Woman Start-up Grant **EW**

■ Periodic grants totaling fifty thousand dollars awarded to women entrepreneurs

Working Woman magazine and the national accounting firm Deloitte & Touche sponsor this grant competition. Judged by business experts, your application will be judged on how innovative and feasible your idea is. One or more winners are selected from a pool of regional semifinalists. A one-page summary of your idea and a three-year financial projection are required for entry. The *Working Woman* grant is awarded to for-profit entities.

How to Proceed

For more information about eligibility and entry requirements, contact:

> Entrepreneurial Grant Program
> Working Woman
> 230 Park Ave.
> New York NY 10169
> (212) 551-9500

AT&T Capital Corporation

■ Grant awards for socially responsible businesses

AT&T Capital Corporation and the American Institute of Certified Public Accountants have teamed up to foster socially responsible business development. This program, funded on an annual basis, awards its grant to for-profit entities only.

How to Proceed

Contact AT&T Capital Corp. at (800) 235-4288 for information about the status of the program and for an application when grants are being awarded.

Catalog of Federal Domestic Assistance

■ Directory of more than twelve hundred federal grants and assistance programs

This comprehensive listing includes information about how to apply for federal grants and assistance programs in every field imaginable, from health care and community development to environmental protection and vocational training. An annual subscription ($53) includes a mid-year supplement. (The catalog is sent in a three-ring binder so that supplements can be easily added.)

How to Proceed

Because the number of entries that relate to your interests will be small, check public or academic libraries in your area to see if this publication is available (or can be requested through interlibrary loan). For more information or to order, contact the U.S. Government Bookstore in your area (see page 223), or contact:

Superintendent of Documents
U.S. Government Printing Office
Mail Stop SM
Washington DC 20401
(202) 512-1800

Selling to the Government

You might think that selling to the government is only for big business, but it's not. The federal government purchases nearly two hundred billion dollars worth of goods and services—from pencils and janitorial services to new building construction—from U.S. businesses. That's a big market, and the federal government has special programs in place to help women business owners get a piece of it.

Historically, women have not fared well when the federal procurement pie has been sliced. For example, despite the fact that women own at least one-third of all U.S. businesses, they receive contracts for less than three billion dollars annually. However, the Federal Acquisition Streamlining Act of 1994 has established new guidelines and procedures designed to improve this picture as well as make the whole federal procurement process more manageable for all business owners.

Every year, the SBA works with all departments in the federal government to set annual goals for purchasing from woman-owned businesses and to identify businesses that can fulfill specific contracts. As a result of the Streamlining Act, all federal agencies must now set a minimum annual goal of purchasing at least 5 percent of needed goods and services from woman-owned enterprises. In addition, a special contract category for purchases of one hundred thousand dollars or less, called *small business set-asides*, requires federal agencies to purchase goods and services from small businesses. Since many woman-owned enterprises fall into the small business category, set-asides also help level the playing field for women business owners.

Procurement and *contracting* are the official terms used to describe the process of selling to the government, because purchasing agents contract with you to "procure" your company's goods or services. (There are also purchasing agents in state, county, and municipal governments and private companies.)

Included in this chapter is information about federal, state, and private resources to help you get started. Only brief references to sponsoring agencies have been included so that you don't get bogged down in unnecessary details. For more information about the federal agencies involved, see "A Guide to Federal Agencies" on page xiii. A review of the definitions of common terms on page xvi may also be helpful to you as you read this chapter. Listings with this symbol **EW** describe programs or resources that are specifically for women.

SELLING TO THE FEDERAL GOVERNMENT

Get Started at the Small Business Administration **EW**

- Publications and women's representatives get you started on the right track
- Sponsored by: SBA's Office of Women's Business Ownership (OWBO)

OWBO can provide you with a wealth of information about procurement and a copy of the SBA publication *Women Business Owners: Selling to the Federal Government*. In addition to information about procurement procedures, this publication includes lists of contracting specialists across the country who can help you sell to federal offices in your area. SBA women's representatives in district offices can also provide guidance on procurement issues, directing you to appropriate federal agencies and purchasing agents who might be interested in your company's products or services.

Women's representatives also coordinate specialized training seminars for women business owners on how to sell to the federal government.

How to Proceed

To order a copy of *Women Business Owners: Selling to the Federal Government,* contact OWBO at the number on the following page, or order a copy from the Government Printing Office (see page 51 for ordering information).

Office of Women's Business Ownership
Small Business Administration
409 Third St. SW, 6th Floor
Washington DC 20416
(202) 205-6673

For information about upcoming specialized training seminars and for guidance in locating appropriate purchasing agents, contact your regional SBA district office (see page 192).

Register with the Procurement Automated Source System (PASS)

■ A special database of small businesses keeps you in the running for contracting dollars

The PASS system, a computerized directory of small businesses interested in bidding for federal contracts, was set up to help small businesses get a fair share of federal procurement dollars. When you register, a profile of your company will be included in the directory. Federal purchasing agents and prime contractors will see your profile when they use the system to identify companies capable of bidding for particular contracts. The PASS system is free to both small businesses and purchasing agents.

As part of the Streamlining Act described in the introduction to this chapter, the SBA is developing an electronic system for all federal commerce. This system, projected to be up and running by the end of 1997, will provide businesses with current information on contract opportunities, consistent and simplified procedures for applying for contracts, and the opportunity to submit bids electronically.

How to Proceed
To register with PASS, you must fill out a one-page self-mailer application form available from your regional SBA office or by writing to:

Procurement Automated Source System Program
Small Business Administration
Mail Code 6256
409 Third St. SW
Washington DC 20416

Office of Government Contracting

- SBA publications that provide practical information and answers to common questions
- Sponsored by: SBA

The SBA Office of Government Contracting has two free publications that you shouldn't miss: *Procurement Assistance: A Practical Guide for Businesses Seeking Federal Contracts* and *The 25 Most-Asked Questions About Federal Procurement.* (This office works primarily on procurement policy and research and is not set up to work directly with business owners. However, staff will provide these excellent publications and help you locate resources if other offices have not been able to answer your questions.)

How to Proceed

Call the office at (202) 205-6460 to request publications.

Office of Small and Disadvantaged Business Utilization (OSDBU)

- Special offices to help women business owners sell to the federal government
- Sponsored by: All major federal agencies

If you want to turn the federal government into a customer, the Office of Small and Disadvantaged Business Utilization (OSDBU) is a resource you won't want to miss. An OSDBU office has been set up in every major department in the federal government to help minorities, women, and small business owners gain access to the federal procurement process.

You can contact the small business specialist or the women's business specialist in each department's OSDBU to determine if your products or services can fulfill any of their procurement requirements. Once you identify which agencies you might do business with, ask for the forms necessary to be added to their solicitation mailing lists. Also request a list of each agency's procurement offices and purchasing agents so you can begin marketing to them.

Two federal departments, the Department of Transportation and NASA, earmark specific dollar amounts annually for woman-owned businesses. Those would be good doors to knock on first.

To give you an idea of what sort of assistance is available, the Department of Commerce, which runs an active women's program, is profiled below.

PROFILE

U.S. Department of Commerce

The Department of Commerce's OSDBU is responsible for ensuring that small, minority, and women-owned businesses receive a fair share of all federal contracts. As a part of that effort, the department has increased its purchases from women-owned enterprises by more than $31 million since the early 1980s, when it purchased approximately $2.8 million annually.

Through its women's program, the department sponsors conferences and publishes directories, handbooks, and bibliographies specifically for women business owners. In addition, women are actively sought to serve on the department's advisory boards and in technical programs.

Each year, the Commerce Department's fourteen bureaus, agencies, and offices purchase everything from direct-mail advertising services to X-ray equipment. Through its OSDBU office, which includes a women's business specialist, the department offers personal counseling to women interested in selling to the federal government and the Department of Commerce specifically.

The free publication *How to Sell to the United States Department of Commerce* is a good introduction to this market. It includes step-by-step information about how to get in the department's procurement pipeline and whom to contact for different types of information. It also includes lists of what each bureau in the department purchases. (By checking this list, you will be able to determine if you can provide a service or product that the Department of Commerce needs.)

How to Proceed

For more information about selling to the U.S. Department of Commerce and to receive a copy of *How to Sell to the United States Department of Commerce,* contact the women's business specialist at:

> **Office of Small and Disadvantaged Business Utilization**
> **U.S. Department of Commerce**
> Fourteenth St. and Constitution Ave. NW, Room H6411
> Washington DC 20230
> (202) 482-1472

For information about selling to other federal agencies, contact the OSDBU in each federal agency or department and ask for the small business specialist or women's business specialist. (For a list of OSDBUs in all major federal agencies, see page 268.)

Certification Program for Women Business Owners EW

- Become eligible for procurement dollars that are earmarked for woman-owned businesses

- Sponsored by: State Department of Transportation

Odd as it may seem, your State Department of Transportation is a good office to contact for Women's Business Enterprise (WBE) certification. WBE certification takes place at the state level because a special program through the Federal Department of Transportation (DOT) earmarks contracting dollars for woman-owned businesses. Each year, the federal DOT works with state transportation departments to set goals for awarding construction contracts to individual states' woman-owned businesses.

As a part of this process, the state transportation departments began certifying businesses that are owned 51 percent or more by women. This certification is always accepted by transportation department programs, most federal agencies, and, in some states, by other state and municipal agencies. Even if you are not in the construction business, it's worthwhile to investigate the program. Companies providing related services and products, such as environmental cleanup, landscaping, and highway maintenance and a host of others are eligible for certification and contracting opportunities.

How to Proceed

See page 274 for a state-by-state listing of transportation departments. Also check the listing of first-stop state offices on page 225. Many of them are involved in WBE certification as well.

If you are interested in learning more about the federal DOT contracting programs, contact the Department of Transportation OSDBU at (800) 532-1169. Another valuable source of information about DOT activities and programs is a newsletter, *The Transportation Link,* produced for the DOT OSDBU by:

The Interracial Council for Business Opportunity
51 Madison Ave., Suite 2212
New York NY 10010
(800) 326-7328

Office of Federal Procurement Policy (OFPP)

■ Office whose sole function is to study procurement policy

This office studies critical issues in establishing and carrying out fair, effective contracting guidelines and legislation. Policies about subcontracting, prime contracting, purchasing goals, and related topics are the focus. As a part of the Federal Acquisition Streamlining Act of 1994, this office is also studying the issue of standardizing definitions of woman-owned businesses and procedures for certifying them. As part of their review of this issue, OFPP staff met with women business owners and representatives of women's business organizations. This office can be contacted directly for the most current information on procurement policy.

Executive Office of the President
Office of Federal Procurement Policy
New Executive Office Building, Room 9013
725 Seventeenth St. NW
Washington DC 20503
(202) 395-3501

Small Business Technology Programs

■ Specialized contracting opportunities for technology companies

■ Sponsored by: SBA and other federal agencies

For companies involved in innovative technology research and development or commercialization, three programs are available: the Small Business Innovation and Research program, the Small Business Technology Transfer program, and the R & D Goaling program. Each program emphasizes either research and development or the application of technologies to the specific needs of federal agencies such as NASA, the Department of Defense, and the Department of Energy, among others. These agencies provide more than two billion dollars in contracts annually.

How to Proceed

For more information about small business technology programs, call your district SBA office (see page 192) or contact:

> The Office of Innovation, Research, and Technology
> 409 Third St. SW, Suite 8150
> Washington DC 20416
> (202) 205-6450

Registration on the Automated Business Locator System (ABELS)

■ An electronic database lets purchasing agents know about your business

■ Sponsored by: U.S. Department of Commerce Minority Business Development Agency

The Automated Business Locator System (ABELS) is an on-line computer directory set up to help purchasing agents in private businesses, state or municipal governments, and the federal government identify minority businesses that can meet their needs for goods and services. ABELS is a free service to minority businesses and to companies or government agencies using the database.

How to Proceed

To register with ABELS, you need to fill out an ABELS Registration/Certification Form and return it to the U.S. Department of Commerce MBDA address that follows. Registration forms are available from your regional MBDA office (see page 218) or from:

Minority Business Development Agency
U.S. Department of Commerce
Information Technology Branch, Room H5712
Fourteenth St. and Constitution Ave. NW
Washington DC 20230
(202) 582-1958

Commerce Business Daily: News on Selling Opportunities

■ Commerce Department publication to keep you current on procurement opportunities

Commerce Business Daily (CBD), published by the Department of Commerce, is a comprehensive source of information about upcoming opportunities to sell to the government. Included in each listing are the name and address of the agency looking for contractors, the service or product desired, the proposal deadline, and phone numbers to request contract specifications information.

CBD also includes information about companies that have recently received large government contracts. These large contractors, referred to as *prime contractors,* subcontract parts of their work out, thus making opportunities available to smaller companies.

An annual subscription to CBD is approximately $250. Depending on your company's procurement potential, a subscription may or may not be a good investment. The state Procurement Technical Assistance Centers (see page 280) subscribe to CBD and can make it available to you. Also check the section under private resources in this chapter; CBD information targeted to your company's needs may be available at a more reasonable price from private information brokers (page 155).

How to Proceed

To subscribe or to get an information booklet about CBD, contact:

Superintendent of Documents
U.S. Government Printing Office
Washington DC 20402
(202) 512-1800

Government Printing Office Procurement Publications

■ Low-cost guides to the world of government contracting

In addition to the publication (*Women Business Owners: Selling to the Federal Government*) described earlier, many other useful government publications on procurement are available. *Doing Business with the Federal Government* is a good place to get a general overview. Combined with more specialized books on a variety of topics (selling to the military, for instance), these publications can be an inexpensive way to educate yourself on how to succeed in the government contracting arena. Also available is a catalog, *Selling to the Government*, which includes leads on people and agencies to contact when looking for specific kinds of contracting opportunities.

How to Proceed

To get more information about procurement booklets, call or visit a government bookstore in your area (see page 223). To receive a brochure that includes a list of publications about selling to the government, contact:

> Superintendent of Documents
> U.S. Government Printing Office
> Washington DC 20402
> (202) 512-1800

More Tips on How to Get Started

The information here is just the beginning—the first of many things you will need to get your foot in the door. Find out as much as you can about government purchasing needs by talking to procurement specialists and purchasing agents, reading each department's guidelines, and attending training sessions on selling to the government. Also, there will be many regional and departmental procurement specialists listed in publications you receive from the SBA, the U.S. Department of Commerce, and other offices. Contact those that are appropriate, either because they work specifically in your geographic area or because you can fulfill their needs.

The most important thing, though, is to make yourself known to the purchasing agents. Contact them personally if you have determined you have something they need.

Send your product or service information to them, attend procurement fairs where you will meet purchasing agents, and register with PASS (see page 145) and, if you are a minority business owner, ABELS (see page 150).

SELLING TO STATE GOVERNMENTS

Women's Business Enterprise (WBE) Certification Program EW

- Grants eligibility for state, local, and private procurement dollars set aside for woman-owned businesses
- Sponsored by: State departments of transportation and first-stop offices

WBE certification can help you get contracts from state, county, and local agencies (as well as private companies) interested in purchasing services and products from woman-owned businesses. In the previous section, "Selling to the Federal Government," an explanation is provided for why WBE certification often occurs on the state level and is handled by state transportation departments (page 148). Certification by your state transportation department is necessary to participate in that department's small-business set-asides for highway construction, maintenance, and related services. (Many transportation departments also publish a state directory of WBE-certified businesses that is used by purchasing agents to identify vendor businesses.) In some states, DOT certification is accepted by certain other agencies also, but not all.

Your state's first-stop office is also a good resource for WBE certification. Many first-stop offices offer their own certification program. Completion of the program through this office, if available, will make you eligible for many contracting opportunities, not only those related to transportation projects.

How to Proceed

If your company can provide goods or services needed in highway construction and maintenance, contact your state's department of transportation about contracting opportunities or to pursue WBE certification. For a state-by-state listing of transportation departments, see page 274. If your state's first-stop office (see page 225) is involved in WBE certification, consider going through its program so you will be eligible to bid on all appropriate state contracts.

Procurement Technical Assistance Centers

- Agencies across the country that provide contracting assistance close to home
- Sponsored by: State and federal governments

If you want to get in on selling to state and municipal agencies in your area, as well as to federal offices, there is help right in your backyard. Almost every state has at least one Procurement Technical Assistance Center to help educate business owners about contracting opportunities at the federal, state, and local levels.

The programs and services offered vary by state, but to give you an idea of what resources you might find, a description follows of the program in Oregon, where there are five assistance center offices.

PROFILE

Oregon's Procurement Technical Assistance Program

The Oregon program is comprehensive, helping businesses to find contracting opportunities, meet bidding and agency requirements, prepare proposals, and even collect payment for completed work. The offices offer workshops, seminars, and individual training in all aspects of the procurement process.

Oregon has developed its own procurement database and electronic bulletin board. Procurement specialists use this database in conjunction with *Commerce Business Daily* and other resources to hook clients up with the right opportunities. Clients can also get information from the system by logging on with a computer and modem.

In Oregon, there has been a strong effort to help businesses sell to their state, county, and local government agencies. The packet of material from Oregon's program, which includes registration forms and an overview of the program, also lists purchasing agents in state, county, and municipal offices.

How to Proceed

Contact the office closest to you in your state. See page 280 for a state-by-state listing of assistance centers. Reviewing the list, you will see that some offices specialize in certain areas (such as Indian affairs or defense purchasing). If there is more than one office in your area, select one that is appropriate for your interests.

PRIVATE SOURCES OF PROCUREMENT INFORMATION

Women Business Owners Corporation (WBOC) **EW**

■ Provides uniform certification for WBOs and procurement technical assistance for woman-owned firms and purchasing agents

What is a woman-owned business? If one is certified by one agency, should other agencies accept the certification? Should corporate purchasing agents accept certification by governmental bodies? A lack of answers to these questions has caused confusion and duplication of effort, resulting in lost contracts for women and fewer purchasing agents buying from women. WBOC's mission is to overcome these pitfalls. Working closely with government agencies and private organizations, WBOC is developing national programs to streamline women's access to procurement opportunities and purchasing agents' access to woman-led firms. WBOC's top goals and activities include a national certification program for woman-owned businesses; the WBOC Internet Network, where procurement information and a national database of certified women-owned businesses can be found; technical assistance for government and corporate purchasing agents; and the WBOC Procurement Institute to help women suppliers understand and participate in government and corporate purchasing opportunities. A participant in the SBA demonstration site program (see page 90), WBOC is establishing a national consortium of women's organizations to help with cooperative resource development.

How to Proceed

For more information about certification or WBOC activities, or to participate in the consortium, contact:

> **Women Business Owners Corporation**
> 18 Encanto Dr.
> Palos Verdes CA 90274-4215
> (310) 530-7500

National Directory of Women-Owned Business Firms `EW`

- Free listing to help purchasing agents find you
- Published by: Business Research

Federal, state, and corporate purchasing agents use this directory to identify woman-owned firms that can fulfill their service and product needs. For more information and a free listing form, contact:

> **Business Research**
> 4201 Connecticut Ave. NW, Suite 610
> Washington DC 20008-1158
> (800) 845-8420

Electronic Information Brokers

Information about opportunities to sell to federal agencies, including news from *Commerce Business Daily,* is available in electronic and printed form from a number of private companies. Information about state and local government contracts is also available from some of the services. The information provided—and the procedures for obtaining it—vary from company to company, so check with each one.

Some companies can search for contract opportunities in the private and public sector that specifically request proposals from woman-owned businesses. To give you an idea of how these services work, one company is profiled below.

PROFILE

Softshare Government Information Services

Softshare makes information available in electronic or printed form to subscribers. An interactive on-line system is available twenty-four hours a day, as well as an electronic system which keeps you informed of contract opportunities that match key search terms you have selected (such as "woman-owned" or "office supplies"). Softshare staff members are available to help you design an effective search strategy. The Softshare database includes information on federal, state, local, and foreign market opportunities.

In addition to search services, Softshare offers a reporting system called SMART that provides market information about your industry's activity in federal contracting. With SMART, you can find out who is buying how much from what companies and base your marketing strategy on that information.

In cases in which an agency accepts electronic submission of proposals, Softshare can help you submit them properly, thus ensuring that your response is received before bid deadlines.

How to Proceed

Request information from the companies listed here, and select the one most appropriate for your needs.

Alden Electronics
40 Washington St.
Westboro MA 01581
(800) 876-1232

Knight-Ridder Information Services Inc.
2440 El Camino Real
Mountain View CA 94040
(800) 334-2564

United Communications Group
11300 Rockville Pike Station, Suite 1100
Rockville MD 20852
(800) 223-4551

Government Access and Information Network (GAIN)
(For more information about this interactive fax service, see page 52.)

Lexis Nexis
P.O. Box 933
Dayton OH 45401
(800) 543-6862

Mercury Computer Services
222 S. Market St., Suite 104
Elizabethtown PA 17022
(800) 669-2441

Sales Opportunity Services
1538 Rear East Pleasant Valley Blvd.
Altoona PA 16602
(800) 225-6853

Softshare Government Information Services
136 W. Canon Perdido, Suite C
Santa Barbara CA 93101
(800) 346-6703

National Minority Business Council (NMBC)

■ Ongoing assistance and resources for an annual membership fee

NMBC provides training and procurement assistance to minority-owned businesses. Women are not specifically included in the organization's primary definition of *minority*, but businesses owned by minority women are eligible for membership.

Membership benefits include international trade assistance, referral of your business to buying agents through a computerized directory, a free listing in the *Corporate Purchasing Directory*, a subscription to the bimonthly *NMBC Business Report*, and discounts on business travel services.

How to Proceed

Call or write the council at:

National Minority Business Council
235 E. Forty-second St.
New York NY 10017
(212) 573-2385

Contract Services Association (CSA)

- Membership organization that serves as an advocate for businesses that contract with the federal government

CSA is a nonprofit membership organization offering advocacy and networking opportunities for its members. It serves as a watchdog in Washington, D.C., monitoring policies and legislation and keeping members informed through reports on issues that affect them. The association maintains a close relationship with many federal agencies to keep abreast of contracting opportunities and program changes, and it works to protect and increase these opportunities. The organization serves all businesses, not just those owned by women, but it does have women- and minority-owned businesses in its membership. As part of the membership requirements, all member businesses must agree to adhere to the organization's code of ethics. For more information, contact:

Contract Services Association
1200 G St. NW, Suite 750
Washington DC 20005-3802
(202) 347-0600

Membership Organizations

By identifying and joining organizations that match your interests, you can tap into a large network of like-minded businesswomen, receive regular association magazines and newsletters, and take advantage of educational and professional development opportunities on a national and regional level. This chapter includes names, addresses, and phone numbers for three types of national organizations:

- Women's business organizations

- Women's professional organizations

- General business associations

When contacting organizations that sound interesting, ask for samples of their publications and flyers about past conferences so you can determine if the organization's focus and activities match your needs. Some associations offer subscriptions and conference attendance to nonmembers, so also ask about these options if you like some aspects of the organization but don't want to make a membership commitment.

WOMEN'S BUSINESS ORGANIZATIONS EW

The organizations included in this section operate specifically to meet the needs of women business owners and entrepreneurs. Each organization has a different focus, designed to meet the needs and interests of particular segments within the women's business ownership community.

American Business Women's Association (ABWA)

P.O. Box 8728
Kansas City MO 64114-0728
(816) 361-6621

With a membership of more than one hundred thousand businesswomen in the United States and Puerto Rico, ABWA brings together women of diverse backgrounds to provide professional and personal development opportunities. Membership benefits include *Women in Business* magazine; national and regional conferences; discounts on travel, prescriptions, and other products; accidental death or dismemberment insurance; and no-annual-fee credit cards.

American Women in Enterprise (AWE)

71 Vanderbuilt Ave., Suite 320
New York NY 10169
(212) 692-9100

AWE membership benefits include access to a telephone hotline for up to ten minutes of expert advice on an urgent issue, a subscription to the *Women in Enterprise* newsletter, networking events, an annual conference, and a variety of purchasing opportunities including access to a buying service for major purchases such as business equipment and cars. Membership also includes discounts on services from the American Women's Economic Development Corporation (AWED), an entrepreneurial training center that offers expert training and counseling in every phase of business growth, development, and management. Program participants have access to courses and personal and telephone counseling.

Association of Black Women Entrepreneurs Inc. (ABWE)

P.O. Box 49368

Los Angeles CA 90049

(213) 624-8639

ABWE provides members with business and educational support through networking, referrals, joint ventures, mentoring opportunities, a quarterly newsletter, seminars, and one annual phone consultation.

The Committee of 200

625 N. Michigan Ave., Suite 500

Chicago IL 60611

(312) 751-3477

Members of The Committee of 200 are presidents, owners, or high-level decision-makers from companies with annual revenues typically exceeding ten million dollars.

The organization has established a foundation dedicated to recognizing and fostering entrepreneurship in women. Through this foundation, scholarships, outreach seminars, and other activities are provided to women in business.

The International Alliance (TIA)

8600 LaSalle Rd., Suite 617

Baltimore MD 21286

(410) 472-4221

TIA serves as a central forum for women's networks across the country by providing members with leadership and skill training, by promoting greater recognition of women's achievements, and by helping public and private organizations identify female expertise. The association sponsors an annual conference, network meetings, and a speaker's bank, and it also publishes a bimonthly newsletter and membership directory.

The Mother's Home Business Network

P.O. Box 423
East Meadows NY 11554
(516) 997-7394

Founded by a woman who has worked at home for fifteen years while raising her children, this group provides support, guidance, and information for mothers working at home—or those who would like to be.

Membership benefits include a subscription to the network's newsletter, *Homeworking Mothers,* which includes inspiring home-business stories, advice, book reviews, a regular feature on dealing with business and kids under the same roof, and a classified ad section. Members also receive an information kit and a copy of *Mother's Money Making Manual.*

National Association of Female Executives (NAFE)

30 Irving Pl., 5th Floor
New York NY 10003
(212) 477-2200

NAFE, a networking and professional development organization, offers contacts and support across the country through its extensive network of local member groups. NAFE offers an array of member benefits, including satellite conferences, access to a loan and venture-capital fund, career assistance, and an excellent full-color magazine, *Executive Female.* NAFE also offers members benefits in the form of financial services, discount purchasing, travel and car rental discounts, travel services, insurance, and health benefits.

National Association of Women Business Owners (NAWBO)

1377 K St. NW, Suite 637
Washington DC 20005
(301) 608-2590

NAWBO, the official U.S. member of the World Association of Women Entrepreneurs, is the only national organization that represents all women business owners. Its membership benefits include national and international networking, management and technical assistance at the local chapter level, newsletters, a full-color magazine, and access to an "angel" network of members interested in investing in woman-owned businesses. In 1995, NAWBO also launched a loan fund with Wells Fargo Bank for all women business owners (see page 127). Opportunities to learn about and participate in international trade missions and international conferences are provided. Members also receive access to product and service discount purchasing.

NAWBO founded the National Foundation for Women Business Owners (see page 62), a nonprofit organization that collects and reports data on women's business-ownership issues and develops women's business-training programs.

National Chamber of Commerce for Women

10 Waterside Plaza, Suite 6H
New York NY 10010
(212) 685-3454

The chamber makes a variety of resources and services available to working and self-employed women through participation on four committees that target members' needs. The committees are The Business Owner's Advisory, The Home-Based Committee, The Productivity Improvement Network, and The World of Women's Business Committee. Assistance is provided through a combination of mentoring, phone counseling, access to information banks, a venture-capital fund, and attendance at free workshops. For more specific information about the committees and services, see page 105.

National Federation of Black Women Business Owners (NFBWB)

1500 Massachusetts Ave. NW, Suite 22
Washington DC 20005
(202) 833-3450

NFBWB works to improve African American women business owners' opportunities to participate fully in the economy with an emphasis on purchasing and contracting activities. The federation offers educational opportunities through seminars, conferences, and trade fairs, and it provides management and technical assistance to members on specific business-development issues (such as finding capital or writing a business plan). The federation maintains a database of its members for purchasing agents and advocates for members in the public and private sector.

Member benefits include participation in training and technical assistance programs, a newsletter, access to the federation's information clearinghouse on contracting issues, and networking opportunities with other members.

National Federation of Business and Professional Women's Clubs (BPW)

2012 Massachusetts Ave. NW
Washington DC 20036
(202) 293-1100

This is an advocacy and educational organization for working women, including business owners. The organization runs the BPW Foundation, a nonprofit research and educational organization, and the BPW Political Action Committee, which provides contributions to and endorses women and pro-women candidates.

Membership benefits include *National Business Woman* magazine, advocacy in Washington and assistance in developing advocacy programs, a legislative hotline, skill-building programs, annual conventions, access to loan funds, and discounts on insurance and other products and services.

National Women's Economic Alliance Foundation (NWEAF)

1440 New York Ave. NW, Suite 300
Washington DC 20005
(202) 393-5257

NWEAF addresses issues of professional, economic, and career development of executive-level men and women in the free-enterprise system. The organization conducts research, provides a placement service, and offers leadership training. Members receive a semiannual newsletter, periodic policy papers, and an annual directory of new women entrepreneurs.

Organization of Women in International Trade (OWIT)

1377 K St. NW, Suite 857
Washington DC 20005
(301) 953-0676 (voice-mail referral only)

An educational, networking, and professional-development organization, OWIT offers annual conferences, periodic seminars and workshops, international networking, and trade missions for women involved in all aspects of international trade, including consulting, agricultural trade, import and export, manufacturing, transportation, and related fields such as sales and marketing, finance, and customs.

Wider Opportunity for Women (WOW)

815 Fifteenth St. NW, Suite 916
Washington DC 20005
(202) 638-3143

WOW works to achieve economic independence and equality of opportunity for women and girls, advocating nontraditional work opportunities for women in every state and the District of Columbia. WOW leads the Women's Work Force Network of more than five hundred independent women's employment programs. A membership branch provides career development, training, and other work-related assistance services.

Women in Franchising (WIF)

53 W. Jackson St., Suite 205
Chicago IL 60604
(800) 222-4943
(312) 431-1467

This organization serves as an information resource for women interested in franchising. To receive information from companies in your area of interest that are looking for women to buy franchises, you must complete a questionnaire about your franchise interests, business background, areas of expertise, ability to purchase a franchise, and income goals. That and $12 buys you a year's worth of information.

Women's Economic Round Table (WERT)

1633 Broadway
New York NY 10017
(212) 759-4360

This organization works to inform and educate its members and the public about important economic issues of our times and to encourage its members to actively influence policy makers. To further its mission, WERT sponsors public forums and member seminars, participates in media coverage of economic issues, and serves as a resource center to business, government, and academia.

Women's Franchise Network

The International Franchise Association
1350 New York Ave. NW, Suite 900
Washington DC 20005
(202) 628-8000 ext. 7788

The International Franchise Association sponsors regional annual conferences for women who are interested in learning more about franchising and networking with women franchise owners.

Women Incorporated (WI)

1401 Twenty-first St., Suite 310
Sacramento CA 95814
(800) 930-3993

This organization's primary mission is to increase women's access to capital. Members have access to a loan pool of $150 million through WI's partnerships with the Money Store and other lenders. In addition, WI provides a wide range of membership benefits, including product and service discounts; health insurance; discounts with business service providers such as Federal Express and Kinko's; travel discounts; access to the Women's Leadership Connection, an on-line service; an excellent full-color magazine; and much more. The new-member kit alone contains a wealth of information. It includes contact information for the organization's vice president of product development (who is available to provide customized help for marketing and management questions), as well as fact sheets on marketing, employee management, and other business topics.

FINDING ORGANIZATIONS IN YOUR AREA

This chapter focuses on national organizations. Although many such organizations have state and local chapters, independent local groups are another excellent source of support and information. To identify local and state women's business organizations and networking groups:

- Contact your SBA women's business representative (see page 192). The SBA district offices work closely with many business groups and may be familiar with an organization in your local area.

- Contact your state women's commission (see page 240). Most commissions serve as clearinghouses for women's resources in their states and maintain databases of women's organizations as a part of that function.

- Check the weekly listing of meetings that appears in most local newspapers.

- Contact The Business Women's Network in Washington, D.C., at (800) 48-WOMEN. This organization researches and publishes *The Business Women's Network Directory*, a comprehensive directory of national, state, and local women's organizations across the country. A referral and research nonprofit organization, The Business Women's Network will refer women to appropriate resources and organizations. For more information about the network and its activities, see page 60.

WOMEN'S PROFESSIONAL ORGANIZATIONS **EW**

The professional groups listed here provide a way for women in specific fields to network with their colleagues, attend seminars and conferences within their industry, and receive publications of interest in specific fields of expertise.

American Agri-Women (AAW)

11841 N. Mt. Vernon Rd.
Shannon IL 61078
(815) 864-2359

AAW, a coalition of farm, ranch, and agribusiness women's organizations, works to educate consumers and policy makers about the value and status of the American farm. AAW addresses issues of food safety, health care, natural resources, water management, and business and tax matters related to successful agricultural management. AAW offers members educational programs and opportunities to influence policy and to network with other women in agriculture and related industries. The coalition has many state affiliates and publishes a bimonthly newsletter, *The Voice of American Agri-Woman*.

American Society of Women Accountants (ASWA)

1755 Lynnfield Rd., Suite 222
Memphis TN 38119-7235
(800) 326-2163
(901) 680-0470

ASWA offers its members an array of professional development opportunities through annual and regional conferences, job referral, career counseling, leadership training, and mentoring. Members receive a monthly newsletter, a membership directory, and discounts on products and services (such as subscriptions and car rentals), and they are eligible for the member loan program. Educational scholarships are also available to support women interested in entering the accounting field.

American Women in Radio and Television (AWRT)

1650 Tyson Blvd., Suite 200
McClean VA 22102
(703) 506-3290

AWRT serves as an educational, advocacy, and referral organization for women in electronic media and related fields. Membership benefits include a newsletter, educational and networking opportunities at regional conferences, and a national convention. Members receive a membership directory; have access to Careerline, a national listing of job openings; are eligible for a variety of awards; and can participate in state and local chapter activities. AWRT also sponsors a foundation that is involved in philanthropic activities designed to promote educational, literary, and charitable activities in the broadcast industry.

American Women's Society of CPAs (AWSCPA)

401 N. Michigan Ave.
Chicago IL 60611
(800) 297-2721

AWSCPA provides networking, advocacy, education, and leadership training for women accountants. These programs are designed to foster professional development and gender equity in the field. Additional membership benefits include travel and phone discounts; business, life, and medical insurance; pension planning services; college scholarships; disability and cancer insurance; and a periodic newsletter.

Association for Women in Computing (AWC)

41 Sutter St., Suite 1006
San Francisco CA 94104
(415) 905-4663

This association works to advance the role of women in the computing industry and to keep its members informed about legal, technical, and other issues related to computing. The association offers opportunities for professional development through technical training, motivational seminars, and networking. Members receive the association quarterly, *NewsBytes*.

Association of Real Estate Women (AREW)

15 W. Seventy-second St., Suite 31G
New York NY 10023-3402
(212) 799-6697

AREW represents women in all fields related to real estate—from architecture and appraisal to finance and sales. An educational and networking organization, AREW sponsors seminars, workshops, and luncheons, and it publishes *AREW News,* a monthly newsletter for members.

Federation of Organizations for Professional Women

1825 I St., Suite 400
Washington DC 20006
(202) 328-1415

The federation is an affiliation of organizations committed to improving the status of professional women in all fields. Membership benefits include seminars and conferences, networking opportunities, a newsletter, a directory of women's organizations, and a variety of other publications, including one specifically for women interested in starting their own businesses. The federation also maintains a legal fund to support business and professional women who have experienced discrimination.

Financial Women International (FWI)

7910 Woodmont Ave., Suite 1430
Bethesda MD 20814-3015
(301) 657-8288

FWI, the largest individual membership organization of women financial executives today, works to keep its members in touch with every facet of the financial industry and in step with local, national, and global economic trends. Each member receives a free annual portfolio review that helps her to assess her strengths and weaknesses and to set goals and explore ways to achieve them. The organization offers continuing-education self-study courses and management and leadership training. Included in the cost of membership are subscriptions to the organization's publications, *FWI Management Quarterly* and *Financial Women Today.*

International Network of Women in Technology (WITI)

4641 Burnet Ave.
Sherman Oaks CA 91403
(818) 990-6705

WITI works to improve the status and increase recognition of the contributions of women in all disciplines and industries who work with technology. Membership benefits include access to the WITI e-mail network, participation in specialized professional development activities, a subscription to the organization's newsletter, *The Strategist*, and an opportunity to attend WITI's annual conference.

International Women's Writing Guild (IWWG)

P.O. Box 810
Gracie Station
New York NY 10028
(212) 737-7536

For women in the writing profession and those who aspire to be writers, the guild provides a combination of practical benefits such as health insurance for the self-employed; an IWWG Mastercard; a subscription to the bimonthly newsletter, *Network;* and a variety of educational events, including the Skidmore Summer Writing Conference and an open house twice a year in New York City where writers can meet agents. The guild also provides guidance in how to set up "zip code parties" that put you in touch with other members in your area.

National Association of Black Women Attorneys, Inc. (NABWA)

3711 Macomb St. NW
Washington DC 20016
(202) 966-9693

This association's primary missions are to address the special problems of being an African American woman attorney and to help female African American law students through a scholarship fund. Although NABWA is a professional organization, its membership is open to non-lawyers interested in helping advance the organization's purpose.

National Association of Women Artists (NAWA)

41 Union Square W, Room 906
New York NY 10003

NAWA's mission is to support women in the fine arts by making exhibit space available and by increasing public awareness of women artists through increased exhibitions. The association has a permanent collection on exhibit in New York; annual traveling exhibitions hosted by art centers, museums, and universities across the country; and international exhibitions. Videos, lectures, and other support materials and activities accompany many of the exhibitions. Based in New York, the association has regional chapters and is working to expand with more. To receive membership information, send NAWA a self-addressed stamped envelope.

National Association of Women Health Professionals (NAWHP)

175 W. Jackson Blvd., Suite A1711
Chicago IL 60604-2801
(312) 786-1468

NAWHP is the only national organization for health-care practitioners (men and women) who provide health-care services for women. Members support the premise that women should be informed decision-makers in their own health care.

The association offers educational opportunities through its conferences and extensive product line of publications, audiotapes, and videos on health care management and practice. The association newsletter, *Focus,* covers research, legislative issues, trends, and health care practices.

National Association of Women in Construction (NAWIC)

327 S. Adams St.
Fort Worth TX 76104
(800) 552-3506
(817) 877-5551

This group works to promote acceptance and advancement of women in the construction industry and educates members in new construction techniques. National and local scholarships are available for engineering construction or architecture students. Members receive the monthly association magazine.

National Association of Women in Insurance (NAWI)

P.O. Box 4410
Tulsa OK 74159
(800) 766-6249
(918) 744-5195

A professional development and networking organization, NAWI's primary mission is to increase the number of women in leadership positions in the insurance industry. It accomplishes these goals through public relations efforts, leadership training, and certification of individual members as Certified Professional Insurance Women.

Membership benefits include subscriptions to *Today's Insurance Woman* and *Leadership News,* a toll-free answer line, educational publications and meetings, and discounts on products and services.

National Association of Women Lawyers (NAWL)

American Bar Center
750 N. Lake Shore Dr.
Chicago IL 60611
(312) 988-6186

Affiliated with the American Bar Association, the International Bar Association, and the International Federation of Women Lawyers, NAWL works to advance the role of women in the legal profession and the judiciary. The association selects and endorses qualified lawyers for public office and all levels of the judiciary. It has a voting delegate in the House of Delegates of the American Bar Association and works through a variety of commissions and federations to improve the status of women in the profession (and women in the legal system in general). Membership benefits include a mentorship program for recently admitted attorneys, educational opportunities at annual regional meetings, and a subscription to the *President's Newsletter* and the quarterly *Women Lawyers Journal.*

National Network of Commercial Real Estate Women (NNCREW)

3115 W. Sixth St., Suite C122
Lawrence KS 66049
(913) 832-1808

A federation of almost thirty independent local organizations, NNCREW provides a national communication vehicle for all women in commercial real estate and related fields such as architecture, property management, interior design, construction, and institutional lending. NNCREW sponsors an annual conference and several regional conferences, and publishes the *National Network News* to help members stay up-to-date on industry issues and member news. Members receive a membership directory.

Roundtable for Women in Food Service, Inc.

425 Central Park West, Suite 2A
New York NY 10025-4323
(212) 865-8100

This organization is open to all professionals in the food-service, beverage, and hospitality industries. It offers a wide range of member benefits, including three national educational events each year, a membership directory, and a quarterly newsletter. Women new to the industry can choose to have a mentor and participate in networking activities at the national and local chapter levels. A special small business membership category is available to owners of businesses with no more than fifty employees.

Society of Women Engineers (SWE)

120 Wall St.
New York NY 10005
(212) 509-9577

This nonprofit organization is made up of graduate engineers and men and women with equivalent engineering experience. The specific objectives of the society are: to inform young women, their parents, counselors, and the general public of the qualifications and achievements of women engineers and the opportunities open to them; to assist women engineers in readying themselves for a return to active work after temporary retirement; to serve as a center of information on women in engineering; and to encourage women engineers to attain high levels of education and professional achievement. The society sponsors an annual convention and student conference that includes technical sessions, workshops, tours, and industrial exhibits.

Women Construction Owners and Executives, USA (WCOE)

1000 Duke St.
Alexandria VA 22314
(703) 684-6060
(800) 788-3548

WCOE serves as an advocacy and professional-development organization for women owners and executives in the construction industry. Membership benefits include attendance at annual conferences, WBE certification assistance, bonding and legal advice, and access to a credit union and business networking opportunities. Members also receive a membership directory and WCOE's newsletter, *The Turning Point.*

Women's Council

National Association of Home Builders
1201 Fifteenth St. NW
Washington DC 20005-2800
(800) 368-5254 ext. 433
(202) 822-0433

The council serves as an educational and professional development organization for women in the home-building industry. Three national conferences each year offer opportunities for networking, leadership training, and attendance at seminars on specific industry topics. The bimonthly newsletter, the *Networker,* includes information on business management, the building industry, and member activities. The council also produces videos and other educational publications for its members, many of which can be rented through its resource library.

Women in Agribusiness (WIA)

P.O. Box 10241
Kansas City MO 64111
(No telephone number available)

This organization's purpose is to organize women in agribusiness and to provide a forum on relevant issues in their field. Membership benefits include a newsletter, a membership directory, and networking opportunities.

Women in Aerospace (WIA)

922 Pennsylvania Ave. SE
Washington DC 20003
(202) 547-9451

The only professional organization that provides a formal network for women working in the aerospace field, WIA works to expand women's advancement opportunities in the field and to increase their visibility as aerospace professionals. Membership benefits include a quarterly newsletter, a membership directory, site visits, and an annual conference.

Women in Cable & Telecommunications

230 W. Monroe, Suite 730
Chicago IL 60606
(312) 634-2330

This organization works to improve economic and career opportunities for women in telecommunications and other closely related industries by serving as an advocacy group, providing educational opportunities, and offering specialized training in leadership and executive development. The annual National Management Conference focuses on real-life cable-management issues using case studies to help foster new skills and problem-solving abilities.

Women in Communications, Inc. (WICI)

10605 Judicial Dr., Suite A-4
Fairfax VA 22030-5167
(703) 359-9000

This organization offers educational and networking opportunities to professional communicators in print and broadcast journalism, public relations, marketing, advertising, publishing, technical writing, film, and design (as well as to educators in the communications field). Members receive the association magazine, *The Professional Communicator*, access to a toll-free job hotline, a membership and resource directory, and a variety of publications, professional development kits, and resource materials.

Women in Film and Video (WIFV)

P.O. Box 19272
Washington DC 20036
(202) 232-2254

WIFV works to help women in the film, video, and related industries by providing professional and educational development opportunities, educating the public about women's achievements in the field, and serving as an information clearinghouse. The organization sponsors an annual women's film festival, offers technical and professional workshops, and sponsors an annual awards event. Specialized committees focus on specific topics, including mentoring and internships, professional development, outreach, and publicity. In addition, a special events committee organizes public screenings of members' work and a "Women Make Movies" film festival. Members receive a lively newsletter that includes technical tips, member news, profiles, and a calendar of events.

Women in Information Processing (WIP)

Lock Box 39173
Washington DC 20016
(202) 328-6161

WIP provides a forum for professionals in the computer, robotics, and telecommunications fields and related disciplines. Membership benefits include access to a speaker's bureau, monthly seminars, résumé guidance, a scholarship program, and the organization's annual "Salary and Perception Survey."

Women in Management (WIM)

30 N. Michigan Ave., Suite 508
Chicago IL 60602
(312) 263-3636

This organization provides professional development, networking, and educational opportunities for women in leadership and management roles. Membership benefits include a newsletter subscription, attendance at special presentations, management conferences, and leadership training events.

Women Life Underwriters Confederation (WLUC)

17 S. High St., Suite 1200
Columbus OH 43215
(800) 776-3008

Women in the insurance field are eligible for this group's membership benefits, which include a mentorship program, accredited continuing education, leadership training, regional retreats, and educational conferences.

Women's Council of Realtors (WCR)

430 N. Michigan Ave.
Chicago IL 60611-4093
(312) 329-8483

The only professional women's group of the National Association of Realtors, the council offers members opportunities for professional development through a four-part leadership training course, referral and relocation certification courses, educational conferences, and a monthly magazine, *Communiqué*. Members also have access to discount buying services, a speaker's bureau, financial planning seminars, and a national referral network.

Check the tips on page 169 to locate independent professional groups in your area.

GENERAL BUSINESS ASSOCIATIONS

The membership organizations included here are not specifically for women, but they offer excellent learning opportunities, access to business information, and participation in discount buying services.

American Entrepreneurs Association (AEA)

2392 Morse Ave.
Irvine CA 92714
(714) 261-2325

Affiliated with *Entrepreneur* magazine, this organization offers discounts on a subscription to *Entrepreneur,* business publications and software, and seminars around the country. Discount buying services for travel, car rental, and other types of services are also available. Members receive an association newsletter in addition to the magazine.

American Management Association (AMA)

135 W. Fiftieth St.
New York NY 10020
(212) 586-8100

The AMA offers a wide range of educational and professional-development opportunities through attendance at conferences, enrollment in AMA courses on specialized management topics, and self-study courses. Members are eligible for reduced purchase and rental rates on a variety of books, publications, and training videos and receive the association publications *Management Review* and *Forum.* Members have access to The Information Resource Center in New York City and free use of state-of-the-art meeting facilities at Management Centers in New York, Chicago, Atlanta, and Washington, D.C. A membership category has been established to meet the special needs of growing companies.

Home Office Association of America (HOAA)

909 Third Ave., Suite 990
New York NY 10022-4731
(800) 809-4622

The association offers a wide range of member benefits through its affiliations with other organizations and businesses. These include health insurance, prescription purchasing, collection services, nationwide messaging, and product and service discounts. Members also receive *Home Office Connections,* written by home-business experts who address topics of particular concern to home-business owners—from purchasing equipment and software to successfully handling zoning problems. Additionally, HOAA works on the political front through lobbying and advocacy efforts in Washington, D.C.

National Alliance of Business (NAB)

National Headquarters
1201 New York Ave. NW, Suite 700
Washington DC 20005-3917
(202) 289-2888

NAB works toward development of national strategies and programs to improve the quality of the American work force by bringing together leaders in government, business, education, and labor. This alliance offers conferences, technical assistance services (such as on-site training and help in accessing public and private business resources), and publications and videos on work, management, and training issues. Members receive alliance publications *WorkAmerica* and *Business Currents,* as well as periodic technical reports. NAB has six service centers around the country. For more information about NAB and to be directed to the service center that serves your area, contact the national headquarters.

National Association for the Cottage Industry (NACI)

P.O. Box 14850
Chicago IL 60614
(312) 472-8116

This organization offers people who work from their homes access to information on business organizational methods, marketing and promotion, zoning, taxes, licensing requirements, and other topics of interest.

National Association for the Self Employed (NASE)

P.O. Box 612067
Dallas TX 75261-9968
(800) 232-6273

This association has a full-time staff dedicated to negotiating deals on high-value benefits such as financial services and health care, publications, travel savings, and family-fun discounts. Members receive the NASE newspaper, *Self-Employed America.*

National Association of Private Enterprise (NAPE)

P.O. Box 612147

Dallas TX 75261-2147

(800) 223-6273

(817) 428-4200

NAPE is the *small* small business owners association. Set up to serve businesses with ten or fewer employees, the association represents small business in Washington, D.C.; provides free consulting on tax, legal, marketing, and other issues; sponsors educational scholarships; and provides access to medical insurance and discounts on a variety of business services and products, including long-distance, office supplies, and credit-card processing.

National Business Association (NBA)

P.O. Box 870728

Dallas TX 75287

(800) 456-0440

(214) 991-5381

This association provides entrepreneurs and small business owners with an array of services and products to help them run their businesses more effectively and to enjoy their time away from work. It provides services and products for business management and financial planning, education, health and personal fitness, and lifestyle management. Products range from productivity software and health insurance to financial products and travel discounts. Members also receive the association newsletter, *National Business News.*

National Federation of Independent Businesses (NFIB)

53 Century Blvd., Suite 3000

Nashville TN 37214

(615) 872-5312

Serving as the small business owner's political voice, this federation represents small-business interests to state and federal legislators and other decision-making bodies through lobbying efforts and research. The organization's track record includes influencing passage of laws that simplified payroll-tax deposit procedures and gave small businesses phase-in and tax-credit options to meet new disability laws. Legislative positions of the organization are determined by a membership vote.

National Minority Business Council (NMBC)

235 E. Forty-second St.
New York NY 10017
(212) 573-2385

The council provides training and procurement assistance to minority-owned businesses. Women are not specifically included in the organization's primary definition of *minority,* but all women-owned minority businesses are eligible for membership. Benefits include international trade assistance, referral of your business to buying agents through a computerized directory, free listing in the Corporate Purchasing Directory, a subscription to the bimonthly *NMBC Business Report,* and discounts on business-travel services.

National Small Business United (NSBU)

1155 Fifteenth St. NW, Suite 710
Washington DC 20005
(800) 345-NSBU (6728)

NSBU's primary mission is to represent small business owners in Washington to ensure that their needs are understood by policy makers and government officials. Members also receive *Small Business USA* and *Capitol Focus,* to keep them informed about congressional activities and current business legislation. Other membership benefits include a variety of health and life insurance plans, product and service discounts, and credit-card programs.

Renaissance Business Associates (RBA)

P.O. Box 26510
Colorado Springs CO 80936-6510
(719) 495-9617

An international organization for businesspeople committed to ethical, socially responsible business practices, this association sponsors an annual conference, local and regional seminars, a mentoring program, and a speaker's bureau. Members receive a bimonthly newsletter called *Business Dynamics*.

The Leads Club

P.O. Box 279
Carlsbad CA 92018
(800) 783-3761
(619) 729-7797

The Leads Club is a networking organization that provides services and education through its national office and business-building opportunities through local networking groups designed to generate business referrals and leads. Originally for women only, most chapters are now coed. Members receive a regular newsletter from headquarters that provides marketing tips, inspiration, and success stories.

7

Resource, Program, and Agency Listings

The listings in this chapter are all referred to in other parts of this guide. As stand-alone lists, they will not be of much use, but the rest of this guide makes reference to every list included here. As you begin to get a feel for the kinds of help a particular agency can offer, you will be able to use the listings independently from the rest of the book.

The Quick-Find Guide on the next page is designed to help you locate the agency or office you are looking for without having to check back to the original reference in a previous chapter.

In general, individuals' names have not been included in the listings because they change so frequently. When necessary, suggestions are provided at the beginning of some lists to help steer you to the right information or person. In two cases (SCORE Women's Coordinators and Women's Business Advocates), names are included because you must contact specific individuals for assistance.

QUICK-FIND GUIDE

SBA REGIONAL OFFICES

There are ten SBA regions, each served by a head office and a number of field offices. Contact the office that serves your state to find out about general SBA services in your area and to be directed to appropriate field offices and personnel. For more information about the SBA and its programs, review "A Guide to Federal Agencies" (page xiii) and the sections on federal resources in Chapters 2, 3, and 4.

REGION 1

Maine, Vermont, Massachusetts, New Hampshire, Connecticut, Rhode Island

Small Business Administration
10 Causeway St., Suite 812
Boston MA 02222-1093
(617) 565-8415

REGION 2

New York, New Jersey, Puerto Rico, Virgin Islands

Small Business Administration
26 Federal Plaza, Room 3108
New York NY 10278
(212) 264-1450

REGION 3

Pennsylvania, Delaware, Maryland, Virginia, Washington, D.C., West Virginia

Small Business Administration
475 Allendale Rd., Suite 201
King of Prussia PA 19406
(610) 962-3700

REGION 4

North Carolina, South Carolina, Kentucky, Tennessee, Georgia, Alabama, Mississippi, Florida

Small Business Administration
1720 Peachtree Rd. NW, Suite 496
Atlanta GA 30309
(404) 347-4999

REGION 5

Minnesota, Wisconsin, Michigan, Ohio, Indiana, Illinois

Small Business Administration
300 S. Riverside Plaza, Suite 1975 S
Chicago IL 60606-6617
(312) 353-0357

REGION 6

New Mexico, Texas, Oklahoma, Arkansas, Louisiana

Small Business Administration
8625 King George Dr., Building C
Dallas TX 75235-3391
(214) 767-7633

REGION 7

Kansas, Missouri, Iowa, Nebraska

Small Business Administration
323 W. Eighth St., Suite 307
Kansas City MO 64106
(816) 374-6380

REGION 8

Montana, North Dakota, South Dakota, Wyoming, Utah, Colorado

Small Business Administration
633 Seventeenth St., 7th Floor
Denver CO 80202
(303) 294-7186

REGION 9

California, Nevada, Arizona, Hawaii

Small Business Administration
71 Stevenson St., 20th Floor
San Francisco CA 94105-2939
(415) 975-4859

REGION 10

Washington, Oregon, Idaho, Alaska

Small Business Administration
1200 Sixth Ave., Suite 1805
Seattle WA 98121
(206) 553-5676
TTY: (206) 553-2872

SBA DISTRICT OFFICES AND WOMEN'S BUSINESS REPRESENTATIVES

Each of the district offices listed here has a women's business representative on staff. Contact the closest office in your region for information about women's business ownership programs and other SBA services in your area. For more information about the Office of Women's Business Ownership and its programs, review "A Guide to Federal Agencies" (page xiii) in the introduction and the beginning of the sections on federal resources in Chapters 2 and 3.

REGION 1

Maine, Vermont, Massachusetts, New Hampshire, Connecticut, Rhode Island

Small Business Administration
330 Main St., 2nd Floor
Hartford CT 06106
(203) 240-4700

Small Business Administration
10 Causeway St., Room 265
Boston MA 02222-1093
(617) 565-5590

Small Business Administration
87 State St., Room 205
Montpelier VT 05602
(802) 828-4422

Small Business Administration
40 Western Ave., Room 512
Augusta ME 04330
(207) 622-8378

Small Business Administration
380 Westminister Mall, 5th Floor
Providence RI 02903
(401) 528-4561

Small Business Administration
143 N. Main St., Suite 202
Concord NH 03301
(603) 225-1400

Small Business Administration
1550 Main St., Room 212
Springfield MA 01103
(413) 785-0268

REGION 2

New York, New Jersey, Puerto Rico, Virgin Islands

Small Business Administration
26 Federal Plaza, Suite 31-00
New York NY 10278
(212) 264-2454

Small Business Administration
100 S. Clinton St., Room 1071
Syracuse NY 13260
(315) 448-0423
(607) 734-8142

Small Business Administration
Two Gateway Center, 4th Floor
Newark NJ 07102
(201) 645-2434

Small Business Administration
111 W. Huron St., Room 1311
Buffalo NY 14202
(716) 551-4301

Small Business Administration
252 Ponce De Leon Blvd., Suite 201
Hato Rey PR 00918
(809) 766-5001

REGION 3

Pennsylvania, Delaware, Maryland, Virginia, Washington, D.C., West Virginia

Small Business Administration
475 Allendale Rd., Suite 201
King of Prussia PA 19406
(610) 962-3800

Small Business Administration
960 Penn Ave., 5th Floor
Pittsburgh PA 15222
(412) 644-2780

Small Business Administration
1504 Santa Rosa Rd., Suite 200
Richmond VA 23229
(804) 771-2400

Small Business Administration
10 S. Howard St., Suite 6220
Baltimore MD 21201-2525
(401) 962-6149 ext. 338

Small Business Administration
1110 Vermont Ave. NW, Suite 900
Washington DC 20005
(202) 606-4000

Small Business Administration
168 W. Main St., 5th Floor
Clarksburg WV 26301
(304) 623-5631

REGION 4

North Carolina, South Carolina, Kentucky, Tennessee, Georgia, Alabama, Mississippi, Florida

Small Business Administration
1375 Peachtree Rd. NW, Suite 496
Atlanta GA 30309
(404) 347-4749

Small Business Administration
7825 Bay Meadows Way, Suite 100B
Jacksonville FL 32256-7504
(904) 443-1900

Small Business Administration
2121 Eighth Ave., Suite 200
Birmingham AL 35203-2398
(205) 731-1344

Small Business Administration
600 Dr. Martin Luther King Jr. Place
Room 188
Louisville KY 40202
(502) 582-5971

Small Business Administration
200 N. College St., Suite A2015
Charlotte NC 28202-2173
(704) 344-6563

Small Business Administration
50 Vantage Way, Suite 201
Nashville TN 37228-1500
(615) 736-5881

Small Business Administration
1835 Assembly St., Room 358
Columbia SC 29201
(803) 765-5377

Small Business Administration
101 W. Capitol St., Suite 400
Jackson MS 39201
(601) 965-4378

REGION 5

Minnesota, Wisconsin, Michigan, Ohio, Indiana, Illinois

Small Business Administration
300 S. Riverside Plaza, Suite 1975 S
Chicago IL 60606-6617
(312) 353-0357

Small Business Administration
212 E. Washington Ave., Room 213
Madison WI 53703
(608) 264-5261

Small Business Administration
Two Nationwide Plaza, Suite 1400
Columbus OH 43215-2592
(614) 469-6860

Small Business Administration
477 Michigan Ave., Room 515
Detroit MI 48226
(313) 226-6075

Small Business Administration
429 N. Pennsylvania St., Suite 100
Indianapolis IN 46204-1873
(317) 226-7272

Small Business Administration
100 N. Sixth St., Suite 612
Minneapolis MN 55403
(612) 370-2324

Small Business Administration
1111 Superior Ave., Suite 630
Cleveland OH 44114-2507
(216) 522-4180

REGION 6

New Mexico, Texas, Oklahoma, Arkansas, Louisiana

Small Business Administration
2120 Riverfront Dr., Suite 100
Little Rock AR 72202
(501) 324-5871

Small Business Administration
222 E. Van Buren St., Suite 500
Harlingen TX 78550-6855
(210) 427-8625

Small Business Administration
625 Silver Ave. SW, Room 320
Albuquerque NM 87102
(505) 766-1870

Small Business Administration
1611 Tenth St., Suite 200
Lubbock TX 79401-2693
(806) 743-7462

Small Business Administration
9301 SW Freeway, Suite 550
Houston TX 77074-1591
(713) 773-6500

Small Business Administration
365 Canal St., Suite 2250
New Orleans LA 70130
(504) 589-6685

Small Business Administration
210 Park Ave., Suite 1300
Oklahoma City OK 73102
(405) 231-5521

Small Business Administration
727 Durango Blvd., Room A-527
San Antonio TX 78206
(210) 229-5900

Small Business Administration
10737 Gateway West, Suite 320
El Paso TX 79935
(915) 540-5676

Small Business Administration
4300 Amon Carter Blvd., Suite 114
Fort Worth TX 76155
(817) 885-6500

REGION 7

Kansas, Missouri, Iowa, Nebraska

Small Business Administration
323 W. Eighth St., Suite 501
Kansas City MO 64105
(816) 374-6708

Small Business Administration
11145 Mill Valley Rd.
Omaha NE 68154
(402) 221-4691

Small Business Administration
100 E. English, Suite 510
Wichita KS 67202
(316) 269-6616

Small Business Administration
815 Olive St., Suite 242
St. Louis MO 63101
(314) 539-6600

Small Business Administration
210 Walnut St., Room 749
Des Moines IA 50309-2186
(515) 284-4422

Small Business Administration
215 Fourth Ave. SE, Suite 200
Cedar Rapids IA 52401
(319) 362-6405

REGION 8

Montana, North Dakota, South Dakota, Wyoming, Utah, Colorado

Small Business Administration
633 Seventeenth St., 7th Floor
Denver CO 80202
(303) 294-7186

Small Business Administration
125 S. State St., Room 2237
Salt Lake City UT 84138-1195
(801) 524-6804

Small Business Administration
301 S. Park Ave., Room 334
Helena MT 59626
(406) 441-1081

Small Business Administration
657 Second Ave. North, Room 219
Fargo ND 58108
(701) 239-5131

Small Business Administration
100 E. B St., Room 4001
Casper WY 82602
(307) 261-6500

Small Business Administration
101 S. Phillips Ave., Suite 200
Sioux Falls SD 57102
(605) 330-4231

REGION 9

California, Nevada, Arizona, Hawaii

Small Business Administration
71 Stevenson St., 20th Floor
San Francisco CA 94105-2939
(415) 975-4859

Small Business Administration
330 N. Brand Blvd., Suite 1200
Glendale CA 91203-2304
(818) 552-3210

Small Business Administration
2719 N. Air Fresno Dr., Suite 107
Fresno CA 93727-1547
(209) 487-5189

Small Business Administration
211 Main St., 4th Floor
San Francisco CA 94105-1988
(415) 744-6820

Small Business Administration
2828 N. Central Ave., Suite 800
Phoenix AZ 85004-1093
(602) 640-2316

Small Business Administration
300 Ala Moana, Room 2214
Honolulu HI 96850-4981
(808) 541-2990

Small Business Administration
550 W. C St., Suite 550
San Diego CA 92188-3540
(619) 557-7250

Small Business Administration
301 E. Stewart Ave., Room 301
Las Vegas NV 89125-2527
(702) 388-6611

Small Business Administration
200 W. Santa Ana Blvd., Suite 700
Santa Ana CA 92701
(714) 550-7420

Small Business Administration
660 J St., Suite 215
Sacramento CA 95814-2413
(916) 498-6410

REGION 10

Washington, Oregon, Idaho, Alaska

Small Business Administration
1200 Sixth Ave., Suite 1805
Seattle WA 98101-1128
(206) 553-5676

Small Business Administration
1200 Sixth Ave., Suite 1700
Seattle WA 98101-1128
(206) 553-7310

Small Business Administration
222 SW Columbia Ave., Room 500
Portland OR 97201-6695
(503) 326-2682

Small Business Administration
W. 601 First Ave., 10th Floor East
Spokane WA 99204-0317
(509) 353-2810

Small Business Administration
222 W. Eighth Ave., Room A36
Anchorage AK 99513
(907) 271-4022

Small Business Administration
1020 Main St., Suite 290
Boise ID 83702-5745
(208) 334-1696

WOMEN'S BUSINESS DEVELOPMENT CENTERS
(OWBO Demonstration Sites)

Check the listing for your state to see if there is a training site in your area. For more information about these programs, see page 90. If the contact information has changed for a site in your area, check with your SBA District Office (see page 192) or call the Office of Women's Business Ownership in Washington, D.C., at (202) 205-6673. (This list includes sites that may not currently receive SBA funding but have in the past and are still operating and offering assistance to women business owners.)

ALABAMA

Women's Business Assistance Center (WBAC)
1301 Azalea Rd., Suite 111-A
Mobile AL 36693
(205) 660-2725

ALASKA

No sites currently in this state.

ARIZONA

National Center For American Indian Enterprise Development (NCAIED)
953 E. Juanita Ave.
Mesa AZ 85204
(602) 831-7524
(Serves Arizona, Washington, and California. See California and Washington listings for contact information in those states.)

ARKANSAS

No sites currently in this state.

CALIFORNIA

National Center for American Indian
Enterprise Development (NCAIED)
Northwest Region
9650 Flair Dr., Suite 303
El Monte CA 91731
(818) 442-3701

American Women's Economic
Development Corp. (AWED)
100 W. Broadway, Suite 500
Long Beach CA 90802
(310) 983-3747

American Women's Economic
Development Corp. (AWED)
2301 Campus Dr., Suite 20
Irvine CA 92715
(714) 474-2933

WEST Company (previously funded)
367 N. State St., Suite 206
Ukiah CA 95482
(707) 468-3553

WEST Company
340 N. Main St.
Fort Bragg CA 95437
(707) 964-7571

WEST Company
367 N. State St., Suite 208
Ukiah CA 95482
(707) 964-7571

Women's Initiative for Self Employment (WISE) (previously funded)
450 Mission St., Suite 402
San Francisco CA 94102
(415) 247-9473

Women's Initiative for Self Employment (WISE)
519 Seventeenth St., Suite 520
Oakland CA 94612
(510) 208-9473

Women Business Owners Corp.
(WBOC)
18 Encanto Dr.
Palos Verdes CA 90274-4215
(310) 530-7500

COLORADO

Mi Casa Business Center for Women
571 Galapaga St.
Denver CO 80204
(303) 573-1302

CONNECTICUT

American Women's Economic
Development Corp. (AWED)
2001 W. Main St., Suite 140
Stamford CT 06902
(203) 326-7914

FLORIDA

Women's Business Development
Center
Florida International University, OET-3
Miami FL 33199
(305) 348-3951/3903

GEORGIA

Coalition of 100 Black Women
The Candler Building
127 Peachtree St. NE, Suite 700
Atlanta GA 30303
(404) 659-4008

HAWAII

No sites currently in this state.

IDAHO

No sites currently in this state.

ILLINOIS

Women's Business Development
Center (WBDC) (previously funded)
8 S. Michigan Ave., Suite 400
Chicago IL 60603
(312) 853-3477

IOWA

No sites currently in this state.

KENTUCKY

Kentucky Mainstream Alliance
c/o Venture Concepts
Chamber of Commerce, Boyd/Brenap
Counties, Inc.
Ashland KY 41105
(606) 324-5111

LOUISIANA

Women Entrepreneurs for Economic
Development (WEED)
1683 N. Clairborne Ave.
New Orleans LA 70116
(504) 947-8522

Women Entrepreneurs for Economic
Development (WEED)
2245 Peters Rd.
Harvey LA 70050
(504) 365-3866

MAINE

Coastal Enterprises, Inc.
P.O. Box 268
Wiscasset ME 04578
(207) 882-7552

MARYLAND

No sites currently in this state.

MASSACHUSETTS

Center for Women and Enterprise, Inc.
45 Broomfield St., 6th Floor
Boston MA 02108
(617) 423-3001

MICHIGAN

Ann Arbor Community Development Corp.
2008 Hogback Rd., Suite 2A
Ann Arbor MI 48105
(313) 677-1400

Grand Rapids Opportunities for
Women (GROW)
25 Sheldon SE, Suite 210
Grand Rapids MI 49503
(616) 458-3403

EXCEL! Midwest Women Business
Owners Development Team
301 W. Fulton
Eberhard Center, Room 718-S
Grand Rapids MI 49504-6495
(616) 771-6639

EXCEL! Midwest Women Business
Owners Development Team
600 W. Lafayette
Detroit MI 48226
(313) 961-4748

MINNESOTA

Women in New Development (WIND)
P.O. Box 579
Bemidji MN 56601
(218) 751-4631

Women's Business Center White Earth
Reservation Tribal Council
N. Main St.
P.O. Box 478
Mahnomen MN 56557
(218) 935-2827

MISSISSIPPI

National Council of Negro Women
10001 G St. NW, Suite 800
Washington DC 20001
(202) 628-0015 ext. 20
(Provides services to rural Mississippi.)

MISSOURI

NAWBO of St. Louis
222 S. Bemiston, Suite 216
St. Louis MO 63105
(314) 863-0046

MONTANA

Montana Women's Capital Fund
302 N. Last Chance Gulch
Helena MT 59624
(406) 443-3144

Women's Opportunity and Resource
Development Inc.
127 N. Higgins
Missoula MT 59802
(406) 543-3550

NEBRASKA

No sites currently in this state.

NEVADA

Nevada Self-Employment Trust
560 Mill St.
Reno NV 89502
(702) 329-6789

Nevada Self-Employment Trust
1600 E. Desert Inn Rd., #209E
Las Vegas NV 89109
(702) 734-3555

NEW HAMPSHIRE

No sites currently in this state.

NEW JERSEY

New Jersey NAWBO EXCEL
225 Hamilton St.
Bound Brook NJ 08805-2042
(908) 560-9607

NEW MEXICO

Women's Economic Self-Sufficiency
Team (WESST Corp.)
414 Silver Southwest
Albuquerque NM 87.102-3239
(505) 848-4760

WESST Corp.
Box 5007 NDCBU
Taos NM 87517
(505) 522-3707

WESST Corp.
500 W. Main
Farmington NM 87401
(505) 325-0678

NEW YORK

American Women's Economic
Development Corp.
71 Vanderbilt Ave., Suite 320
New York NY 10169
(212) 692-9100

Asian Women in Business
134 Spring St., Suite 203
New York NY 10012
(212) 226-1737

NORTH CAROLINA

No sites currently in this state.

NORTH DAKOTA

Women's Business Institute
901 Page Dr.
Fargo ND 58106
(701) 235-6488

OHIO

Ohio Women's Business Resource
Network (OWBRN)
77 S. High St., 28th Floor
Columbus OH 43266
(614) 466-2682

*All sites that follow for Ohio are members of the
Ohio Women's Business Resource Network
and offer business assistance at the local level.
Some are not SBA-funded.*

Women's Development Center
300 N. Abbe Rd.
Elyria OH 44035
(216) 366-0770

Enterprise Center/Women's Business
Center
129 E. Main St.
Hillsboro OH 45133
(513) 393-9599

Northwest Ohio Women's
Entrepreneurial Network
300 Madison Ave., Suite 200
Toledo OH 43604
(419) 243-8191

Women Entrepreneurs, Inc.
Bartlett Building
36 E. Fourth St.
Cincinnati OH 45202
(513) 684-0700

EMPOWER **Pyramid Career Services**
2400 Cleveland Ave. NW
Canton OH 44709
(330) 453-3767

Women's Business Resource Program of Southeast Ohio
Technology and Enterprise Building
20 E. Circle Dr., Suite 190
Athens OH 45701
(614) 593-1797

Women's Entrepreneurial Growth Organization (WEGO)
P.O. Box 544
Akron OH 44309
(330) 972-5179

Women's Network, Inc.
1540 W. Market St., Suite 100
Akron OH 44313
(330) 864-5636

The Cushwa Center for Industrial Development
Youngstown University
410 Wick Ave.
Youngstown OH 44555-3495
(216) 742-3495

OKLAHOMA

Working Women's Money University
3501 NW Sixty-third, Suite 609
Oklahoma City OK 73116
(405) 842-1196

OREGON

Southern Oregon Women's Access to Credit
33 N. Central, Suite 410
Medford OR 97510
(503) 779-3992

PENNSYLVANIA

National Association of Women Business Owners Pittsburgh
5604 Solway St., Suite 207
Pittsburgh PA 15217
(412) 521-4735 ext. 4736

Women's Business Development Center
1315 Walnut St., Suite 1116
Philadelphia PA 19107
(215) 790-WBDC (9232)

RHODE ISLAND

No sites currently in this state.

SOUTH CAROLINA

No sites currently in this state.

SOUTH DAKOTA

The Entrepreneur's Network for
Women
100 S. Maple, P.O. Box 81
Watertown SD 57201
(701) 882-5080

TENNESSEE

No sites currently in this state.

TEXAS

Center for Women's Business
Enterprise
2425 W. Loop S., Suite 1004
Houston TX 77027
(713) 552-1267

Center for Women's Business
Enterprise
508 Ladin Lane
Austin TX 78734
(512) 261-8525

North Texas Women's Business
Development Center, Inc.
Bill J. Priest Institute for Economic
Development
1402 Corinth St.
Dallas TX 75215-2111
(214) 428-1177

UTAH

Utah Technology Finance Corp.
177 E. 100 S.
Salt Lake City UT 84111
(801) 364-4346

VERMONT

No sites currently in this state.

VIRGINIA

No sites currently in this state.

WASHINGTON

National Center for American Indian
Enterprise Development
NCAIED Pacific Region
Women's Business Assistance Project
1000 W. Harrison, S. Tower - Suite 530
Seattle WA 98119
(206) 285-2190

WASHINGTON, D.C.

American Women's Economic
Development Corp. (AWED)
1250 Twenty-fourth St. NW, Room 120
Washington DC 20037
(202) 857-0091

Venture Concepts (previously funded)
709 Second St. NE, Suite 100
Washington DC 20002
(202) 543-1200

WEST VIRGINIA

No sites currently in this state.

WISCONSIN

Wisconsin Women's Business Initiative Corp. (WWBIC)
1915 N. Dr. Martin Luther King Jr. Dr.
Milwaukee WI 53212
(414) 372-2070

Wisconsin Women Entrepreneurs, Inc.
6949 N. 100th St.
Milwaukee WI 53224
(414) 358-9260

WYOMING

No sites currently in this state.

SMALL BUSINESS DEVELOPMENT CENTERS

Call the office listed here for your state, and a staff member will direct you to the SBDC closest to you. In Texas, call the regional office closest to you. For more information about training and counseling opportunities at SBDCs, see page 94.

ALABAMA

Alabama SBDC Consortium
University of Alabama at Birmingham
Medical Towers Building
1717 Eleventh Ave., Suite 419
Birmingham AL 35294
(205) 934-7260

ALASKA

Alaska SBDC
University of Alaska at Anchorage
430 W. Seventh Ave., Suite 110
Anchorage AK 99501
(907) 274-7232

ARIZONA

Arizona SBDC Network
2411 W. Fourteenth St., Suite 132
Tempe AZ 85251
(602) 731-8720

ARKANSAS

Arkansas SBDC
University of Arkansas at Little Rock
100 S. Main, Suite 401
Little Rock AR 72201
(501) 324-9043

CALIFORNIA

California SBDC **Program**
Department of Commerce
801 K St., Suite 1700
Sacramento CA 95814
(916) 324-5068

COLORADO

Colorado SBDC
Colorado Office of Business
Development
1625 Broadway, Suite 1710
Denver CO 80202
(303) 892-3809

CONNECTICUT

Connecticut SBDC
University of Connecticut
2 Boutne Place, U-94
Storrs CT 06269-5094
(203) 486-4135

DELAWARE

Delaware SBDC
University of Delaware
Purnell Hall, Suite 005
Newark DE 19716-2711
(302) 831-2747

FLORIDA

Florida SBDC **Network**
University of West Florida
19 W. Garden St., Suite 300
Pensacola FL 32501
(904) 444-2060

GEORGIA

Georgia SBDC
University of Georgia
Chicopee Complex, 1180 E. Broad St.
Athens GA 30602-5412
(706) 542-5760

HAWAII

Hawaii SBDC **Network**
University of Hawaii at Hilo
520 W. Kiwili
Hilo HI 96720
(808) 933-3515

IDAHO

Idaho SBDC
Boise State University
1910 University Dr.
Boise ID 83725
(208) 385-1640

ILLINOIS

Illinois SBDC
Department of Commerce and
Community Affairs
620 E. Adams St., 3rd Floor
Springfield IL 62701
(217) 524-5856

INDIANA

Indiana SBDC
Economic Development Council
One N. Capitol, Suite 420
Indianapolis IN 46204
(317) 264-6871

IOWA

Iowa SBDC
Iowa State University
137 Lynn Ave.
Ames IA 50014
(515) 292-6351

KANSAS

Kansas SBDC
Wichita State University
1845 Fairmount
Wichita KS 67260-0148
(316) 689-3193

KENTUCKY

Kentucky SBDC
University of Kentucky
Center for Business Development
225 Business and Economics Building
Lexington KY 40506-0034
(606) 257-7668

LOUISIANA

Louisiana SBDC
Northeast Louisiana University
College of Business Administration
700 University Ave.
Monroe LA 71209-6435
(318) 342-5506

MAINE

Maine SBDC
University of Southern Maine
96 Falmouth St.
Portland ME 04103
(207) 780-4420

MARYLAND

Maryland SBDC
Department of Economic and Employment Development
217 E. Redwood St., 10th Floor
Baltimore MD 21202
(410) 333-6995

MASSACHUSETTS

Massachusetts SBDC
University of Massachusetts-Amherst
Room 205, School of Management
Amherst MA 01003
(413) 545-6301

MICHIGAN

Michigan SBDC
Wayne State University
2727 Second Ave.
Detroit MI 48201
(313) 964-1798

MINNESOTA

Minnesota SBDC
500 Metro Square
121 Seventh Pl. East
St. Paul MN 55101-2146
(612) 297-5770

MISSISSIPPI

Mississippi SBDC
University of Mississippi
Old Chemistry Building, Suite 216
University MS 38677
(601) 232-5001

MISSOURI

Missouri SBDC
University of Missouri
300 University Place
Columbia MO 65211
(314) 882-0344

MONTANA

Montana SBDC
Montana Department of Commerce
1424 Ninth Ave.
Helena MT 59620
(406) 444-4780

NEBRASKA

Nebraska SBDC
University of Nebraska at Omaha
Sixtieth and Dodge Sts., CBA Room 407
Omaha NE 68182
(402) 554-2521

NEVADA

Nevada SBDC
University of Nevada: Reno
College of Business Administration-
032, Room 411
Reno NV 89557-0100
(702) 784-1717

NEW HAMPSHIRE

New Hampshire SBDC
University of New Hampshire
108 McConnell Hall
Durham NH 03824
(603) 862-2200

NEW JERSEY

New Jersey SBDC
Rutgers University
Graduate School of Management
180 University Ave.
Newark NJ 07102
(201) 648-5950

NEW MEXICO

New Mexico SBDC
Santa Fe Community College
P.O. Box 4187
Santa Fe NM 87502-4187
(505) 438-1362

NEW YORK

New York SBDC
State University of New York
State University Plaza, S-523
Albany NY 12246
(518) 443-5398

NORTH CAROLINA

North Carolina SBDC
University of North Carolina
4509 Creedmoor Rd., Suite 201
Raleigh NC 27612
(919) 571-4154

NORTH DAKOTA

North Dakota SBDC
University of North Dakota
118 Gamble Hall, UND, Box 7308
Grand Fork ND 58202
(701) 777-3700

OHIO

Ohio SBDC
77 S. High St.
P.O. Box 1001
Columbus OH 43226-0101
(614) 466-2711

OKLAHOMA

Oklahoma SBDC
Southeastern Oklahoma State
University
P.O. Box 2584, Station A
Durant OK 74701
(405) 924-0277

OREGON

Oregon SBDC
Lane Community College
44 W. Broadway, Suite 501
Eugene OR 97401-3021
(503) 726-2250

PENNSYLVANIA

Pennsylvania SBDC
The Wharton School
University of Pennsylvania
444 Vance Hall, 3733 Spruce St.
Philadelphia PA 19104-6374
(215) 898-1219

PUERTO RICO

Puerto Rico SBDC
University of Puerto Rico
P.O. Box 5253 College Station
Mayaguez PR 00681
(809) 833-5822

RHODE ISLAND

Rhode Island SBDC
Bryant College
1150 Douglas Pike
Smithfield RI 02917
(401) 232-6111

SOUTH CAROLINA

South Carolina SBDC
University of South Carolina
College of Business Administration
Columbia SC 29201-9980
(803) 777-4907

SOUTH DAKOTA

South Dakota SBDC
University of South Dakota
414 E. Clark
Vermillion SD 57069
(605) 677-5279

TENNESSEE

Tennessee SBDC
Memphis State University
Building 1, South Campus
Memphis TN 38152
(901) 678-2500

TEXAS

North Texas-Dallas SBDC
Bill J. Priest Institute for Economic
Development
140 Corinth St.
Dallas TX 75215
(214) 565-5831

University of Houston SBDC
University of Houston
1100 Louisiana, Suite 500
Houston TX 77002
(713) 752-8444

NW Texas SBDC
Texas Tech University
2579 S. Loop 289, Suite 114
Lubbock TX 79423
(806) 745-3973

University of Texas South Texas
Border SBDC
UTSA Downtown Center
1222 N. Main St., Suite 450
San Antonio TX 78212
(210) 558-2464

UTAH

Utah SBDC
University of Utah
102 W. 500 S., Suite 315
Salt Lake City UT 84101
(801) 581-7905

VERMONT

Vermont SBDC
Vermont Technical College
P.O. Box 422
Randolph VT 05060
(802) 728-9101

VIRGIN ISLANDS

UVI Small Business Development
Center
University of the Virgin Islands
Sunshine Mall, Suite 104
Frederiksted, St. Croix USVI 00840
(809) 776-3206

VIRGINIA

Virginia SBDC
901 E. Byrd St., Suite 1800
Richmond VA 23219
(804) 371-8253

WASHINGTON

Washington SBDC
Washington State University
Kruegel Hall, Suite 135
Pullman WA 99164-4727
(509) 335-1576

WASHINGTON, D.C.

District of Columbia SBDC
Howard University
Sixth and Fairmont Sts. NW
Room 128
Washington DC 20059
(202) 806-1550

WEST VIRGINIA

West Virginia SBDC
950 E. Kanawha Blvd.
Charleston WV 25301
(304) 558-2960

WISCONSIN

Wisconsin SBDC
University of Wisconsin
432 N. Lake St., Room 423
Madison WI 53706
(608) 263-7794

WYOMING

WSBDC **State Network Office**
P.O. Box 3275
Laramie WY 82071-3275
(307) 766-3505

SCORE WOMEN'S BUSINESS OWNERSHIP COORDINATORS

To find a retired woman executive who will provide free counseling on a range of business start-up and management issues, contact the coordinator that serves your state. For more information about SCORE, see page 93.

These volunteer coordinators change frequently. If the coordinator on this list is no longer serving your area, contact the national SCORE coordinator for women's programs or the SBA Office of Women's Business Ownership for current information.

NATIONAL PROGRAM COORDINATOR

Florence Alberts
60 Edgehill Way
San Francisco CA 94127
(415) 566-1975

NATIONAL SBA LIAISON

SBA **Office of Women's Business Ownership**
409 Third St. SW, 6th Floor
Washington DC 20416
(202) 205-6673

REGION 1

Maine, Vermont, Massachusetts, New Hampshire, Connecticut, Rhode Island

Position vacant at press time. Contact the regional SCORE office at:

SCORE Director
R.R. 1, Box A39
Gove Hill Rd.
Thetford Center VT 05075
(802) 785-2596

REGION 2

New York, New Jersey, Puerto Rico, Virgin Islands

Ria Riley
465 Summerhaven Dr.
East Syracuse NY 13057
(315) 637-4195

REGION 3

Pennsylvania, Delaware, Maryland, Virginia, Washington, D.C., West Virginia

Beatrice Checket
907 Sextant Way
Annapolis MD 21401
(410) 266-8746

REGION 4

North Carolina, South Carolina, Kentucky, Tennessee, Georgia, Alabama, Mississippi, Florida

Position vacant at press time. Contact the regional SCORE office at:

SCORE Director
15791 Loch Maree Lane
Delray Beach FL 33446
(407) 495-9623

REGION 5

Minnesota, Wisconsin, Michigan, Ohio, Indiana, Illinois

Gwen Arnold
2614 Traver Blvd.
Ann Arbor MI 48105
(313) 994-7483

REGION 6

New Mexico, Texas, Oklahoma, Arkansas, Louisiana

Doris Bentley
222 Amelia St.
Lafayette LA 70506
(318) 232-2970

REGION 7

Kansas, Missouri, Iowa, Nebraska

Betty Finnell
7640 N. Lucern Ct.
Kansas City MO 64151
(816) 741-5997

REGION 8

Montana, North Dakota, South Dakota, Wyoming, Utah, Colorado

Bernice Zeiler
1020 Burlington Ave.
Billings MT 59102
(406) 259-1779

REGION 9

California, Nevada, Arizona, Hawaii

Willeen H. Hasler
276-25 N. El Camino Real
Oceanside CA 92054
(619) 439-6243

REGION 10

Washington, Oregon, Idaho, Alaska

Diana Wilhite
617 N. Helena
Spokane WA 99202
(509) 534-9001

BUSINESS INFORMATION CENTERS (BICs)

Use the SBA regional maps to find the closest BIC in your area. In addition to up-and-running centers, we have included centers planned to open in the near future as of press time and centers in the planning stages. If any contact information has changed and you cannot get through to a center, contact the SBA Office of Business Initiatives in Washington, D.C., at (202) 205-6665. Check with the Office of Initiatives or your SBA District Office (see page 192) for opening dates of planned centers. For more information about the services and resources offered by BICs, see pages 48 and 95.

REGION 1

Maine, Vermont, Massachusetts, New Hampshire, Connecticut, Rhode Island

SBA **District Office**
10 Causeway St., Room 265
Boston MA 02222-1093
(617) 565-5615

Small Business Administration
380 Westminister Mall, Room 511
Providence RI 02903
(401) 528-4583

Vermont Technical College
Business Information Center
Main St.
Randolph Center VT 05061
(802) 728-3391 ext. 231

Small Business Administration
40 Western Ave., Room 512
Augusta ME 04330
(Contact the SBA Office of Initiatives for a phone number.)

A center is also planned for Hartford, Connecticut.

REGION 2

New York, New Jersey, Puerto Rico, Virgin Islands

Small Business Administration
2 Gateway Center, 4th Floor
Newark NJ 07102
(201) 645-3580

REGION 3

Pennsylvania, Delaware, Maryland, Virginia, Washington, D.C., West Virginia

SBA/Bell Atlantic Business
Information Center
SBA District Office
1110 Vermont Ave. NW, Suite 900
Washington DC 20043-4500
(202) 606-4000 ext. 266

SBA/WVHTC Foundation
Business Information Center
200 Fairmont Ave., Suite 100
Fairmont WV 26554
(304) 366-2577

SBA/NationsBank/Bell Atlantic Small
Business Resource Center
3 W. Baltimore St.
Baltimore MD 21201
(410) 605-0990

Centers are also planned for Wilmington, Delaware; and Richmond, Virginia.

REGION 4

North Carolina, South Carolina, Kentucky, Tennessee, Georgia, Alabama, Mississippi, Florida

SBA **District Office**
1720 Peachtree Rd. NW, 6th Floor
Atlanta GA 30309
(404) 347-2355

SBA/**NationsBank**/MBDA
Small Business Resource Center
3401 W. End Ave.
Nashville TN 37203
(615) 749-4000

SBA/**NationsBank**/MBDA
BellSouth—College of Charleston
Small Business Resource Center
284 King St.
Charleston SC 29401
(803) 853-3900

SBA
200 N. College St., Suite 2015
Charlotte NC 28202-2137
(704) 344-9797

Centers are also planned for Atlanta, Georgia; Miami, Florida; and Louisville, Kentucky.

REGION 5

Minnesota, Wisconsin, Michigan, Ohio, Indiana, Illinois

SBA **District Office**
500 Madison St., Suite 1250
Chicago IL 60661-2511
(312) 353-1825

A center is also planned for Minneapolis, Minnesota.

REGION 6

New Mexico, Texas, Oklahoma, Arkansas, Louisiana

Small Business Administration
First Oklahoma Tower
210 Park Ave., Suite 1300
Oklahoma City OK 73102
(405) 231-4494

Small Business Administration
625 Silver Ave. SW, Suite 320
Albuquerque NM 87102
(505) 766-1887

SBA District Office
9301 SW Freeway, Suite 550
Houston TX 77074-1591
(713) 773-6518

Small Business Administration
Fort Worth Business Assistance Center
100 E. Fifteenth St., Suite 400
Fort Worth TX 76102
(817) 871-6000

SBA/Greater El Paso Chamber of Commerce
Business Information Center
Ten Civic Center Plaza
El Paso TX 79901
(915) 534-0531

REGION 7

Kansas, Missouri, Iowa, Nebraska

Business Information Center
121 S. Meramec Ave., Lobby Level
St. Louis MO 63105
(314) 854-6861

Small Business Administration
11145 Mill Valley Rd.
Omaha NE 68154
(401) 221-3622

SBA District Office
323 W. Eighth St., Suite 104
Kansas City MO 64105
(816) 374-6675

REGION 8

Montana, North Dakota, South Dakota, Wyoming, Utah, Colorado

Small Business Administration
721 Nineteenth St., Suite 426
Denver CO 68154
(303) 844-4028

Centers are also planned for Salt Lake City, Utah; and Helena, Montana.

REGION 9

California, Nevada, Arizona, Hawaii

SBA Business Information Center
3600 Wilshire Blvd., Suite L100
Los Angeles CA 90010
(213) 751-7253

SBA District Office
550 W. C St., Suite 550
San Diego CA 92101
(619) 557-7252

Small Business Administration
211 Main St., 4th Floor
San Francisco CA 94105-1988
(Contact the SBA Office of Initiatives
for a phone number.)

A center is also planned for Honolulu,
Hawaii.

REGION 10

Washington, Oregon, Idaho, Alaska

SBA District Office
1200 Sixth Ave., Suite 1700
Seattle WA 98101
(206) 553-7310

SBA/Spokane Chamber of
Commerce
Business Information Center
1020 W. Riverside Dr.
Spokane WA 99201
(509) 535-2800

Confederated Tribes of Warm Springs
Economic Development Office
1103 Wasco St.
Warm Springs OR 97761
(541) 553-3592

Confederated Tribes of the
Grande Ronde Community
9615 Grand Ronde Rd.
Grand Ronde OR 97347
(541) 879-2475

The Klamath Tribes
414 Chocktoot St.
Chiloquin OR 97624
(541) 783-2219

SBA District Office
1020 Main St.
Boise ID 83702-5745
(208) 334-9077

MINORITY BUSINESS DEVELOPMENT AGENCY (MBDA) REGIONAL OFFICES

To find out about minority business assistance in your area, contact the office that serves your state or area. For general information about MBDA programs, contact the Washington, D.C., office and review the information on MBDAS on page 97.

FOR GENERAL INFORMATION:

U.S. Department of Commerce
Minority Business Development Agency
Public Affairs, Room 6707
Washington DC 20230
(202) 482-5196

ATLANTA REGION

Alabama, Florida, Georgia, Kentucky, Mississippi, North Carolina, South Carolina, Tennessee

MBDA **Regional Office**
401 W. Peachtree St. NW, Suite 1930
Atlanta GA 30308-3516
(404) 730-3300

MBDA **Miami District Office**
51 Southwest First Ave., Room 1314
Miami FL 33130
(305) 536-5054

CHICAGO REGION

Illinois, Indiana, Iowa, Kansas, Michigan, Minnesota, Missouri, Nebraska, Ohio, Wisconsin

MBDA **Regional Office**
55 E. Monroe St., Suite 1440
Chicago IL 60603
(312) 353-0182

DALLAS REGION

Arkansas, Colorado, Louisiana, Montana, New Mexico, North Dakota, Oklahoma, South Dakota, Texas, Utah, Wyoming

MBDA **Regional Office**
1100 Commerce St., Room 7B23
Dallas TX 75242
(214) 767-8001

SAN FRANCISCO REGION

Alaska, American Samoa, Arizona, California, Hawaii, Idaho, Nevada, Oregon, Washington

MBDA **Regional Office**
221 Main St., Room 1280
San Francisco CA 94105
(415) 744-3001

MBDA **Los Angeles District Office**
977 N. Broadway, Suite 201
Los Angeles CA 90012
(213) 894-7157

WASHINGTON REGION

Delaware, Maryland, Pennsylvania, Virginia, Washington, D.C., West Virginia

MBDA **Regional Office**
1255 Twenty-second St. NW, Suite 701
Washington DC 20036
(202) 377-1356

MBDA **Philadelphia District**
Federal Office Building
600 Arch St., Room 10128
Philadelphia PA 19106
(215) 597-9236

NEW YORK REGION

Connecticut, Maine, Massachusetts, New Hampshire, New Jersey, New York, Puerto Rico, Rhode Island, Vermont, Virgin Islands

MBDA **Regional Office**
26 Federal Plaza, Room 3720
New York NY 10278
(212) 264-3262

MBDA **Boston District Office**
10 Causeway St., Room 418
Boston MA 02222-1041
(617) 565-6850

WOMEN'S BUREAU: U.S. DEPARTMENT OF LABOR REGIONAL OFFICES

For information about bureau programs in your area, contact the regional office that serves your state. For general information about the bureau, contact the Washington, D.C., office listed here. For more information about the bureau, see page 99.

FEDERAL OFFICE

Women's Bureau, Office of the Secretary
U.S. Department of Labor
200 Constitution Ave. NW
Washington DC 20210
(800) 827-5335

REGION 1

Maine, Vermont, Massachusetts, New Hampshire, Connecticut, Rhode Island

Women's Bureau
One Congress S., 11th Floor
Boston MA 02114
(617) 565-1988

REGION 2

New York, New Jersey, Puerto Rico, Virgin Islands

Women's Bureau
201 Varick St., Room 601
New York NY 10014
(212) 337-2389

REGION 3

Pennsylvania, Delaware, Maryland, Virginia, Washington, D.C., West Virginia

Women's Bureau
Gateway Building, Room 2450
3535 Market St.
Philadelphia PA 19104
(215) 596-1183

REGION 4

North Carolina, South Carolina, Kentucky, Tennessee, Georgia, Alabama, Mississippi, Florida

Women's Bureau
1371 Peachtree St. NE, Room 323
Atlanta GA 30367
(404) 347-4461

REGION 5

Minnesota, Wisconsin, Michigan, Ohio, Indiana, Illinois

Women's Bureau
230 S. Dearborn St., Room 1022
Chicago IL 60604
(312) 353-6985

REGION 6

New Mexico, Texas, Oklahoma, Arkansas, Louisiana

Women's Bureau
Federal Building
525 Griffin St., Suite 731
Dallas TX 75202
(214) 767-6985

REGION 7

Kansas, Missouri, Iowa, Nebraska

Women's Bureau
Center City Square Building
1100 Main St., Suite 1230
Kansas City MO 64106
(816) 426-6108

REGION 8

Montana, North Dakota, South Dakota, Wyoming, Utah, Colorado

Women's Bureau
1801 California St., Suite 905
Denver CO 80202-2614
(303) 391-6756

REGION 9

California, Nevada, Arizona, Hawaii

Women's Bureau
71 Stevenson St., Suite 927
San Francisco CA 94105
(415) 975-4750

REGION 10

Washington, Oregon, Idaho, Alaska

Women's Bureau
1111 Third Ave., Room 885
Seattle WA 98101-3211
(206) 553-1534

U.S. GOVERNMENT BOOKSTORES

You can purchase any government publication from stores in your regional area or from the national office in Washington, D.C. References to useful government publications are sprinkled throughout this guide, but for an overview of the federal government's publication lists and services, see page 51.

ALABAMA

U.S. Government Bookstore
O'Neill Building
2021 Third Ave. N
Birmingham AL 35203
(205) 731-1056

CALIFORNIA

U.S. Government Bookstore
ARCO Plaza, C-Level
505 S. Flower St.
Los Angeles, CA 90071
(213) 239-9844

U.S. Government Bookstore
Room 1023, Federal Building
450 Golden Gate Ave.
San Francisco CA 94102
(415) 252-5334

COLORADO

U.S. Government Bookstore
Room 117, Federal Building
1961 Stout St.
Denver CO 80294
(303) 844-3964

U.S. Government Bookstore
Norwest Banks Building
201 W. Eighth St.
Pueblo CO 81003
(719) 544-3142

FLORIDA

U.S. Government Bookstore
100 W. Bay St., Suite 100
Jacksonville FL 32202
(904) 353-1280

GEORGIA

U.S. Government Bookstore
First Union Plaza
999 Peachtree St. NE, Suite 120
Atlanta GA 30309-3964
(404) 347-1900

ILLINOIS

U.S. Government Bookstore
One Congress Center
401 S. State St., Suite 124
Chicago IL 60605
(312) 353-5133

MARYLAND

U.S. Government Bookstore
Warehouse Sales Outlet
8660 Cherry Lane
Laurel MD 20707
(301) 953-7974

MASSACHUSETTS

U.S. Government Bookstore
Thomas P. O'Neil Building, Room 169
Boston MA 02222
(617) 720-4180

MICHIGAN

U.S. Government Bookstore
Suite 160, Federal Building
477 Michigan Ave.
Detroit MI 48226
(313) 226-7816

MISSOURI

U.S. Government Bookstore
120 Bannister Mall
5600 E. Bannister Rd.
Kansas City MO 64137
(816) 767-2256

NEW YORK

U.S. Government Bookstore
Room 110, Federal Building
26 Federal Plaza
New York NY 10278
(212) 264-3825

OHIO

U.S. Government Bookstore
Room 1653, Federal Building
1240 E. Ninth St.
Cleveland OH 44199
(216) 522-4922

U.S. Government Bookstore
Room 207, Federal Building
200 N. High St.
Columbus OH 43215
(614) 469-6956

OREGON

U.S. Government Bookstore
1305 SW First Ave.
Portland OR 97201-5801
(503) 221-6217

PENNSYLVANIA

U.S. Government Bookstore
Robert Morris Building
100 N. Seventeenth St.
Philadelphia PA 19103
(215) 597-0677

U.S. Government Bookstore
Room 118, Federal Building
1000 Liberty Ave.
Pittsburgh PA 15222
(412) 644-2721

TEXAS

U.S. Government Bookstore
Room 1C50, Federal Building
1100 Commerce St.
Dallas TX 75242
(214) 767-0076

U.S. Government Bookstore
Texas Crude Building
801 Travis St., Suite 120
Houston TX 77002
(713) 228-1187

WASHINGTON

U.S. Government Bookstore
Room 194, Federal Building
915 Second Ave.
Seattle WA 98174
(206) 553-4270

WASHINGTON, D.C.

U.S. Government Printing Office
710 N. Capitol St. NW
Washington DC 20401
(202) 512-0132

U.S. Government Bookstore
1510 H St. NW
Washington DC 20005
(202) 653-5075

WISCONSIN

U.S. Government Bookstore
Reuss Federal Plaza, Suite 150
310 W. Wisconsin Ave.
Milwaukee WI 53203
(414) 297-1304

FIRST-STOP STATE OFFICES

Contact the office in your state for information about local and state business development opportunities. For more information about what first-stop offices do, see page 53. If there is not a first-stop office in your state, there may still be some excellent business assistance resources available through the Small Business Development Center network, your state Department of Economic Development, and other organizations in your area.

ALABAMA

The State of Alabama offers no specific programs for women-owned business enterprises but does assist them through its minority business assistance program.

Department of Economic and Community Affairs
Office of Minority Business
401 Adams Ave., Suite 570
Montgomery AL 36130
(800) 447-4191
(334) 242-2220

ALASKA

The State of Alaska has no specific office of women's business ownership assistance. The University of Alaska Small Business Development Center does offer several programs for women business owners, including an annual women's business conference.

University of Alaska Small Business Development Center
430 W. Seventh Ave., Suite 110
Anchorage AK 99501
(907) 274-7232

ARIZONA

Governor's Office for Women
1700 W. Washington #240
Phoenix AZ 85007
(602) 542-1755

Arizona Department of Commerce Minority and Women's Business Services
Small Business Assistance Center
3800 N. Central, Suite 1400
Phoenix AZ 85012
(800) 542-5684
(602) 280-1476

CALIFORNIA

Office of Small and Minority Business
1531 I St., 2nd Floor
Sacramento CA 95814-2016
(916) 322-1847

COLORADO

Office of Business Development
The Women's Business Office
1625 Broadway, Suite 1710
Denver CO 80282
(303) 892-3840

CONNECTICUT

The Connecticut Department of Economic Development provides assistance to WBES and administers a program to encourage the participation of WBES in state procurement.

Connecticut Department of Economic Development
Connecticut Economic Resource Center
865 Brook St.
Rocky Hill CT 06067-3405
(800) 392-2122

DELAWARE

The State of Delaware has no specific office for women-owned businesses, but the Small Business Development Center network offers some programs for women, including cosponsorship of an annual Entrepreneurial Women's Expo.

North Delaware
(302) 831-1555 (Newark)

Central Delaware
(302) 678-1555 (Dover)

South Delaware
(302) 856-1555 (Georgetown)

FLORIDA

The State of Florida has no specific office for women-owned businesses, but the Minority Business Advocacy and Assistance Office encourages minority- and women-owned businesses to participate in state contracting opportunities.

Commission on Minority and Economic Business Development
Small and Minority Business Advocacy Office
107 W. Gaines St.
201 Collins Building
Tallahassee FL 32399-2005
(904) 922-6852

GEORGIA

The State of Georgia has no specific programs for women business owners. However, the Georgia Department of Administrative Services sponsors a program to encourage the participation of women and minority businesses in state procurement.

Small and Minority Business Program
Georgia Department of Administrative Services
200 Piedmont Ave., Suite 1302
Atlanta GA 30334
(404) 656-6315

HAWAII

The State of Hawaii has no specific programs for women business owners. However, the Office of Small Business Information Services can provide women with general information on state resources for business start-up and expansion. This office does compile data on women business owners in the state and can refer callers to a privately published directory of women-owned businesses.

Department of Business and Economic Development
Business Development Division
737 Bishop St., Suite 1900
Honolulu HI 96813
(808) 586-2590

ILLINOIS

Illinois Department of Commerce and Community Affairs
Office of Women's Business Development
100 W. Randolph St., Suite 3-400
Chicago IL 60601
(312) 814-7176

INDIANA

Indiana Small Business Development Corp.
Office of Women and Minorities in Business
One N. Capitol Ave., Suite 1275
Indianapolis IN 46204
(317) 264-2820

IOWA

Iowa Department of Economic Development
The Targeted Small Business Program
200 E. Grand Ave.
Des Moines IA 50309
(515) 242-4721

KANSAS

Kansas Department of Commerce
Business Development Division
Office of Minorities and Women
700 SW Harrison, Suite 1300
Topeka KS 66603-3712
(913) 296-5298

KENTUCKY

Kentucky Cabinet for Economic Development
Small and Minority Business Division
Capitol Plaza Tower, 23rd Floor
Frankfort KY 40601
(800) 626-2930

LOUISIANA

The State of Louisiana does not have a specific office to assist women business owners, but the Department of Economic Development offers some WBE programs.

Department of Economic Development
P.O. Box 94185
Baton Rouge LA 70804
Certification: (504) 342-5373
Specialized loans: (504) 342-5675

MAINE

The State of Maine does not have a state-sponsored agency or program to assist women business owners. The Women's Business Development Corporation, a private nonprofit organization, serves as an information resource to women business owners in the state.

The Women's Business Development Corp.
P.O. Box 658
Bangor ME 04402-0658
(207) 974-5990

MARYLAND

The State of Maryland offers no programs specifically to assist women business owners.

MASSACHUSETTS

The Massachusetts State Office of Minority and Women's Business Assistance offers several programs to assist women business owners.

Office of Minority and Women Business Assistance (certification)
100 Cambridge St., Room 1305
Boston MA 02202
(617) 727-8692

Minority Business Assistance Center
University of Massachusetts
Boston College of Management
5th Floor
Boston MA 02125-3393
(617) 287-7750

Office of Business Development
Minority and Women's Business
Ownership Specialist
1 Ashburton Place, Room 2101
Boston MA 02108
(800) 522-7482

MICHIGAN

The State of Michigan has no specific
programs to assist women business
owners.

MINNESOTA

Minnesota has special programs to
encourage WBE participation in state
contracting.

Department of Administration
Customer and Vendor Services
Targeted Small Business Program
112 Administration Building
50 Sherburne Ave.
St. Paul MN 55155
(612) 296-2000

MISSISSIPPI

**Mississippi Department of Economic
and Community Development**
Office of Minority Business Enterprise
Minority and Women's Advocacy
Program
Box 849
Jackson MS 39205
(601) 359-3448

MISSOURI

The State of Missouri has no specific
programs for women, but the council
refers women to appropriate resources
in the community.

**Council on Women's Economic
Development**
Missouri Department of Economic
Development
P.O. Box 1157
Jefferson City MO 65102-1157
(314) 751-3237

MONTANA

The State of Montana has no specific
programs to assist women business
owners.

NEBRASKA

Nebraska has no specific programs for
women business owners, but the
Department of Economic Development
does maintain a directory of women-
owned businesses.

**Nebraska Department of Economic
Development**
Existing Business Assistance Division
P.O. Box 94666
Lincoln NE 68509
(800) 426-6505
(402) 471-3782

NEVADA

Department of Business and Industry
Center for Business Advocacy and
Services
Women's Business Advocacy Program
Office of Small Business
2501 E. Sahara, Suite 202
Las Vegas NV 89104
(702) 486-4335

NEW JERSEY

The New Jersey Division of Women and
Minority Businesses provides certifica-
tions for state set-aside contracts.

**New Jersey Department of Commerce
and Economic Development**
Division of Development for Small,
Women and Minority Businesses
20 W. State St., CN 835
Trenton NJ 08625-0835
(609) 292-3860

NEW MEXICO

The State of New Mexico sponsors
a program to encourage women
business owners to participate in state
procurement.

**State of New Mexico General Services
Department**
State Purchasing Division
Procurement Assistance Program
1100 St. Francis Dr., Room 2006
Santa Fe NM 87503
(505) 827-0425

NEW YORK

The New York Office of Women's Business Development assists women business owners and administers a statewide
unified women's business certification
program.

**New York State Office of Minority and
Women's Business Development**
1 Commerce Plaza
Albany NY 12245
(518) 474-6346

NORTH CAROLINA

The North Carolina Small Business
Development Technology Center works
closely with minority- and women-
owned firms.

**Small Business Development
Technology Center**
333 Fayetteville Mall, Suite 1150
Raleigh NC 27601
(800) 258-0862
(919) 571-7272

OHIO

The State of Ohio offers comprehensive
assistance to women business owners
through its Women's Business Resource
Program.

Ohio Department of Development
77 S. High St., 28th Floor
Columbus OH 43266-0413
(800) 848-1300
(614) 466-4945

OKLAHOMA

Oklahoma Department of Commerce Business Development Division
Office of Women-Owned Business Assistance
P.O. Box 26980
Oklahoma City OK 73126-0980
(405) 841-5242

OREGON

Office of Minority, Women and Emerging Small Business
155 Cottage St. NE, 3rd Floor
Salem OR 97310
(541) 378-5651

PENNSYLVANIA

Entrepreneurial Assistance Office
Women's Business Advocate
400 Forum Building
Harrisburg PA 17120
(800) 280-3801
(717) 787-3339

Pennsylvania Office of Minority and Women Business Enterprise
Room 502, North Office Building
Harrisburg PA 17125
(717) 787-7380

RHODE ISLAND

Department of Administration
Office of Minority Business Enterprise
7 Jackson Walkway
Providence RI 02903
(401) 277-6253

SOUTH CAROLINA

The State of South Carolina has no specific programs, but the Office of Small and Minority Business Assistance does provide resources to women business owners.

Office of the Governor
Office of Small and Minority Business Assistance
1205 Pendleton St.
Columbia SC 29201
(803) 734-0657

SOUTH DAKOTA

The State of South Dakota has no specific office to assist women business owners.

TENNESSEE

The State of Tennessee offers no specific programs. The Office of Minority Business Enterprise does assist women as part of its disadvantaged business program.

Department of Economic and Community Development
Office of Minority Business Enterprise
Rachel Jackson Building, 7th Floor
320 Sixth Ave. North
Nashville TN 37243-0405
(615) 741-2545

TEXAS

The State of Texas has no specific office of women's business ownership. Several state offices do sponsor programs to assist women business owners in competing for procurement contracts.

State of Texas Department of Commerce
State Purchasing and General Services Commission
P.O. Box 13047
Austin TX 78711-3047
(512) 463-3416

UTAH

The Utah Women's Business Development Council and the Utah Small Business Development Center offer special assistance to encourage the development of women-owned businesses.

Utah Small Business Development Center
Women's Business Development Council
102 W. 500th St. S., Suite 315
Salt Lake City UT 84104
(801) 581-7905

The Utah Technology Finance Corp. (UTFC) operates the Utah Office of Women's Business Ownership, offering training in Salt Lake City and outlying areas of the state. UTFC also administers the SBA demonstration site and microloan programs in the state.

Utah Technology Finance Corp.
177 E. 100th S.
Salt Lake City UT 84111
(801) 364-4364

VERMONT

There are no specific statewide programs in Vermont designed to assist women business owners. However, the State and the City of Burlington in partnership with Trinity College jointly fund the Women's Small Business Project.

The Women's Small Business Project
Trinity College
208 Colchester Ave.
Burlington VT 05401
(802) 658-0337

VIRGINIA

Department of Economic Development
Small Business Development Division
Women's Business Enterprise Coordinator
901 E. Byrd St.
Richmond VA 23219
(804) 371-8253

WASHINGTON

State of Washington Office of Minority and Women's Business Enterprises
406 S. Water
P.O. Box 41160
Olympia WA 98504-1160
(360) 753-9693

Business Assistance Center (BAC)
Minority and Women's Business
Development Program
2001 Sixth Ave., Suite 2700
Seattle WA 98121
(206) 389-2561

WASHINGTON, D.C.

Minority Business Development Office
441 Fourth St. NW, Suite 970N
Washington DC 20001

WEST VIRGINIA

The State of West Virginia has no specific office to assist women business
owners, but the Small Business Development Center works with women business owners, publishes a directory of
women business owners in the state,
and organizes special events, expos, and
conferences.

Small Business Development Center
Women and Minority Business
Development Specialists
950 Kanawha Blvd. E.
Charleston WV 25305
(304) 558-2960

WISCONSIN

The State of Wisconsin assists women
business owners through its Department of Development. Within the
Department, the Office of Women's
Business Services serves as an advocate
for women's business issues and offers
resources and financial programs
designed to assist WBES.

Department of Development
Bureau of Business and Industry
Development
Women's Business Services
123 W. Washington Ave.
Madison WI 53707
(608) 266-0593

WYOMING

The State of Wyoming has no specific
programs for women business owners.

STATE ECONOMIC DEVELOPMENT DEPARTMENTS

State economic development departments offer specialized business assistance and referral to meet the needs of their state. For more information about services and programs typically offered, see pages 54 and 124.

ALABAMA

Department of Economic and
Community Affairs
Development Council
P.O. Box 5690
Montgomery AL 36103
(334) 242-0893

ALASKA

Department of Commerce and
Economic Development
Division of Trade and Development
3601 C St., Suite 700
Anchorage AK 99503-5934
(907) 269-8110

ARIZONA

Department of Commerce
Business Connection Program
3800 N. Central Ave., Suite 1500
Phoenix AZ 85012
(800) 542-5684

ARKANSAS

Industrial Development Commission
1 Capitol Mall, Room 4C-300
Little Rock AR 72201
(501) 682-1121

CALIFORNIA

California Trade and Commerce
Agency
Office of Small Business
801 K St., Suite 1700
Sacramento CA 95814
(800) 303-6600
(916) 327-HELP (4357)

COLORADO

Office of Business Development
1625 Broadway, Suite 1710
Denver CO 80202
(800) 333-7798
(303) 892-3840

CONNECTICUT

Department of Economic
Development
Connecticut Economic Resource
Center (CERC)
805 Brook St., Building #4
Rocky Hill CT 06067-3405
(800) 392-2122

DELAWARE

Delaware Development Office
99 Kings Highway
P.O. Box 1401
Dover DE 19903
(302) 739-4271

FLORIDA

Department of Commerce
Division of Economic Development
107 W. Gaines St., Room 443
Collins Building
Tallahassee FL 32399-2000
(800) 342-0771
(904) 488-9357

GEORGIA

Department of Industry, Trade and
Tourism
285 Peachtree Center Ave. NE
Suite 1100
Atlanta GA 30303
(404) 656-3573

HAWAII

Department of Business, Economic
Development and Tourism
Business Development Division
737 Bishop St., Suite 1900
Honolulu HI 96813
(808) 586-2590

IDAHO

Department of Commerce
Division of Economic Development
P.O. Box 83720
Boise ID 83720-0090
(208) 334-2470

ILLINOIS

Department of Commerce and
Community Affairs
620 E. Adams St.,
Springfield IL 62701
(800) 252-2923

INDIANA

Department of Commerce
Business Development and Marketing
Group
1 N. Capitol St., Suite 700
Indianapolis IN 46204
(800) 45-STATE (457-8283)
(317) 232-0159

IOWA

Department of Economic
Development
200 E. Grand
Des Moines IA 50309
(515) 242-4700

KANSAS

Department of Commerce and
Housing
Business Development Division
700 SW Harrison, Suite 1300
Topeka KS 66603-3712
(913) 296-3805

KENTUCKY

Economic Development Cabinet
2300 Capital Plaza Tower
500 Mero St.
Frankfort KY 40601
Referral to business development specialist: (800) 626-2930
Business Information Clearinghouse:
(800) 626-2250

LOUISIANA

Department of Economic
Development
P.O. Box 94185
Baton Rouge LA 70804-9185
(504) 342-5388

MAINE

Department of Economic and Community Development
Business Answers
59 State House Station
Augusta ME 04333-0059
(207) 287-8103

MARYLAND

Department of Business and
Economic Development
Division of Regional Development
217 E. Redwood St.
Baltimore MD 21202
(410) 767-0095

MASSACHUSETTS

Massachusetts Office of Business
Development
1 Ashburton Place, Room 2101
Boston MA 02108
(800) 522-7482
(617) 727-3206

MICHIGAN

Michigan Jobs Commission
Industry and Investment Relations
Customer Assistance Office
201 N. Washington Square
Lansing MI 48913
(517) 373-9808

MINNESOTA

Economic Development Division
Small Business Assistance Office
500 Metro Square
121 Ninth Place E
St. Paul MN 55101-2146
(800) 657-3858

MISSISSIPPI

Department of Economic and
Community Development
P.O. Box 849
Jackson MS 39205-0849
(601) 359-3449

MISSOURI

Department of Economic
Development
301 W. High St.
Jefferson City MO 65102
(800) 523-1434
(314) 751-3237

MONTANA

Economic Development Division
1424 Ninth Ave.
Helena MT 59620
(406) 444-4780

NEBRASKA

Department of Economic Development
One-Stop Business Assistance Center
301 Centennial Mall S.
Lincoln NE 68509-4666
(800) 426-6505

NEVADA

Department of Business and Industry
Center for Business Advocacy and
Services
2501 E. Sahara, Suite 202
Las Vegas NV 89104
(702) 486-4335

NEW HAMPSHIRE

Department of Resources and
Economic Development
Office of Business and Industrial
Development
P.O. Box 1856
Concord NH 03302
(603) 271-2591

NEW JERSEY

Department of Commerce and
Economic Development
Division of Economic Development
20 W. State St., CN823
Trenton NJ 08625
(800) 533-0186
(609) 292-7757

NEW MEXICO

Economic Development Department
Joseph Montoya Building
1100 St. Francis Dr.
Santa Fe NM 87503
(505) 827-0300

NEW YORK

Empire State Development
633 Third Ave.
New York NY 10017
(800) STATE NY (782-8369)

NORTH CAROLINA

Department of Commerce
Business and Industry Development
430 N. Salisbury St.
Raleigh NC 27603-5900
(919) 733-9205
(for expansion and relocation)

Small Business Development
Technology Center
333 Fayette St. Mall, Suite 1150
Raleigh NC 27601
(800) 258-0862
(919) 715-7272
(for start-up)

NORTH DAKOTA

Department of Economic
Development and Finance
1833 E. Bismark Expressway
Bismark ND 58504
(701) 328-5300

OHIO

Department of Development
77 S. High St., 29th Floor
Columbus OH 43266-0101
(800) 345-OHIO (6446)
(614) 644-9389

OKLAHOMA

Department of Commerce
P.O. Box 26980
Oklahoma City OK 73126-0980
(800) 879-6552
(405) 843-9770

OREGON

Department of Economic
Development
775 Summer St. NE
Salem OR 97310
(800) 442-UASK (8275)
(541) 986-0123

PENNSYLVANIA

Department of Commerce
Entrepreneurial Development Division
Small Business Resource Center
433 Forum Building
Harrisburg PA 17120
(800) 280-3801

RHODE ISLAND

Economic Development Corp.
7 Jackson Walkway
Providence RI 02903
(401) 277-2601

SOUTH CAROLINA

Department of Commerce
P.O. Box 927
Columbia SC 29202
(803) 737-0400

SOUTH DAKOTA

Governor's Office of Economic
Development
Capitol Lake Plaza
711 E. Wells Ave.
Pierre SD 57501
(605) 773-5032

TENNESSEE

Department of Economic and
Community Development
320 Sixth Ave., 8th Floor
Nashville TN 37243-0405
(615) 741-1888

TEXAS

Department of Commerce
Business Development Division
Information Resources for Business
1700 Congress Ave., Suite 1146
Austin TX 78701
(512) 936-0172

UTAH

Department of Community and
Economic Development
Division of Business and Economic
Development
324 S. State St., 5th Floor
Salt Lake City UT 84111
(801) 538-8700

VERMONT

Department of Economic
Development
109 State St.
Montpelier VT 05602
(802) 828-3221

VIRGINIA

Department of Economic
Development
Small Business Development Division
901 E. Byrd St.
Richmond VA 23219
(804) 371-8252

WASHINGTON

Department of Community Trade and
Economic Development
Business Assistance Center
919 Lakeridge Way SW, Suite A
Olympia WA 98504-2516
(800) 237-1233
(360) 664-9501

WASHINGTON, D.C.

Economic Development Office of
the Mayor
441 Fourth St. NW
11th Floor, Suite 1140
Washington DC 20001
(202) 727-6365

WEST VIRGINIA

Development Office
Small Business Development Center
Building 6, Room B504
1900 Kanawha Blvd. E.
Charleston WV 25305
(304) 558-2969

WISCONSIN

Department of Development
Bureau of Business Development
123 W. Washington Ave.
Madison WI 53703
(608) 267-9552

WYOMING

Department of Commerce
Division of Economic and Community
Development
6101 Yellowstone Rd., 4th Floor
Cheyenne WY 82002
(307) 777-7284

STATE WOMEN'S COMMISSIONS

Women's Commissions work to improve the economic, educational, and employment status of women in their state. For more information about the commissions, see page 55.

ALABAMA

Alabama Women's Commission
200 S. Franklin Dr.
Troy AL 36081-4508
(205) 566-8744

ALASKA

Office of the Governor
3601 State St., Suite 742
Anchorage AK 99503
(907) 561-4227

ARIZONA

Governor's Office for Women
1700 W. Washington, 4th Floor
Phoenix AZ 85007
(800) 253-0883
(602) 542-1755

ARKANSAS

No commission currently in place.

CALIFORNIA

Commission on the Status of Women
1303 J St., Suite 400
Sacramento CA 95814-2900
(916) 445-3173

COLORADO

No commission currently in place.

CONNECTICUT

Permanent Commission on the
Status of Women
90 Washington St.
Hartford CT 06106
(203) 566-5702

DELAWARE

Commission for Women
Carvel State Office Building
820 N. French St., 6th Floor
Wilmington DE 19801
(302) 577-2660

FLORIDA

Commission on the Status of Women
Department of Legal Affairs
Office of the Attorney General
The Capitol
Tallahassee FL 32399-1050
(904) 922-0252

GEORGIA

No commission currently in place.

HAWAII

Commission on the Status of Women
Department of Human Services
335 Merchant St., Room 253
Honolulu HI 96813
(808) 586-5758

IDAHO

Commission on Women's Programs
Towers Building, 10th Floor
450 W. State St.
Boise ID 83720
(208) 334-4673

ILLINOIS

Assistant Chief of Staff
Office of the Governor
2 ½ State House
Springfield IL 62706
(217) 785-8652

INDIANA

Commission for Women
Civil Rights Division
100 N. Senate Ave.
Indianapolis IN 46204
(317) 233-6549

IOWA

Commission on the Status of Women
Department of Human Rights
Lucas State Office Building, 1st Floor
Des Moines IA 50319
(515) 281-4467

KANSAS

No commission currently in place.

KENTUCKY

Commission on Women
614A Shelby St.
Frankfort KY 40601
(502) 564-6643

LOUISIANA

Office of Women's Services
Office of the Governor
P.O. Box 94095
Baton Rouge LA 70804-9095
(504) 922-0960

MAINE

No commission currently in place.

MARYLAND

Maryland Commission for Women
Department of Human Resources
311 W. Saratoga St., Room 232
Baltimore MD 21201
(410) 767-7137

MASSACHUSETTS

Chief Policy Advisor
Office of the Governor
State House, Room 360
Boston MA 02133
(617) 727-6250

MICHIGAN

Michigan Women's Commission
611 W. Ottawa St., 3rd Floor
Lansing MI 48933
(517) 373-2884

MINNESOTA

Commission on the Economic Status
of Women
85 State Office Building
St. Paul MN 55155
(612) 296-8590

MISSISSIPPI

No commission currently in place.

MISSOURI

Missouri Women's Council
Department of Economic
Development
1442 Aaron Court, Suite E
Jefferson City MO 65102
(314) 751-0810

MONTANA

Women in Employment Advisory
Council
Mitchel Building
Helena MT 59624
(406) 444-3111

NEBRASKA

Commission on the Status of Women
P.O. Box 94985
Lincoln NE 68509-4985
(402) 471-2039

NEVADA

No commission currently in place.

NEW HAMPSHIRE

Commission on the Status of Women
State House Annex, Room 334
25 Capitol St.
Concord NH 03301
(603) 271-2660

NEW JERSEY

Division on Women
Department of Community Affairs
101 S. Broad St., CN 801
Trenton NJ 08625-0801
(609) 292-8840

NEW MEXICO

Commission on the Status of Women
4001 Indian School Rd., Suite 220
Albuquerque NM 87110
(505) 841-4665

NEW YORK

New York State Division for Women
2 World Trade Center, 57th Floor
New York NY 10047
(212) 417-5842

NORTH CAROLINA

Council on Status for Women
Department of Administration
526 N. Wilmington St.
Raleigh NC 27604
(919) 733-2455

NORTH DAKOTA

Commission on the Status of Women
Department of Economic Development
1833 E. Bismark
Bismark ND 58501-4004
(701) 328-5301

OHIO

Women's Policy and Research
Commission
30 E. Broad St., Suite 2701
Columbus OH 43266-0920
(614) 466-5580

OKLAHOMA

Governor's Commission on the
Status of Women
3112 NW 26th St.
Oklahoma City OK 73107

OREGON

Commission for Women
Portland State University
Smith Center, Room M315
Box 751
Portland OR 97207
(541) 725-5889

PENNSYLVANIA

Commission for Women
Office of the Governor
209 Finance Building
Harrisburg PA 17120
(717) 787-8128

RHODE ISLAND

Advisory Commission on Women
260 W. Exchange St.
Providence RI 02903
(401) 277-6105

SOUTH CAROLINA

Division on Women
Office of the Governor
2221 Devine St., Suite 408
Columbia SC 29205
(803) 734-9144

SOUTH DAKOTA

No commission currently in place.

TENNESSEE

No commission currently in place.

TEXAS

Commission on Women
Office of the Governor
Box 12428, Capitol Station
Austin TX 78711
(512) 475-2615

UTAH

Commission on Women and
Children
1124 State Office Building
Salt Lake City UT 84114
(801) 538-1736

VERMONT

Governor's Commission on the
Status of Women
126 State St.
Montpelier VT 05633-6801
(802) 828-2851

VIRGINIA

Division of Health and Human
Services
Governor's Cabinet
622 Ninth St. Office Building
Richmond VA 23219
(804) 786-7765

WASHINGTON

Interagency Committee on the Status
of Employed Women
P.O. Box 47450
Olympia WA 98504-7450
(360) 753-5540

WASHINGTON, D.C.

Commission for Women
2000 Fourteenth St. NW, Room 354
Washington DC 20009
(202) 939-8083

WEST VIRGINIA

Women's Commission
Building Six, Room 637
Charleston WV 25305
(304) 558-0070

WISCONSIN

Wisconsin Women's Council
16 N. Carroll St., Suite 720
Madison WI 53702
(608) 266-2219

WYOMING

Department of Employment
Council for Women's Issues
Herschler Building, 2nd Floor E
Cheyenne WY 82002
(307) 777-7671

NATIONAL ASSOCIATION OF WOMEN'S YELLOW PAGES

Check the state-by-state listing below to see if there is a *Women's Yellow Pages* publisher in your area. For more information about the *Women's Yellow Pages,* see page 67.

ALABAMA

Women's Yellow Pages of the
Gulf Coast
P.O. Box 6021
Mobile AL 36660
(800) 378-7461
(334) 660-2725

Women's Yellow Pages of Greater
Birmingham
P.O. Box 20824
Birmingham AL 35216
(205) 967-0085

ALASKA

No yellow pages currently in Alaska.

ARKANSAS

No yellow pages currently in Arkansas.

ARIZONA

Today's Arizona Woman Business
Directory
4425 N. Saddlebag Trail
Scottsdale AZ 85251
(602) 945-5000

CALIFORNIA

Women's Yellow Pages and Referral
Service
13601 Ventura Blvd., #374
Sherman Oaks CA 91423
(818) 995-6646

Women's Business Network, Inc.
P.O. Box 108
Berkeley CA 94710
(415) 326-0212

Sacramento Women's Yellow Pages
3104 O St., Suite 255
Sacramento CA 95816
(916) 452-3264

COLORADO

Colorado Woman Publishing, Inc.
P.O. Box 22274
Denver CO 80222
(916) 452-3264

CONNECTICUT

No yellow pages currently in
Connecticut.

DELAWARE

No yellow pages currently in Delaware.

FLORIDA

The Women's Network, Inc.
4524 Curry Ford Rd., #280
Orlando FL 32812-2774
(407) 896-4444

Today's Florida Business Woman
P.O. Box 7223
St. Petersburg FL 33734-7223
(813) 825-0018

GEORGIA

**Women's Yellow Pages of Greater
Atlanta**
180 Allen Rd., N. Building, #303
Atlanta GA 30328
(404) 255-4144

HAWAII

No yellow pages currently in Hawaii.

IDAHO

No yellow pages currently in Idaho.

ILLINOIS

**Women in Business Yellow Pages of
Metro Chicago and Springfield**
7358 N. Lincoln, Suite 150
Chicago IL 60646
(708) 679-7800

INDIANA

No yellow pages currently in Indiana.

IOWA

No yellow pages currently in Iowa.

KANSAS

No yellow pages currently in Kansas.

KENTUCKY

No yellow pages currently in
Kentucky.

LOUISIANA

No yellow pages currently in Louisiana.

MAINE

No yellow pages currently in Maine.

MARYLAND

Women's Yellow Pages of Maryland
c/o The Annapolis Publishing Co.
114 West St.
Annapolis MD 21401
(410) 267-0886

MASSACHUSETTS

No yellow pages currently in
Massachusetts.

MICHIGAN

No yellow pages currently in
Michigan.

MINNESOTA

No yellow pages currently in
Minnesota.

MISSISSIPPI

No yellow pages currently in
Mississippi.

MISSOURI

**The Women's Yellow Pages of Greater
St. Louis**
222 S. Meramec, Suite 209
St. Louis MO 63105
(314) 725-1452

MONTANA

No yellow pages currently in Montana.

NEBRASKA

No yellow pages currently in Nebraska.

NEVADA

Women's Yellow Pages of S. Nevada
3021 Valley View, Suite 209
Las Vegas NV 89102
(702) 362-6507

NEW HAMPSHIRE

No yellow pages currently in
New Hampshire.

NEW JERSEY

No yellow pages currently in
New Jersey.

NEW MEXICO

**Albuquerque Women in Business
Directory**
P.O. Box 12955
Albuquerque NM 87195
(505) 247-9195

NEW YORK

Ask-Women for Success Guide
93 Fruehauf Ave.
Snyder NY 14226-3805
(716) 839-0855

NORTH CAROLINA

Directory of Women-Owned Businesses
P.O. Box 156571
Durham NC 27704
(919) 220-8177

Women's Yellow Pages of the Greater Charlotte Area
5567 Robinhood Rd.
Charlotte NC 28211
(704) 364-0225

NORTH DAKOTA

No yellow pages currently in North Dakota.

OHIO

No yellow pages currently in Ohio.

OKLAHOMA

No yellow pages currently in Oklahoma.

OREGON

No yellow pages currently in Oregon.

PENNSYLVANIA

The Greater Philadelphia Women's Yellow Pages
P.O. Box 1002
Havertown PA 19083
(215) 446-4747

Greater Pittsburgh Women's Yellow Pages
1133 Greenlawn Dr.
Pittsburgh PA 15220
(412) 561-4313

RHODE ISLAND

No yellow pages currently in Rhode Island.

SOUTH CAROLINA

No yellow pages currently in South Carolina.

SOUTH DAKOTA

No yellow pages currently in South Dakota.

TENNESSEE

No yellow pages currently in Tennessee.

TEXAS

Women Mean Business Directory
14275 Midway Rd., Suite 220
Dallas TX 75244
(214) 687-9020

UTAH

No yellow pages currently in Utah.

VERMONT

No yellow pages currently in Vermont.

VIRGINIA

The Women's Yellow Pages Directory of
Hampton Road
416 Oakmears Crescent
Virginia Beach VA 23462
(804) 499-3543

WASHINGTON

Women's Business and Resource
Directory
P.O. Box 58876
Renton WA 98058
(206) 726-9687

WASHINGTON, D.C.

No yellow pages currently in
Washington, D.C.

WEST VIRGINIA

No yellow pages currently in
West Virginia.

WISCONSIN

Women's Yellow Pages of Greater
Milwaukee
P.O. Box 13827
Milwaukee WI 53213
(414) 789-1346

WYOMING

No yellow pages currently in Wyoming.

SBA MICROLENDERS

SBA Microlenders are nonprofit organizations that serve as intermediaries for microloan
funds made available by the SBA. The lenders on the list provide microloans and technical
assistance to loan recipients in their state or region. (Some SBA program participants provide technical assistance only.) If the contact information is no longer accurate or to find
out if there is a new microlender in your area, contact your SBA District Office (see page
192) or the SBA Office of Financial Assistance at (202) 205-6490. For more information
about the SBA microloan program, see page 122.

ALABAMA

Elmore Community Action
Committee, Inc.
1011 W. Tallassee, P.O. Drawer H
Wetumpka AL 36092
(334) 567-4361

ALASKA

Southeast Alaska Small Business
Development Center
400 Willoughby Ave., Suite 211
Juneau AK 99801-1724
(907) 463-3789
(Provides technical assistance only.)

ARIZONA

Chicanos por la Causa, Inc.
1112 E. Buckeye Rd.
Phoenix AZ 85034
(602) 257-0700

PPEP Housing Development Corp.
Micro Industry Credit Rural
Organization
802 E. Forty-sixth St.
Tucson AZ 85713
(602) 622-3553

ARKANSAS

Arkansas Enterprise Group
605 Main St., Suite 203
Arkadelphia AR 71923
(501) 246-9739

Delta Community Development Corp.
675 Eaton Rd.
Forrest City AR 72335
(501) 633-9113

**White River Planning and
Development District**
1652 White Dr.
Batesville AR 72503
(501) 793-5233

CALIFORNIA

Arcata Economic Development Corp.
100 Ericson Court, Suite 100
Arcata CA 95521
(707) 822-4616

**Center for SE Asian Refugee
Resettlement**
875 O'Farrel St.
San Francisco CA 94109
(415) 885-2743

**Coalition for Women's Economic
Development**
315 W. Ninth St., Suite 705
Los Angeles CA 90015
(213) 489-4995

Valley Rural Development Corp.
3417 W. Shaw, Suite 100
Fresno CA 93711
(209) 271-9030

**Women's Initiative for
Self Employment**
450 Mission St., Suite 402
San Francisco CA 94105
(415) 247-9473

COLORADO

**Greater Denver Local Development
Corp.**
P.O. Box 2135
Denver CO 80201-2135
(303) 296-9535

Region 10 LEAP Inc.
P.O. Box 849
Montrose CO 81402
(303) 249-2436

CONNECTICUT

New Haven Community Investment Corp.
809 Chapel St., 2nd Floor
New Haven CT 06510
(203) 776-6172

DELAWARE

Wilmington Economic Development Corp.
605-A Market St. Mall
Wilmington DE 19801
(302) 571-9088

FLORIDA

Community Equity Investments, Inc.
302 N. Barcelona St.
Pensacola FL 32501
(904) 444-2234

United Gainesville Community Development Corp., Inc.
505 NW Second Ave.
Gainesville FL 32602
(904) 376-8891

Lee County Employment and Economic Development Corp.
2121 W. First St., Rear
P.O. Box 2285
Fort Myers FL 33902-2285
(813) 337-2300
(Provides technical assistance only.)

GEORGIA

Fulton Community Development Corp., Inc.
Greater Atlanta Small Business Project
10 Park Place S., Suite 305
Atlanta GA 30303
(404) 659-5955

Small Business Assistance Corp.
31 W. Congress St., Suite 100
Savannah GA 31401
(912) 232-4700

HAWAII

The Immigrant Center
720 N. King St.
Honolulu HI 96817
(808) 845-3918

IDAHO

Panhandle Area Council
11100 Airport Dr.
Hayden ID 83835-9743
(208) 772-0584

ILLINOIS

Greater Sterling Development Corp.
1741 Industrial Dr.
Sterling IL 61081
(815) 625-5255

Illinois Development Finance Authority
233 S. Wacker Dr., Suite 5310
Chicago IL 60606
(312) 793-5586

Economic Development Council for the Peoria Area
124 SE Adams St., Suite 300
Peoria IL 61602
(309) 676-7500

The Neighborhood Institute and Women's Self Employment Project
20 N. Clark St., Suite 400
Chicago IL 60602
(312) 606-8255

Women's Business Development Center
8 S. Michigan Ave., Suite 400
Chicago IL 60603
(312) 853-3477
(Provides technical assistance only through this SBA program, but also has a microloan program.)

INDIANA

Eastside Community Investments Inc.
26 N. Arsenal Ave.
Indianapolis IN 46201
(317) 637-7300

Metro Small Business Assistance Corp.
1 NW Martin Luther King Jr. Blvd.
Evansville IN 47708-1869
(812) 426-5857

Hoosier Valley Economic Development Corp.
1613 E. Eighth St.
P.O. Box 843
Jeffersonville IN 47131-0843
(812) 288-6451

IOWA

Siouxland Economic Development Corp.
400 Orpheum Electric Building
Sioux City IA 51102
(712) 279-6286

Institute for Social and Economic Development
1901 Broadway, Suite 313
Iowa City IA 52240
(319) 338-2331
(Provides technical assistance only.)

KANSAS

S. Central Kansas Economic Development District
151 N. Volutsia
Wichita KS 67214
(316) 683-4422

Center for Business Innovations, Inc.
4747 Troost Ave.
Kansas City MO 64110
(816) 561-8567

Great Plains Development, Inc.
100 Military Plaza, Suite 128
P.O. Box 1116
Dodge City KS 67801
(316) 227-6406
(Provides technical assistance only.)

KENTUCKY

Community Ventures Corp.
1450 N. Broadway
Lexington KY 40505
(606) 281-5475

Kentucky Highlands Investment Corp.
362 Old Whitley Rd.
London KY 40741
(606) 864-5175

Louisville Central Development Corp.
306 Roy Wilkins Ave.
Louisville KY 40203
(502) 583-8821

Purchase Area Development District
1002 Medical Dr.
Mayfield KY 42066
(502) 247-7171

LOUISIANA

Greater Jennings Chamber of
Commerce
414 Cary Ave.
Jennings LA 70546
(318) 824-0933

MAINE

Coastal Enterprises, Inc.
P.O. Box 268
Water St.
Wiscasset ME 04578
(207) 882-7552

N. Maine Regional Planning
Commission
2 S. Main St.
Caribou ME 04736
(207) 743-7716

MARYLAND

Council for Equal Business
Opportunity, Inc.
The Park Plaza
800 N. Charles St., Suite 300
Baltimore MD 21201
(410) 576-2326

MASSACHUSETTS

Economic Development Industrial
Corp. of Lynn
37 Central Square, 3rd Floor
Lynn MA 01901
(617) 592-2361

Jewish Vocational Service, Inc.
105 Chauncy St., 6th Floor
Boston MA 02111
(617) 451-8147

Jobs for Fall River, Inc.
1 Government Center
Fall River MA 02722
(508) 324-2620

Springfield Business Development
Fund
36 Court St., Room 222
Springfield MA 01103
(413) 787-6050

Western Massachusetts Enterprise
Fund
324 Wells St.
Greenfield MA 01301
(413) 787-6050

MICHIGAN

Ann Arbor Community
Development Corp.
2008 Hogback Rd., Suite 2A
Ann Arbor MI 48105
(313) 677-1400

Detroit Economic Growth Corp.
150 W. Jefferson, Suite 1500
Detroit MI 48226
(313) 677-1400

Community Capital Development
Corp.
The Walter Reuther Center
711 N. Saginaw St., Suite 123
Flint MI 48503
(810) 239-5847

Northern Economic Initiative Corp.
1009 W. Ridge St.
Marquette MI 49855
(906) 228-5571

Cornerstone Alliance
185 E. Main
Benton Harbor MI 49022-4440
(616) 925-6100
(Provides technical assistance only.)

MINNESOTA

Northeast Entrepreneurs Fund, Inc.
Olcott Plaza, Suite 140
820 Ninth St. North
Virginia MN 55792
(218) 749-4191

Women Venture
2324 University Ave.
St. Paul MN 55114
(612) 646-3808

Neighborhood Development
Center, Inc.
663 University Ave.
St. Paul MN 55104
(612) 290-8150
(Provides technical assistance only.)

MISSISSIPPI

Delta Foundation
819 Main St.
Greensville MS 38701
(601) 335-5291

Friends of Children of Mississippi, Inc.
4880 McWillie Circle
Jackson MS 39206
(601) 362-1541

MISSOURI

Center for Business Innovations, Inc.
4747 Troost Ave.
Kansas City MO 64110
(816) 561-8567

Community Development Corp. of
Kansas City
2420 E. Linwood Blvd., Suite 400
Kansas City MO 64109
(816) 924-5800
(Provides technical assistance only.)

MONTANA

Capital Opportunities
District IX Human Resource
Development Council, Inc.
321 E. Main St., Suite 300
Bozeman MT 59715
(406) 587-4486

Women's Opportunity and Resource
Development, Inc.
127 N. Higgins Ave.
Missoula MT 59802
(406) 543-3550

Montana Department of Commerce
SBDC Division
1424 Ninth Ave.
P.O. Box 200501
Helena MT 59620-0501
(406) 444-4780
(Provides technical assistance only.)

NEBRASKA

Rural Enterprise Assistance Project
P.O. Box 406
Walthill NE 68067
(402) 846-5428

West Central Nebraska Development
District
201 E. Second St., Suite C
P.O. Box 599
Ogallala NE 69153
(308) 284-6077

Omaha Small Business Network, Inc.
2505 N. Twenty-fourth St.
Omaha NE 68110
(402) 346-8262
(Provides technical assistance only.)

NEVADA

Nevada Women's Fund
201 W. Liberty St., Suite 201
Reno NV 89501
(702) 786-2335

NEW HAMPSHIRE

Institute for Cooperative
Community Development, Inc.
2500 N. River Rd.
Manchester NH 03106
(603) 644-3103

Northern Community
Investment Corp.
20 Main St.
Johnsbury VT 05819
(802) 748-5101

NEW JERSEY

Trenton Business Assistance Corp.
Division of Economic Development
319 E. State St.
Trenton NJ 08608-1866

Greater Newark Business
Development Consortium
1 Newark Center, 22nd Floor
Newark NJ 07102-5265
(201) 242-6237

Union County Economic
Development Corp.
Liberty Hall Corporate Center
1085 Morris Ave., Suite 531
Union NJ 07083
(908) 527-1166

Jersey City Economic Development
Corp.
601 Pavonia Ave.
Jersey City NJ 07306
(201) 420-7755

New Jersey Small Business
Development Center
180 University Ave.
Newark NJ 07102-1895
(201) 648-5950
(Provides technical assistance only.)

NEW MEXICO

Women's Economic Self Sufficiency
Team
414 Silver SW
Albuquerque NM 87102-3239
(505) 848-4760

New Mexico Community
Development Loan Fund
P.O. Box 705
Albuquerque NM 87103-0705
(505) 243-3196
(Provides technical assistance only.)

NEW YORK

Adirondack Economic Development
Corp.
Trudeau Rd., P.O. Box 747
Saranac Lake NY 12983
(518) 891-5523

Hudson Development Corp.
444 Warren St.
Hudson NY 12534
(518) 828-3373

Manhattan Borough Development
Corp.
15 Park Row, Suite 510
New York NY 10038
(212) 791-3660

Rural Opportunities, Inc.
339 East Ave.
Rochester NY 14604
(716) 546-7180

Brooklyn Economic Development
Corp.
30 Flatbush Ave., Suite 420
Brooklyn NY 11217-1197
(718) 522-4600
(Provides technical assistance only.)

NORTH CAROLINA

Self-Help Ventures Fund
413 E. Chapel Hill St.
Durham NC 27701
(919) 956-8526

W.A.M.Y. Community Action
P.O. Box 552
Boone NC 28607
(704) 264-2421

North Carolina Rural Economic
Development Center, Inc.
1300 Saint Mary's St., Suite 500
Raleigh NC 27601
(919) 715-2725
(Provides technical assistance only.)

NORTH DAKOTA

Lake Agassiz Regional Council
417 Main Ave.
Fargo ND 58103
(701) 239-5373

OHIO

Enterprise Development Corp.
900 E. State St.
Athens OH 45701
(614) 592-1188

Columbus Countywide Development
Corp.
941 Chatham Lane, Suite 207
Columbus OH 43221
(614) 645-6171

Hamilton County Development Co.
1776 Mentor Ave.
Cincinnati OH 45212
(513) 632-8292

Women's Entrepreneurial Growth
Organization of NE Ohio
58 W. Center St., Suite 228
Akron OH 44308
(330) 535-4523

Women Entrepreneurs, Inc.
36 E. Fourth St., Suite 925
Cincinnati OH 45202
(513) 684-0700
(Provides technical assistance only.)

OKLAHOMA

Rural Enterprises Inc.
422 Cessna St.
Durant OK 74701
(405) 924-5094

Tulsa Economic Development Corp.
130 N. Greenwood Ave., Suite G
Tulsa OK 74120
(918) 585-8332

OREGON

Cascade West Financial Services, Inc.
408 SW Monroe St.
Corvallis OR 97333
(541) 757-6854

PENNSYLVANIA

The Ben Franklin Technology Center of Southeastern Pennsylvania
3624 Market St.
Philadelphia PA 19104-2615
(215) 382-0380

Washington County Council on Economic Development
703 Courthouse Square
Washington PA 19104-2615
(215) 382-0380

York County Industrial Development Corp.
1 Market Way East
York PA 17401
(717) 846-8879

Philadelphia Commercial Development Corp.
1315 Walnut St., Suite 600
Philadelphia PA 19107
(215) 790-2200
(Provides technical assistance only.)

PUERTO RICO

Corp. for the Economic Development of San Juan City
Avenue Munos Rivera, #1127
Rio Piedras PR 00926
(809) 756-5080

RHODE ISLAND

No sites currently in this state.

SOUTH CAROLINA

Charleston Citywide Local Development Corp.
496 King St.
Charleston SC 29403
(803) 724-3796

Santee Lynches Regional Development Corp.
115 N. Harvin St., 4th Floor
Sumter SC 29151-1837
(803) 775-7381

SOUTH DAKOTA

Lakota Fund
P.O. Box 340
Kyle SD 57752
(605) 455-2500

NE South Dakota Energy Conservation Corp.
414 Third Ave. East
Sisseton SD 57262
(605) 698-7654

TENNESSEE

South Central Tennessee Development District
815 S. Main St.
P.O. Box 1346
Columbia TN 38402
(615) 381-2040

TEXAS

Business Resource Center Incubator
4601 N. Nineteenth St.
Waco TX 76708
(817) 754-8898

Southern Dallas Development Corp.
1402 Corinth, Suite 1150
Dallas TX 75215
(214) 428-7332

Corpus Christi Chamber of Commerce/SBDC
1201 N. Shoreline
P.O. Box 640
Corpus Christi TX 78403
(512) 881-1843
(Provides technical assistance only.)

UTAH

Utah Technology Finance Corp.
177 E. South St.
Salt Lake City UT 84111
(801) 364-4346

VERMONT

Economic Development Council of Northern Vermont, Inc.
155 Lake St.
St. Albans VT 05478
(802) 524-4546

Northern Community Investment Corp.
20 Main St.
Johnsbury VT 05819
(802) 748-5101

Champlain Valley Office of Economic Opportunity, Inc.
191 North St.
Burlington VT 05401
(802) 862-2771

VIRGINIA

Ethiopian Community Development Council, Inc.
1038 S. Highland St.
Arlington VA 22204
(703) 685-0510

Business Development Center, Inc.
147 Mill Ridge Rd.
Lynchburg VA 24502
(804) 582-6100

People, Inc. of Southwest Virginia
988 W. Main St.
Abingdon VA 24210
(703) 628-9188

The Commonwealth of Virginia
Department of Economic Development
1021 E. Cary St.
Richmond VA 23291
(804) 371-8253
(Provides technical assistance only.)

WASHINGTON

Snohomish County Private Industry Council
917 134th St. SE, Suite A-10
Everett WA 98204
(206) 743-9669

Tri-Cities Enterprise Association
2000 Logstron Blvd.
Richland WA 99352
(509) 375-3268

WASHINGTON, D.C.

ARCH Development Corp.
1227 Good Hope Rd. SE
Washington DC 20020
(202) 889-5023

H Street Development Corp.
611 H St. NE
Washington DC 20002
(202) 544-8353

American Women's Economic
Development Corp.
Washington, D.C., Regional Training
Center
1250 Twenty-fourth St. NW, Suite 120
Washington DC 20037
(202) 857-0091

WEST VIRGINIA

Ohio Valley Industrial and Business
Development Corp.
Twelfth and Chapline Sts.
Wheeling WV 26003
(304) 232-7722

WISCONSIN

Advocap, Inc.
19 W. First St.
P.O. Box 1108
Fond du Lac WI 54936
(414) 922-7760

Impact Seven, Inc.
100 Digital Dr.
Clear Lake WI 54005
(715) 263-2532

Northwest Side Community
Development Corp.
5174 N. Hopkins Ave.
Milwaukee WI 53209
(414) 462-5509

Women's Business Initiative Corp.
3112 W. Highland Blvd.
Milwaukee WI 53208
(414) 933-3231

WYOMING

No sites currently in this state.

MICROLENDERS INTERESTED IN WORKING WITH WOMEN

The microlenders included in this listing have indicated an interest in working with women in the start-up or expansion phase. These lenders typically work with businesses in their local area only, but some offer loans throughout their state or in several counties. Call to find out what their service area is. Note that this is not a comprehensive list; check the lists of SBA microlenders (see page 249) and demonstration sites (see page 198) also. Some of the agencies included here offer only technical assistance but are included because they can help you develop a loan application and refer you to appropriate lenders. For more information about how to locate other microlenders, see page 122.

ALABAMA

No sites identified in this state.

ALASKA

Economic Development/Tináa Corp.
320 W. Willoughby, Suite 300
Juneau AK 99801
(907) 463-7122

ARIZONA

No sites identified in this state.

ARKANSAS

The Good Faith Fund
400 Main St., Suite 118
Pine Bluff AR 71603
(501) 535-6233

CALIFORNIA

Banker's Small Business CDC Finance Corp.
5353 Mission Center Rd., Suite 218
San Diego CA 92108
(619) 291-3594

Arcata Economic Development Corp.
100 Ericson Court, Suite 100
Arcata CA 95521
(707) 822-4616

Coalition for Women's Economic Development
315 W. Ninth St., Suite 705
Los Angeles CA 90015
(213) 489-4995

Micro Enterprise Assistance Program of Orange County
c/o Human Relations Commission
1300 S. Grand Ave., Building B
Santa Ana CA 92705
(714) 567-7470

Mid-Peninsula YWCA
Women Entrepreneur Program
4161 Alma St.
Palo Alto CA 94306
(415) 494-0972

San Francisco Renaissance
404 Bryant St.
San Francisco CA 94107
(415) 541-8580

West Company
367 N. State St., Suite 201
Ukiah CA 95482
(707) 468-3553

Women's Economic Growth
1512 S. Oregon St.
Yreka CA 96097
(916) 842-1571

Women's Economic Ventures
1136 E. Montecito St.
Santa Barbara CA 93103
(805) 965-6073

COLORADO

Mi Casa Resource Center for Women
571 Galapago St.
Denver CO 80204
(303) 573-1302

Greater Denver Local Development
Corp.
P.O. Box 2135
Denver CO 80201-2135
(303) 296-9535

CONNECTICUT

Hartford College for Women
Entrepreneurial Center
50 Elizabeth St.
Hartford CT 06105
(860) 768-5617

DELAWARE

No sites identified in this state.

FLORIDA

No sites identified in this state.

GEORGIA

No sites identified in this state.

HAWAII

No sites identified in this state.

IDAHO

Idaho Department of Commerce
Economic Development Division
P.O. Box 83720
Boise ID 83720-0093
(208) 334-2470

Self-Employment Economic
Development Council, Inc.
P.O. Box 98
Clarkston WA 99403
(509) 758-5868
(Serves Idaho)

ILLINOIS

Illinois Development Finance
Authority
Sears Tower
233 S. Wacker Dr., Suite 5310
Chicago IL 60606
(312) 793-5586

Women's Business Development Center
8 S. Michigan Ave.
Chicago IL 60603
(312) 853-3477

Women's Self-Employment Project
20 N. Clark St., Suite 400
Chicago IL 60602
(312) 606-8255

YWCA
229 Sixteenth St.
Rock Island IL 61201
(309) 788-9793

INDIANA

No sites identified in this state.

IOWA

Institute for Social and Economic
Development
1901 Broadway, Suite 313
Iowa City IA 52240
(319) 338-2331

KANSAS

El Dorado Resource Center
613 N. Main St.
El Dorado KS 67042
(316) 321-4030

KENTUCKY

Human/Economic Appalachian
Development Corp.
P.O. Box 504
Berea KY 40403
(606) 986-8423

LOUISIANA

No sites identified in this state.

MAINE

Maine Displaced Homemakers
Program
Stoddard House, University of Maine
Augusta ME 04330
(207) 621-3433

Women's Business Development Corp.
P.O. Box 658
Bangor ME 04402-0658
(207) 234-2019

MARYLAND

Women Entrepreneurs
of Baltimore, Inc.
28 E. Ostend St.
Baltimore MD 21230
(410) 727-4921

MASSACHUSETTS

Women's Institute for Housing and
Economic Development
43 Kingston St.
Boston MA 02111
(617) 423-2296

MICHIGAN

Community Action Agency of South
Central Michigan
P.O. Box 1026
Battle Creek MI 49016
(616) 965-7766

Ann Arbor Community Development
Corp.
2008 Hogback Rd., Suite 2A
Ann Arbor MI 48105
(313) 677-1400

MINNESOTA

Northeast Entrepreneur Fund, Inc.
820 Ninth St. North, Suite 140
Virginia MN 55792
(218) 749-4191

Northwest Minnesota Initiative Fund
72 Paul Bunyun Dr. NW
Bemidji MN 56601
(218) 759-2057

Women Venture
2324 University Ave., Suite 200
St. Paul MN 55114
(612) 646-3808

MISSISSIPPI

No sites identified in this state.

MISSOURI

Green Hills Rural Development, Inc.
909 Main St.
Trenton MO 64683
(816) 359-5086

MONTANA

Montana Department of Commerce
1424 Ninth Ave.
Helena MT 59620
(406) 444-3494

Human Resource Development
Council
321 E. Main St., Suite 300
Bozeman MT 59715
(406) 587-4486

Action for Eastern Montana
111 W. Bell
Glendive MT 59330
(406) 365-3364

Northwest Montana Human
Resources, Inc.
P.O. Box 8300
Kalispell MT 59904
(406) 752-6565

Women's Opportunity and Resource
Development
127 N. Higgins
Missoula MT 59802
(406) 543-3550

NEBRASKA

No sites identified in this state.

NEVADA

No sites identified in this state.

NEW HAMPSHIRE

No sites identified in this state.

NEW JERSEY

No sites identified in this state.

NEW MEXICO

Women's Economic Self-Sufficiency
Team
414 Silver SW
Albuquerque NM 87102-3239
(505) 848-4760

NEW YORK

Accion New York
235 Havemeyer St.
Brooklyn NY 11211
(718) 599-5170

Adirondack Economic Development
Corp.
P.O. Box 747
Saranac Lake NY 12983
(518) 891-5523

Albany-Colonie Regional Chamber
of Commerce
1 Computer Dr. S
Albany, NY 12205
(518) 458-9851

The Entrepreneur Center
311 Turner St., Suite 216
Utica NY 13501
(315) 733-9848

Interracial Council for Business
Opportunity
51 Madison Ave.
New York NY 10010
(212) 779-4360

Orange-Ulster Board of Cooperative
Educational Services
469 Broadway
Newburgh NY 12550
(914) 565-6395

Urban League Business Development
Center
215 Tremont St., Door #4
Rochester NY 14608
(716) 436-4377

NORTH CAROLINA

Mountain Microenterprise Fund
29 ½ Page Ave.
Asheville NC 28801
(704) 253-2834 or 2919

West Greenville Community
Development Corp.
706 W. Fifth St.
P.O. Box 1605
Greenville NC 27835-1605
(919) 752-9277

NORTH DAKOTA

No sites identified in this state.

OHIO

Appalachian Center for Economic
Networks
94 N. Columbus Rd.
Athens OH 45701
(614) 592-3854

Women's Business Development
Center
37 N. High St.
Columbus OH 43215
(614) 221-2936

Columbus Countywide
Development Corp.
941 Chatham Lane
Columbus OH 43221
(614) 645-6171

Pyramid Career Services
2400 Cleveland Ave. NW
Canton OH 44709
(330) 453-3767

Women Entrepreneurs, Inc.
P.O. Box 2662
Cincinnati OH 45201-2662
(513) 684-0700

Women's Business Resource Program
of Southeast Ohio/SBDC
20 E. Circle Dr., Suite 190
Athens OH 45701
(614) 593-1797

Women's Entrepreneurial Growth
Organization
University of Akron SBDC
Buckingham Building, Room 55
Akron OH 44325-3115
(330) 972-5179

OKLAHOMA

No sites identified in this state.

OREGON

Cascade West Financial Services, Inc.
408 SW Monroe
Corvallis OR 97333
(541) 757-6854

PENNSYLVANIA

Ben Franklin Technology Center of
South Eastern Pennsylvania
3624 Market St.
Philadelphia PA 19104-2615
(215) 382-0380

LEAP Program
Chamber of Commerce
238 Market St.
Bloomsburg PA 17815
(717) 784-2522

RHODE ISLAND

No sites identified in this state.

SOUTH CAROLINA

No sites identified in this state.

SOUTH DAKOTA

Community Action Program
Northeast South Dakota Energy
Conservation Corp.
414 Third Ave. East
Sisseton SD 57262
(605) 698-7654

TENNESSEE

No sites identified in this state.

TEXAS

No sites identified in this state.

UTAH

Utah Technology Finance Corp.
177 E. 100 S.
Salt Lake City UT 84111
(801) 364-4346

VERMONT

Northeast Employment and Training
Organization
P.O. Box 584
Newport VT 05885
(802) 334-7378

VIRGINIA

No sites identified in this state.

WASHINGTON

Cascadia Revolving Fund
157 Yesler Way, Suite 414
Seattle WA 98104
(206) 447-9226

**Private Industry Council of
Snohomish County**
917 134th St. SW, A-10
Everett WA 98204
(206) 743-9669

**Self-Employment Economic
Development Council, Inc.**
P.O. Box 98
Clarkston WA 99403
(509) 758-5868

WASHINGTON, D.C.

Accion International
Department of U.S. Operations
733 Fifteenth St. NW, Suite 700
Washington DC 20005
(202) 393-5113

American Woman's Economic Development, Inc.
1250 Twenty-fourth St. NW, Suite 120
Washington DC 20037
(202) 857-0091

Venture Concepts
325 Penny Ave. SE
Washington DC 20003
(202) 543-1200

WEST VIRGINIA

Center for Economic Options
601 Delaware Ave.
Charleston WV 25302
(304) 345-1298

WISCONSIN

West Cap
P.O. Box 308
Glenwood City WI 54013
(715) 265-4271

Women's Business Initiative Corp.
1915 N. Dr. Martin Luther King Jr. Dr.
Milwaukee WI 53212
(414) 372-2070

WYOMING

No sites identified in this state.

OFFICE OF SMALL AND DISADVANTAGED BUSINESS UTILIZATION (OSDBU)

Contact the women's business representative or small business specialist in each of the federal departments listed here for information about selling your goods or services to federal agencies. For more information about OSDBU programs, see page 146.

MAJOR GOVERNMENT DEPARTMENTS

Agriculture Department
Fourteenth St. and
Independence Ave. SW
1323 S. Building
Washington DC 20250-9400
(202) 720-7117

Air Force Department
The Pentagon, Room 5E271
Washington DC 20330-1060
(703) 697-1950

Army Department
The Pentagon, Room 2A712
Washington DC 20301-0106
(703) 697-1950

Commerce Department
Fourteenth St. and Constitution Ave.
NW, H6411
Washington DC 20230
(202) 482-1472

Defense Department
The Pentagon, Room 2A340
Washington DC 20301-3061
(703) 614-1151

Defense Logistics Agency
8725 John J. Kingman Rd.
Suite 2533 DDAS
Fort Belvior VA 22060-6221
(703) 274-6471

Education Department
600 Independence Ave. SW
Room 3120 (ROB #3)
Washington DC 20202-0521
(202) 708-9820

Energy Department
100 Independence Ave. SW, R45-058
Washington DC 20585
(202) 586-7377

Environmental Protection Agency
401 M St. SW, A 1230-C
Washington DC 20460
(703) 305-7777

General Services Administration
Eighteenth and F Sts. NW, Room 6029
Washington DC 20405
(202) 501-1021

Health and Human Services Department
200 Independence Ave. SW
Room 517D
Washington DC 20201
(202) 690-7300

Housing and Urban Development Department
451 Seventh St. SW, Room 10230
Washington DC 20410
(202) 708-1428

Interior Department
1849 C St. NW, Room 2747
Washington DC 20240
(202) 208-3493

Justice Department
1331 Pennsylvania Ave. NW
Room 1010 National Place
Washington DC 20530
(202) 616-0521

Labor Department
200 Constitution Ave. NW
Room C-2318
Washington DC 20210
(202) 219-9148

National Aeronautics and Space Administration (NASA)
300 E St. SW, Room 9K70, Code K
Washington DC 20546
(202) 358-2088

Navy Department
2211 Jefferson Davis Highway
Crystal Plaza, Building 5, Room 120
Arlington VA 20360-5000
(703) 602-8569

State Department
1700 N. Lynn St., Room 633 (SA-6)
Rossyln VA 22209
(703) 875-6824

Transportation Department
400 Seventh St. SW, Room 9414
Washington DC 20590
(202) 366-1930

Treasury Department
1500 Pennsylvania Ave. NW
Room 6100, The Annex
Washington DC 20220
(202) 622-0530

Veteran Affairs Department
801 Vermont Ave. NW
OSDBU 005SB, Room 620
Washington DC 20420
(202) 565-8124

OTHER GOVERNMENT AGENCIES

Administrative Office of U.S. Courts
1120 Vermont Ave. NW, Room 907
Washington DC 20544
(202) 633-6299

Agency for International Development
1100 Wilson Blvd., (SA-14)
Room 1200A
Arlington VA 20523-1414
(703) 875-1551

Consumer Product Safety Commission
4330 East-West Highway, Room 706
Bethesda MD 20814
(301) 504-0570

Corp. of National Service
1201 New York Ave. NW
Washington DC 20525
(202) 606-5000 ext. 320

Corps of Engineers
Pulaski Building, Room 4117
20 Massachusetts Ave. NW
Washington DC 20314
(202) 761-0725

Defense Nuclear Agency
6801 Telegraph Rd.
Alexandria VA 22310-3398
(703) 325-5021

Executive Office of the President
Office of Administration
New Executive Office Building
Room 5001
725 Seventeenth St. NW
Washington DC 20503
(202) 395-7669

Export-Import Bank of the U.S.
811 Vermont Ave. NW, Room 1017
Washington DC 20571
(202) 565-3335

Farm Credit Administration
1501 Farm Credit Dr., Room 1215
McLean VA 22102-5090
(703) 883-4147

Federal Communications Commission
1919 M St. NW, Room 734-C
Washington DC 20554
(202) 418-1100

Federal Emergency Management Agency
Federal Center Plaza
500 C St. SW, Room 350
Washington DC 20472
(202) 646-3743

Federal Maritime Commission
800 N. Capital St., Room 980
Washington DC 20573
(202) 523-5900

Federal Mediation and Conciliation Service
2100 K St. NW, 8th Floor
Washington DC 20427
(202) 606-8150

Federal Trade Commission
Sixth St. and Pennsylvania Ave. NW
Room H-700
Washington DC 20580
(202) 326-2260 or 2258

Federal Transit Administration
400 Seventh St. SW, Room 7412
Washington DC 20590
(202) 366-2285

General Accounting Office
441 G St. NW, Room 6854
Washington DC 20001
(202) 512-7751

Government Printing Office
N. Capitol and H Sts. NW, Room C-897
Washington DC 20401
(202) 512-1365

International Trade Commission
500 E St. SW, 214
Washington DC 20436
(202) 205-2730

Interstate Commerce Commission
Twelfth St. and Constitution Ave. NW
Room 3148
Washington DC 20423
(202) 927-7597

Library of Congress
1701 Brightseat Rd.
Landover MD 20785
(202) 707-8612

Marine Corps
3033 Wilson Blvd.
Clarendon Square Building
Arlington VA 22202
(703) 696-1022

National Academy of Sciences
Office of Contracts and Grants
2101 Connecticut Ave. NW, Room 406
Washington DC 20418
(202) 344-2254

**National Archives and Records
Administration**
Eighth St. and Pennsylvania Ave. NW
Room 403
Washington DC 20408
(202) 501-5110

**National Endowments for the
Humanities**
1100 Pennsylvania Ave. NW, Room 201
Washington DC 20506
(202) 786-0233

National Labor Relations Board
1099 Fourteenth St. NW, Suite 7108
Washington DC 20570
(202) 273-3890

National Science Foundation
4201 Wilson Blvd.
Arlington VA 22230
(703) 306-1391 or 5335

Nuclear Regulatory Commission
Maryland National Bank Building
R7217
7735 Old Georgetown Rd.
Bethesda MD 20555
(301) 415-7380 or 7381

Office of Personnel Management
1900 E St. NW, Room 3B-427
Washington DC 20415
(202) 606-2180

Overseas Private Investment Corp.
1100 New York Ave. NW
Washington DC 20527
(202) 336-8520

Peace Corps
1990 K St. NW, Room 6368
Washington DC 20526
(202) 606-3009

Pennsylvania Ave. Development Corp.
1331 Pennsylvania Ave. NW
Suite 1220-North
Washington DC 20004-1703
(202) 724-9091

U.S. Postal Service
475 L'Enfant Plaza W. SW, Room 3821
Washington DC 20260-5616
(202) 268-6578

Railroad Retirement Board
1310 G St. NW, Suite 500
Washington DC 20005
(202) 272-7742

Resolution Trust Corp.
801 Seventeenth St. NW
Washington DC 20434-0001
(202) 416-6925

Securities and Exchange Commission
450 Fifth St. NW, Room 7201
Washington DC 20549
(202) 942-8945

Small Business Administration
Small Purchase and Contracts
409 Third St. SW, 5th Floor
Washington DC 20416
(202) 205-6822

Smithsonian Institution
915 L'Enfant Plaza SW, Room 3120
Washington DC 20560
(202) 287-3508

Tennessee Valley Authority
20 E. Eleventh St.
Chattanooga TN 37402-2801
(615) 751-6269

U.S. Information Agency
400 Fifth St. NW
Washington DC 20547
(202) 205-9662

Washington Metropolitan Area Transit Authority (METRO)
600 Fifth St. NW
Washington DC 20001
(202) 962-1082

Office of Acquisition Management
Acquisition Services
Fourteenth St. and Constitution
Ave. NW, H6516
Washington DC 20230
(202) 482-1555 or 1472

Patent and Trademark Office
Office of Procurement
2011 Crystal Dr.
Crystal Park #1, Suite 810
Arlington VA 22202
(703) 305-8152

National Oceanic and Atmospheric Administration
System Acquisitions Office
1315 East-West Highway
Room 9626, Code SAO-X2
Silver Spring MD 20910
(301) 713-3478

Census Bureau
Procurement Office
Federal Office Building #3, Room 1551
Suitland MD 20233
(301) 457-1804

National Institute of Standards and Technology (NIST)
Systems Program Office
Acquisition and Assistance Division
Quince Orchard and Hwy. 270
Building 301, Room B-132
Gaithersburg MD 20899
(301) 975-6343

STATE DEPARTMENTS OF TRANSPORTATION

For general information about certification as a women's business enterprise (WBE) and the role of state transportation departments, review Chapter 5. For information about the role of your state department of transportation in certification and helping you sell goods and services to federal, state, and local governments, see page 148. (DBE, which you will see in many of the listings below, refers to disadvantaged business enterprises.)

ALABAMA

State Transportation Department
Equipment and Procurement Office
Bureau of Human Resources
1409 Coliseum Blvd.
Montgomery AL 36130-3050
(800) 247-3618

ALASKA

Department of Transportation
Public Facilities
Statewide DBE/EXEEO Office
P.O. Box 196900
Anchorage AK 99519-6900
(800) 770-6236
(907) 266-1488

ARIZONA

Department of Transportation
Procurement Division
1739 W. Jackson St.
Mail Drop 100P
Phoenix AZ 85007
(602) 255-7211

ARKANSAS

Arkansas State Highway and
Transportation Department
Programs and Contracts Division
P.O. Box 2261
Little Rock AR 72203
(501) 569-2261

CALIFORNIA

California Department of
Transportation
Division of Civil Rights
1120 North St.
P.O. Box 942873
Sacramento CA 94273-0001
(916) 654-4576

COLORADO

Colorado Department of
Transportation
DBE Certification
1560 Broadway, Suite 1530
Denver CO 80202
(303) 894-2355

CONNECTICUT

Department of Transportation
2800 Berlin Turnpike
Newington CT 06111
(203) 594-2163

DELAWARE

Delaware Department of
Transportation
Disadvantaged Business Enterprise
Program
Contracts Administration Building
P.O. Box 778
Dover DE 19903
(302) 739-4359

FLORIDA

Florida Department of
Transportation
Minority Programs Office
3717 Appalachee Parkway, Suite G
Tallahassee FL 32311
(904) 488-3145

GEORGIA

Transportation Department
Contracts Administration Office
2 Capitol Square
Atlanta GA 30334
(404) 656-5325

HAWAII

Department of Transportation
Contracts
869 Punchbowl St., Room 105
Honolulu HI 96813
(808) 587-2130

IDAHO

Idaho Transportation Department
Contract Administration
P.O. Box 7129
Boise ID 83707-1129
(208) 334-8430

ILLINOIS

Illinois Department of
Transportation
Small Business Enterprises
2300 S. Dirksen Parkway, Room 319
DOT Administration Building
Springfield IL 62764
(217) 785-5947

INDIANA

Indiana Department of Highways
Supportive Services
100 N. Senate Ave., Room N855
Indianapolis IN 46204
(317) 232-5093

IOWA

Department of Transportation
Contracts Office
800 Lincoln Way
Ames IA 50010
(515) 239-1414

KANSAS

Kansas Department of
Transportation
Office of Engineering Support
Docking State Office Building
7th Floor
Topeka KS 66612
(913) 296-7940

KENTUCKY

Highway Department
Contracts Procurement Division
501 High St., Room 902
Frankfort KY 40622
(502) 564-3500

LOUISIANA

Department of Transportation and
Development
Compliance Programs Section
P.O. Box 94245
Baton Rouge LA 70804-9245
(504) 379-1382

MAINE

Department of Transportation
Division of Equal Opportunity and
Employee Relations
Transportation Building
State House Station 16
Augusta ME 04333-0016
(207) 287-3576

MARYLAND

Department of Transportation
MBE-EOO
P.O. Box 8755
BWI Airport MD 21240
(410) 859-7327

MICHIGAN

Michigan Department of
Transportation
Office of Equal Employment
Opportunity
2nd Floor Logan Square
322 S. Martin Luther King Jr. Blvd.
Lansing MI 48910
(517) 373-0791

MINNESOTA

Minnesota Department of
Transportation
EEO Contract Management Office
395 John Ireland Blvd., MS 170
St. Paul MN 55155
(612) 297-1376

MISSISSIPPI

Mississippi State Highway Department
Procurement Division
P.O. Box 1850
Jackson MS 39215-1850
(601) 359-7294

MISSOURI

Highway and Transportation
Department
Equipment and Procurement Division
P.O. Box 270
Jefferson City MO 65102
(314) 751-3720

MONTANA

Montana Department of Highways
Civil Rights Bureau
2701 Prospect Ave.
P.O. Box 201001
Helena MT 59620-1001
(406) 444-6337

NEBRASKA

Nebraska Department of Roads
Contracts
Central Complex Headquarters
1500 Highway 2, Room 104
Lincoln NE 68509
(402) 479-4528

NEVADA

Nevada Department of Transportation
Contracts Compliance
1263 S. Stewart St.
Carson City NV 89712
(702) 687-5497

NEW HAMPSHIRE

New Hampshire Department of
Transportation Compliance
P.O. Box 483
Concord NH 03302-0483
(603) 271-6611

NEW JERSEY

Transportation Department
Procurement Division
1035 Parkway Ave., CN 605
Trenton NJ 08625
(609) 530-6355

NEW MEXICO

Highway and Transportation
Department
Procurement Bureau
P.O. Box 1149
Santa Fe NM 87504
(505) 827-5125

NEW YORK

Transportation Department
Contracts Management Bureau
Building 5, Room 108
1220 Washington Ave.
Albany NY 12232-0203
(518) 457-2600

NORTH CAROLINA

Transportation Department
Purchasing Section
P.O. Box 25201
Raleigh NC 27611
(919) 733-7101

NORTH DAKOTA

Department of Transportation
Civil Rights Office
608 E. Boulevard Ave.
Bismarck ND 58505-0700
(701) 328-2500

OHIO

Ohio Department of Transportation
DBE Services
25 S. Front St., Room 108
Columbus OH 43216
(614) 466-1163

OKLAHOMA

Oklahoma Department of
Transportation
DBE Supportive Services
200 NE Twenty-first St.
Oklahoma City OK 73105
(405) 521-3379

OREGON

Transportation Department
DBE Unit
135 Transportation Building
Salem OR 97310
(503) 986-3289

PENNSYLVANIA

Pennsylvania Department of
Transportation
Bureau of Equal Opportunity
Transportation Building, Room 109
Harrisburg PA 17120
(717) 787-5891

RHODE ISLAND

Transportation Department
DBE Program
210 State Office Building
Providence RI 02903
(401) 277-4576

SOUTH CAROLINA

South Carolina Department of
Highways and Public Transportation
Office of Compliance
P.O. Box 191
Columbia SC 29202-0191
(803) 737-1372

SOUTH DAKOTA

Department of Transportation
Civil Rights Program
700 Broadway Ave. E
Pierre SD 57501-2586
(605) 773-4906 or 3284

TENNESSEE

Transportation Department
Contracts Certification Office
505 Deaderick St., Suite 700
Nashville TN 37243
(615) 741-7929

TEXAS

State Department of Highways and
Public Transportation
125 E. Eleventh St.
Austin TX 78701-2483
(512) 463-8870

UTAH

Transportation Department
4501 S. 2700 West
Salt Lake City UT 84119
(801) 965-4063

VERMONT

Transportation Agency
Civil Rights
133 State St.
Montpelier VT 05633
(802) 828-2644

VIRGINIA

Commonwealth of Virginia
Department of Transportation
Office of Equal Opportunity
1401 E. Broad St.
Richmond VA 23219
(804) 786-2935

WASHINGTON

Transportation Department
Office of Equal Opportunity
Transportation Building
P.O. Box 47314
Olympia WA 98504-7314
(206) 705-7090

WEST VIRGINIA

Transportation Department
Highway Division/Procurement
Division
1900 Kanawha Blvd., Room A256
Charleston WV 25305
(304) 558-2908

WISCONSIN

Wisconsin Department of
Transportation
DBE Services
4802 Sheboygan Ave., Room 451
Madison WI 52707-7915
(608) 267-9527

WYOMING

Transportation Department
Purchasing Office
P.O. Box 1708
Cheyenne WY 82003-1708
(307) 777-4395

PROCUREMENT TECHNICAL ASSISTANCE CENTERS

Most states have at least one procurement assistance center to help businesses sell to federal, state, and local agencies. Check the state-by-state listing that follows to see if there is an office in your state. In cases where there is more than one office, contact the one closest to you. Some states with only one office listed have satellite offices, so staff may be able to direct you to an assistance center in your local area. For more information about these centers and how they can help you become involved in government contracting, see page 154.

ALABAMA

University of Alabama at
Birmingham
1717 Eleventh Ave. S., Suite 419
Birmingham AL 35294-4410
(205) 934-7260

ALASKA

University of Alaska Anchorage
Small Business Development Center
430 W. Seventeenth Ave., Suite 110
Anchorage AK 99501
(907) 274-7232

ARIZONA

APTAN, Inc.
1435 N. Hayden Rd.
Scottsdale AZ 85257-3773
(602) 945-5452

National Center for American Indian
Enterprise Development
National Center Headquarters
953 E. Juanita Ave.
Mesa AZ 85204
(602) 545-1298

ARKANSAS

Board of Trustees, University of
Arkansas
Cooperative Extension Service
P.O. Box 391
Little Rock AR 72203
(501) 337-5355

CALIFORNIA

Merced County Department of
Economic and Strategic Development
1632 N St.
Merced CA 95340
(209) 385-7312

Inland Empire Economic Partnership
Small Business Development Center
2002 Iowa Ave., Suite 110
Riverside CA 92507
(909) 781-2345

Riverside Community College District
4800 Magnolia Ave.
Riverside CA 92506-1299
(909) 222-8094

San Diego Incubator Corp.
Contracting Opportunities Center
3350 Market St.
San Diego CA 92102
(619) 595-7055

West Valley Mission Community
College District
1400 Fruitdale Ave.
Saratoga CA 95070-5698
(408) 741-2190

COLORADO

No sites currently available in this state.

CONNECTICUT

Southeast Area Technical
Development Center
1084 Shennecossett Rd.
Groton CT 06340
(203) 449-8777

DELAWARE

Delaware State University
School of Business and Economics
1200 N. Dupont Highway
Dover DE 19901
(302) 739-5146

FLORIDA

University of West Florida
Florida PTA Program
11000 University Parkway
Pensacola FL 32514
(904) 444-2066

GEORGIA

Georgia Technical Research Corp.
400 Tenth St.
Centennial Research Building
Room 246
Atlanta GA 30332-0420
(912) 953-1460

Columbus College
Center for Procurement Technical
Assistance
4225 University Ave.
Columbus GA 31907-5645
(706) 649-1092

HAWAII

COC of Hawaii
1132 Bishop St., Suite 200
Honolulu HI 96813
(808) 545-4301

IDAHO

Idaho Department of Commerce
Procurement Technical Assistance
700 W. State St.
Boise ID 83703
(208) 334-2470

ILLINOIS

**Latin American Chamber of
Commerce**
The Chicago Procurement Assistance
Center
2539 N. Kedzie Ave., Suite 11
Chicago IL 60647
(312) 252-5211

**State of Illinois
Department of Commerce and
Community Affairs**
Procurement Technical Assistance
620 E. Adams St., 3rd Floor
Springfield IL 62701
(217) 785-6310

INDIANA

**Indiana Small Business
Development Corp.**
Government Marketing
Assistance Group
1 N. Capital Ave., Suite 1275
Indianapolis IN 46204-2026
(317) 264-5600

Partners in Contracting Corp.
Procurement Technical Assistance
Center
3510 Calumet, Suite 2B
Hammond IN 46320
(219) 932-7811

IOWA

Iowa Department of Economic
Development
Procurement Technical Assistance
200 E. Grand Ave.
Des Moines IA 50309
(515) 242-4888

KANSAS

There are currently no sites in this state.

KENTUCKY

Cabinet for Economic Development
Department of Community
Development
500 Mero St.
22nd Floor, Capital Plaza
Frankfort KY 40601
(800) 838-3266

LOUISIANA

Louisiana Productivity Center
University of Southwestern Louisiana
241 E. Lewis St.
P.O. Box 44172
Lafayette LA 70504-4172
(318) 482-6767

NW Louisiana Government
Procurement Center
Shreveport COC
400 Edwards St.
P.O. Box 20074
Shreveport LA 71120-0074
(318) 677-2532

MAINE

Eastern Maine Development Corp.
Market Development Center
One Cumberland Place, Suite 300
Bangor ME 04401
(800) 955-6549

MARYLAND

Tri-County Council for Western
Maryland
111 S. George St.
Cumberland MD 21502
(301) 777-2158

MASSACHUSETTS

No sites currently available in this state.

MICHIGAN

CEO Council, Inc.
Southwest Technical Assistance Center
100 W. Michigan, Suite 294
Kalamazoo MI 49007
(616) 342-0000

Downriver Community Conference
Economic Development
15100 Northline
Southgate MI 48195
(313) 281-0700 ext. 190

Genesee County Metropolitan
Planning Commission
Procurement Technical Assistance Center
1101 Beach St., Room 223
Flint MI 48502
(810) 257-3010

Jackson Alliance for Business Development
Procurement Technical Assistance Center
133 W. Michigan Ave.
Jackson MI 49201
(517) 788-4680

Northeast Michigan Consortium
20709 State St.
Onaway MI 49765
(517) 733-8548

NW Michigan Council of Governments
Procurement Technical Assistance Center
P.O. Box 506
Traverse City MI 49685-0506
(616) 929-5036

Saginaw Future Inc.
Procurement Technical Assistance Center
301 E. Genessee Ave., 3rd Floor
Saginaw MI 48607
(517) 754-8222

Schoolcraft College
Procurement Technical Assistance
18600 Haggerty Rd.
Livonia MI 48152-2696
(313) 462-4438

Thumb Area Consortium/Community Growth Alliance
Procurement Technical Assistance Center
3270 Wilson St.
Marlette MI 48453
(517) 635-3561

Warren Center Line
Sterling Heights Chamber of Commerce
30500 Van Dyke, Suite 118
Warren MI 48093
(810) 751-3939

West Central Michigan Employment and Training Consortium
Procurement Technical Assistance Center
110 Elm St.
Big Rapids MI 49307
(616) 796-4891

Marquette County Economic Development Corp.
Upper Peninsula Procurement Technical Assistance Center
198 Airport Rd.
Negaunee MI 49866
(906) 475-4121

MINNESOTA

Minnesota Project Innovation, Inc.
Government Marketing Assistance
111 Third Ave. S., Suite 100
Minneapolis MN 55401-2551
(612) 338-3280

MISSISSIPPI

Mississippi Contract Procurement
Center
1636 Popps Ferry Rd., Suite 229
Biloxi MS 39532
(601) 396-1288

MISSOURI

Curators of University of Missouri
University Extension
310 Jesse Hall
Columbia MO 65211
(314) 882-0344

Missouri Southern State College
3950 E. Newman Rd.
Joplin MO 64801-1595
(417) 625-3001

MONTANA

High Plains Development Authority
2800 Terminal Dr., Suite 209
P.O. Box 2568
Great Falls MT 59404
(406) 454-1934

Montana Trade Port Authority
2722 Third Ave. North, Suite 300 W
Billings MT 59101-1931
(406) 256-6871

NEBRASKA

University of Nebraska at Omaha
Business Development Center
1313 Farnham-on-the Mall, Suite 132
Omaha NE 68182-0248
(402) 595-2381

NEVADA

State of Nevada
Commission on Economic
Development
Capitol Complex
Carson City NV 89710
(702) 687-4325

NEW HAMPSHIRE

State of New Hampshire
Office of Business and Industrial
Development
172 Pembroke Rd.
P.O. Box 856
Concord NH 03302-1856
(603) 271-2591

NEW JERSEY

Foundation at New Jersey Institute of
Technology
Procurement Technical Assistance
Center
University Heights
Newark NJ 07102
(201) 596-3105

Union County Economic
Development Corp.
Procurement Technical Assistance
Center
1085 Morris Ave., Suite 531-LIB Hall
Union NJ 07083
(908) 527-1166

NEW MEXICO

State of New Mexico General
Services Department
Procurement Assistance Program
1100 St. Francis Dr., Room 2006
Santa Fe NM 87503
(505) 827-0425

NEW YORK

Cattaraugus County
Department of Economic
Development and Tourism
303 Court St.
Little Valley NY 14755
(716) 938-9111

New York City Department of
Businesses Services
Procurement Outreach Program
110 William St., 2nd Floor
New York NY 10038
(212) 513-6472

Rockland Economic Development Corp.
Procurement Technical Assistance Center
1 Blue Hill Plaza, Suite 812
Pearl River NY 10965
(914) 735-7040

South Bronx Overall Economic
Development Corp.
Procurement Assistance
370 E. 149th St.
Bronx NY 10455
(718) 292-3113

Long Island Development Corp.
Procurement Technical Assistance
Program
255 Glen Cove Rd.
Carle Place NY 11514
(516) 741-5690

NORTH CAROLINA

University of North Carolina at
Chapel Hill
Small Business and Technology
Development Center
Bynum Hall, Room 300
Chapel Hill NC 27599-4100
(919) 571-4154

NORTH DAKOTA

University of North Dakota
Small Business Development Center
P.O. Box 7308
Grand Forks ND 58202-7308
(701) 237-9678

OHIO

Central State University
Procurement and Technical
Assistance Center
100 Jenkins Hall
Wilberforce OH 45384
(513) 376-6660

Community Improvement Corp. of Lake County
Northeast Ohio Government Contract
Assistance Center
7750 Clocktower Dr.
Kirtland OH 44094-5198
(216) 951-8488

Greater Cleveland Growth Association
Cleveland Area Development Corp.
200 Tower City Center, 50 Public Square
Cleveland OH 44113-2291
(216) 621-3300 ext. 280

Greater Columbus Chamber of Commerce
37 N. High St.
Columbus OH 43215
(614) 225-6952

Lawrence Economic Development Corp.
Procurement Outreach Center
101 Sand and Solida Rds.
P.O. Box 488
South Point OH 45680
(614) 894-3838

Mahoning Valley Economic Development Corp.
Technical Procurement Center
4319 Belmont Ave.
Youngstown OH 44505-1005
(216) 759-3668

Terra Technical College
N. Central Ohio Procurement
Technical Assistance Program
1220 Cedar St.
Fremont OH 43420
(419) 332-1002

University of Cincinnati
CECE-Small Business Development
Center
111 Edison Dr.
Cincinnati OH 45216-2262
(513) 948-2083

Toledo Lucas County Public Library
325 N. Michigan St.
Toledo OH 43624
(419) 259-5244

OKLAHOMA

Department of Vocational and Technical Education
Bid Assistance Center
1500 W. Seventh Ave.
Stillwater OK 74074-4364
(405) 743-5571

Tribal Government Institute
111 N. Peters, Suite 204
Norman OK 73069
(405) 329-5542

OREGON

The Organization for Economic Initiatives
Government Contract Acquisition Program
99 W. Tenth Ave., Suite 337-B
Eugene OR 97401
(541) 344-3537

PENNSYLVANIA

Economic Development Council of Northeast Pennsylvania
Local Development District
1151 Oak St.
Pittston PA 18640
(717) 655-5581

Indiana University of Pennsylvania
College of Business
Robertshaw Building, Room 10
650 S. Thirteenth St.
Indiana PA 15705-1087
(412) 357-7824

Johnstown Area Regional Industries
Defense Procurement Assistance Center
111 Market St.
Johnstown PA 15901
(814) 539-4951

Mon-Valley Renaissance
California University of Pennsylvania
250 University Ave.
California PA 15419
(412) 938-5881

NW Pennsylvania Regional Planning and Development Commission
Procurement Technical Assistance Center
614 Eleventh St.
Franklin PA 16323
(814) 437-3024

North Central Pennsylvania Regional Planning and Development Commission
North Central Business Development Center
651 Montmorenci Ave.
P.O. Box 488
Ridgway PA 15853
(814) 773-3162

Northern Tier Regional Planning and Development Commission
507 Main St.
Towanda PA 18848-1697
(717) 265-9103

Private Industry Council of Westmoreland/Fayette, Inc.
Procurement Assistance Center
531 S. Main St.
Greensburg PA 15601
(412) 836-2600

SEDA-Council of Governments
Procurement Technical Assistance Center
R.R. 1, Box 372
Lewisburg PA 17837
(717) 524-4491

Southern Alleghenies Planning and Development Commission
Procurement Technical Assistance Program
541 Fifty-eighth St.
Altoona PA 16002
(814) 949-6528

University of Pennsylvania-Wharton
Procurement Technical Assistance Program
Philadelphia PA 19104-6374
(215) 898-1219

West Chester University
Center for the Study of Connectivity and Databases
128 Elsie O. Bull Center
West Chester PA 19383
(610) 436-3337

PUERTO RICO

Commonwealth of Puerto Rico
Economic Development Administration
355 Roosevelt Ave.
Hato Rey PR 00918
(809) 753-6861

RHODE ISLAND

Rhode Island Department of Economic Development
7 Jackson Walkway
Providence RI 02903
(401) 277-2601

SOUTH CAROLINA

University of South Carolina
Small Business Development Center
College of Business Administration
Columbia SC 29208
(803) 777-4907

SOUTH DAKOTA

University of South Dakota
Procurement Technical Assistance Center
414 E. Clark Patterson, 11B
Vermillion SD 57069-2390
(605) 367-5252

TENNESSEE

University of Tennessee
Center for Industrial Services
226 Capitol Blvd. Bldg., Suite 606
Nashville TN 37219-1804
(615) 242-2456

TEXAS

Angelina College Procurement Assistance Center
P.O. Box 1768
Lufkin TX 75902
(409) 639-3678

San Antonio Procurement Outreach Program
Economic Development Department
P.O. Box 839966
San Antonio TX 78283
(210) 207-3910

El Paso Community College
Resource Development
P.O. Box 20500
El Paso TX 79998
(915) 594-2283

Northeast Texas Community College
East Texas Procurement Technical
Assistance Program
P.O. Box 1307
Mt. Pleasant TX 75456-1307
(903) 572-1911

**Panhandle Regional Planning
Commission**
Economic Development Unit
P.O. Box 9257
Amarillo TX 79105-9257
(806) 372-3381

University of Houston/TIPS
110 Louisiana, Suite 500
Houston TX 77002
(713) 752-8477

University of Texas at Arlington
Automation and Robotics Research
Center
Office of the President
Box 19125
Arlington TX 76019
(817) 794-5978

Texas Technical University
College of Business Administration
2579 S. Loop 289
Lubbock TX 79423
(806) 745-1637

University of Texas at Brownsville/TSC
Center for Business and Economic
Development
1600 E. Elizabeth St.
Brownsville TX 78520
(210) 548-8713

**Greater Corpus Christi Business
Alliance**
Small Business Development Center
1201 N. Shoreline
Corpus Christi TX 78401
(512) 881-1831

UTAH

**Utah Department of Community and
Economic Development**
Utah Procurement Outreach Program
324 S. State St., Suite 504
Salt Lake City UT 84111
(801) 538-8791

VERMONT

State of Vermont
Department of Economic Development
109 State St.
Montpelier VT 05609
(802) 828-3221

VIRGINIA

**Crater Planning District
Commission**
Procurement Assistance Center
1964 Wakefield St.
P.O. Box 1808
Petersburg VA 23805
(804) 861-1667

George Mason University
Entrepreneurship Center
4400 University Dr.
Fairfax VA 22030
(703) 993-8300

Southwest Virginia Community
College
Economic Development Department
P.O. Box SVCC
Richland VA 24641
(703) 964-7334

WASHINGTON

Economic Development Council of
Snohomish County
917 134th St. SW, Suite 103
Everett WA 98204
(206) 743-4567

WASHINGTON, D.C.

No sites currently in this area.

WEST VIRGINIA

Mid-Ohio Valley Regional Council
Procurement Technical Assistance
Center
P.O. Box 247
Parkersburg WV 26102
(304) 295-8714

Regional Contracting Assistance
Center
1116 Smith St., Suite 202
Charleston WV 25301
(304) 344-2546

WISCONSIN

Madison Area Technical College
Small Business Procurement
Assistance Center
211 N. Carroll St.
Madison WI 53703
(608) 258-2330

Wisconsin Procurement Institute
10437 Innovation Dr., Suite 322
Wauwatosa WI 53226-4815
(414) 443-9744

WYOMING

No sites currently in this state.

Index

SUBMISSION AND CORRECTION FORM

If you would like to have your organization considered for inclusion in the next edition (or have found errors in a current listing) of *The Women's Business Resource Guide*, please fill out a copy of this form and send it along with any printed material you may have to:

The Women's Business Resource Guide
c/o Information Design Northwest
P.O. Box 25505
Eugene OR 97402

Organization: _____

Contact Person: _____

Street Address: _____

City, State, Zip: _____

Telephone: _____ Fax: _____

Please provide a brief description of your organization's activities (or describe the correction and include the page number on which the entry appears):